The
Paleo
Diabetes
Diet Solution

The

Paleo
Diabetes
Diet Solution

Manage Your Blood Sugar with **125 Recipes** Plus a 30-Day Meal Plan

---

Jill Hillhouse, CNP
with Lisa Cantkier, CHN

Robert
ROSE

For complete cataloguing information, see page 288.

Disclaimer
This book is a general guide only and should never be a substitute for the skill, knowledge and experience of a qualified medical professional dealing with the facts, circumstances and symptoms of a particular case. People with diabetes must work closely with their physicians and other health-care professionals before adopting any changes, to monitor any medications they are taking and the effects of any dietary changes they may make. The ideas presented in this book apply specifically to people with insulin resistance and type 2 diabetes, but may also be useful for people with type 1 diabetes.

The nutritional, medical and health information presented in this book is based on the research, training and professional experience of the authors, and is true and complete to the best of their knowledge. However, this book is intended only as an informative guide for those wishing to know more about health, nutrition and medicine; it is not intended to replace or countermand the advice given by the reader's personal physician. Because each person and situation is unique, the authors and the publisher urge the reader to check with a qualified health-care professional before using any procedure where there is a question as to its appropriateness. A physician should be consulted before beginning any exercise program. The authors and the publisher are not responsible for any adverse effects or consequences resulting from the use of the information in this book. It is the responsibility of the reader to consult a physician or other qualified health-care professional regarding his or her personal care.

This book contains references to products that may not be available everywhere. The intent of the information provided is to be helpful; however, there is no guarantee of results associated with the information provided. Use of brand names is for educational purposes only and does not imply endorsement.

The recipes in this book have been carefully tested by our kitchen and our tasters. To the best of our knowledge, they are safe and nutritious for ordinary use and users. For those people with food or other allergies, or who have special food requirements or health issues, please read the suggested contents of each recipe carefully and determine whether or not they may create a problem for you. All recipes are used at the risk of the consumer. We cannot be responsible for any hazards, loss or damage that may occur as a result of any recipe use. For those with special needs, allergies, requirements or health problems, in the event of any doubt, please contact your medical adviser prior to the use of any recipe.

Design and production: Daniella Zanchetta/PageWave Graphics Inc.
Layout: Alicia McCarthy/PageWave Graphics Inc.
Editor: Sue Sumeraj
Recipe editor: Jennifer MacKenzie
Proofreader: Kelly Jones
Indexer: Gillian Watts
Photography: Tango Photography
Food stylist: Éric Régimbald
Props stylist: Véronique Gagnon-Lalanne

Cover images *(from top)*: Jicama, Avocado, Radish and Orange Salad with Cilantro (page 134), Skillet-Grilled Lamb with Avocado Mint Sauce (page 236) and Mexican Chicken Soup (page 118).

The publisher gratefully acknowledges the financial support of our publishing program by the Government of Canada through the Canada Book Fund.

Published by Robert Rose Inc.
120 Eglinton Avenue East, Suite 800, Toronto, Ontario, Canada M4P 1E2
Tel: (416) 322-6552 Fax: (416) 322-6936
www.robertrose.ca

Printed and bound in Canada

1 2 3 4 5 6 7 8 9 FP 24 23 22 21 20 19 18 17 16

Contents

Acknowledgments

The writing of this book has been fueled and inspired by my clients, who have listened, questioned and learned right alongside me. I thank them and congratulate them for seeking to take control of their health.

It takes a team to produce a book and many thanks go to Daniella Zanchetta and Alicia McCarthy of PageWave Graphics, who worked on the design and layout of this book, photographer Pierre Lafrenière and Tango Photography, food stylist Éric Régimbald, props stylist Véronique Gagnon-Lalanne, proofreader Kelly Jones and indexer Gillian Watts. A big thank you also to Marian Jarkovich and Martine Quibell at Robert Rose for their publicity and marketing expertise.

Many thanks to Sue Sumeraj and Jennifer MacKenzie for their editorial guidance and to Bob Dees at Robert Rose for his commitment to this project. A warm and special thank you to my collaborator, Lisa Cantkier, for helping me undertake this venture.

I'd like to thank my invaluable testers and researchers Cristina Tache, Laura De Sanctis and Samantha Lotus, as well as Lisa Danziger, Angela Gruenthal, Samantha Mahfood, Maggie Millwood and Beth Robert. A special thanks to Nancy MacDonald and Anne Langford for their unyielding encouragement.

My greatest appreciation goes to my children, Stewart and Duncan, for always agreeing to try my creations, and finally, to Bob for his steadfast support.

— Jill Hillhouse

I'd like to thank my coauthor, Jill Hillhouse, for asking me to contribute to this book. Living with celiac disease, I have a special interest in the health benefits of the paleo diet, and I am delighted to have been a part of this book. I would also like to sincerely thank the *entire* team that worked tirelessly to make this book become a reality, including and especially Bob Dees. A special thank you to my husband, Nathan, and sons, Elan and Jacob, for their love and support — *I love you more.*

— Lisa Cantkier

Introduction:
A New Perspective

Food is _____. When asked to fill in the blank, many of you will answer "fuel." The analogy of the body as a car and food as the fuel that gives us energy has been around for a long time, and we even use it to make a point in chapter 2. Yes, food is fuel, and it provides nourishment, but it is also so much more. Many of us have spent a considerable amount of time adding up the calories in food and calculating how many we can eat and still lose weight. We are diligent, but we gain weight. Or sometimes we eat more than we "should" but end up losing a few pounds. If the concept of "food as fuel" was all there was to it, we should gain or lose based on the calorie count. From experience, we can attest that it doesn't always happen this way. The body is an incredibly complex and dynamic system of biochemical, hormonal and genetic reactions that respond to the environment. What we put into it is not just fuel, it is information that controls our gene expression, hormones and metabolism.

> If the concept of "food as fuel" was all there was to it, we should gain or lose based on the calorie count. From experience, we can attest that it doesn't always happen this way.

The macronutrients — protein, fat and carbohydrates — are the big pieces that provide calories and energy. Vitamins, minerals and phytochemicals, on the other hand, are the smaller pieces, the micronutrients that are the supporting players in the chemical reactions that make things happen in our bodies. The mineral magnesium, for example, is part of hundreds of enzymatic reactions involved in things like muscle and nerve function, blood pressure regulation and blood sugar control. And flavonoids from plants inhibit the activity of certain enzyme pathways and modify the signaling in other cells. Neither magnesium nor flavonoids provide "fuel," but they do provide information. Information that tells the body to turn on this pathway or release that hormone. Information that sends signals throughout the body to express one gene and not express another. This is the science of epigenetics: the study of how certain things turn genes on and off.

A powerful demonstration of the concept of food as information was the result of the Functional Genomics and Nutrition (FUNGENUT) Study published in *The American Journal of Clinical Nutrition*. The researchers recruited subjects with metabolic syndrome and divided them into two groups. For 12 weeks, both groups ate the same amount of calories, with the same breakdown of protein, fat, carbohydrates and fiber. The only difference between the two groups was the source of the carbohydrates: one group ate oats, wheat and potatoes; the other ate whole-kernel rye bread and rye pasta. In the oat, wheat and potato group, 62 genes that relate to metabolic stress and increased inflammation were up-regulated (turned on), while in the rye bread and pasta group, 71 genes that regulate insulin signaling and apoptosis (programmed cell death) were down-regulated (turned off). In other words, because of the different *type* of carbohydrates the participants ate, their genes were either given information that instructed them to increase inflammation and promote the progression toward type 2 diabetes, or they were given information that allowed the body to turn off the genes associated with increased insulin resistance. Here is the final sentence of the conclusion offered by the researchers. "The changes in gene expression [in this study] suggest that over the long term, such carbohydrate modifications may influence the risk of cardiovascular disease and T2DM [type 2 diabetes mellitus], even in the absence of weight loss."

The mapping of the human genome showed us that there are far fewer genes than we thought, and made us realize that their interaction is far more complex than we thought. The search for a "diabetes gene" has been disappointing, although it has uncovered a number of predisposing genes that can get "turned on" with the right mix of environmental, dietary and lifestyle exposures. This is really important to understand. We can't change our genes, but we can change how they are expressed. Type 2 diabetes is, to a very large extent, a result of our environment and lifestyle choices.

While food is the majority of the blood sugar puzzle, it's not the only piece. Our environment matters too. "Environment" doesn't just mean our physical space, but also the collection of conditions and influences that surround us: our stress levels, our sleep patterns, how much we move, the state of our digestion and the toxins we encounter. All of these things also provide the body and each individual cell within it with information that can turn certain genes on or off and move us along the path of disease or in the direction of health.

The changes over the last 150 years in both the types of foods we eat and the way these foods are processed have been dramatic. In the United States in 1889, 93% of food spending was on food to be eaten at home. By 2009, that percentage had dropped to 51%, and a good proportion of that was actually for commercially prepared food to be eaten at home (takeout). Since 1960, fast-food spending as a percentage of total money spent on food has increased from 2% to over 20%.

Homeostasis
The body is a very complicated, highly connected network that is always seeking a dynamic state of equilibrium called homeostasis. When one system in the body is influenced or disturbed, that message resonates through the entire network, with both foreseen and unforeseen effects. Anything that interferes with the complex mechanisms the body uses to regulate blood sugar may cause or contribute to diabetes.

We can't change our genes, but we can change how they are expressed. Type 2 diabetes is, to a very large extent, a result of our environment and lifestyle choices.

> The information in this book will help you understand how blood sugar works in the body and how the paleo approach to eating can help you restore healthy blood sugar function and halt, if not reverse, the health consequences of blood sugar dysfunction and type 2 diabetes.

One hundred and fifty years is a nanosecond in terms of the ability of our bodies to adapt to startling increases in sugar, refined grains and industrial seed oils. The rise in blood sugar dysfunction and type 2 diabetes is a consequence of the industrialization of our food away from our historical and ancestral norms, augmented by changes in our lifestyle.

The information in the first half of this book will help you understand how blood sugar works in the body and how those ancestral norms — the paleo approach to eating — can help you restore healthy blood sugar function and halt, if not reverse, the health consequences of blood sugar dysfunction and type 2 diabetes. You will also learn how to navigate eating away from home, how to read and understand food labels and how to stock your pantry with foods that will restore your health. The second half of the book ties everything together with delicious paleo-inspired recipes that will leave you satisfied and finally in control of your blood sugar.

One of the key themes of this book is that the food we eat is the single most important influence on our health. Food is so much more than the sum of its parts. It is the environment we surround our cells with multiple times per day. There are millions of molecules of information in every bite of food, information that gets translated into cellular instructions. These instructions control our health and our disease patterns. Every food decision we make relays information, and every food choice is an opportunity to give our bodies information that translates into health and well-being. Let's choose wisely.

Part 1

Managing Diabetes with the Paleo Diet

CHAPTER 1
The Problem of Diabetes

Diabetes is one of our biggest health threats. In North America and around the world, diabetes rates are on a steady and alarming uphill climb. According to the American Diabetes Association, in the United States, 29.1 million people, or 9.3% of the population (all ages), have diabetes, but almost 28% of those people have not yet been diagnosed. In Canada, the overall percentage is the same, and researchers estimate that the number of people with diabetes will grow to over 23% of the population by 2025.

But this isn't the whole story. The U.S. Centers for Disease Control and Prevention estimates that an additional 86 million people — a startling one in three — have prediabetes and don't know it. Their blood sugar and insulin levels are high, with all the accompanying health consequences, just not high enough for the official diagnosis of diabetes.

The Diagnosis of Diabetes

The diagnosis of diabetes is, perhaps, part of the problem. The actual diagnosis is like a line in the sand after which the medical system kicks in and people with diabetes are offered diabetes education sessions and diabetic drugs, taught to follow diabetic diets and instructed to try to achieve certain blood sugar numbers. Up until that point, however, health-care professionals offer only vague warnings of "Your blood sugar number is a little higher than last year" or "Careful, you're getting close to being prediabetic." There is almost a wait-and-see-and-hope-it-doesn't-turn-into-diabetes mindset going on. We hear the terms "insulin resistance," "metabolic syndrome," "obesity" and "prediabetes" mentioned, but we don't really know what they all mean or where we fit in.

When we finally get a diagnosis of type 2 diabetes, many of us are surprised. We are told type 2 diabetes is a chronic progressive disease and that, once you get it, you will always have it and that it will most certainly get worse over time. We don't understand what's actually at stake with unbalanced blood sugar and, until we get that diagnosis, we may cut back a bit and watch what we are eating (whatever that means), but beyond that, we don't really have an action plan.

> We've been hearing the same message for decades — eat less, exercise more — and for the most part it doesn't work.

Once that diagnosis has been made, we are pointed to the clinical guidelines of the American Diabetes Association and the Canadian Diabetes Association, in the section called "Strategies for Preventing or Delaying Type 2 Diabetes." The first recommendation is for health-care providers to refer patients to a structured diet and lifestyle modification program that will help them lose 5% to 7% of their body weight and increase their physical activity to at least 150 minutes of moderate exercise per week. The diet modification programs encourage reducing energy intake (a.k.a. calories) while maintaining a healthful eating pattern to promote weight loss, and following the government food guides.

This is the same message we have been hearing for decades — eat less, exercise more — and for the most part it doesn't work. As a result, diabetes does indeed become chronic and progressive. We maintain and manage the disease state instead of fixing it.

Instead of thinking in terms of having a diagnosis of type 2 diabetes or not, think of blood sugar as a spectrum, or continuum, from optimal blood sugar balance to insulin resistance to metabolic syndrome to prediabetes to full-blown type 2 diabetes. As you can see in the diagram below, anything other than optimal blood sugar control is really prediabetes.

The Blood Sugar Spectrum

Optimal blood sugar   Insulin resistance   Metabolic syndrome   Prediabetes diagnosis   Type 2 diabetes

———————————————— THIS IS ALL PREDIABETES ————————→

How Normal Blood Sugar Works

Let's start at the beginning, with our food. Everything we eat is made up of two classes of nutrients: macronutrients and micronutrients. Micronutrients are the vitamins, minerals and phytochemicals that are abundant in the nutrient-dense foods we'll talk about later. There are three macronutrients: proteins, fats and carbohydrates. When we eat these macronutrients, they are broken down into their component parts by the work of our incredible digestive system. Proteins are broken down into individual amino acids; fats are broken down into individual fatty acids and glycerol; and carbohydrates are broken down into individual glucose (sugar) molecules.

The Role of Insulin

The hormone insulin enables glucose to move from the bloodstream into the body's cells, where it can be used as fuel or stored for later use. Think of insulin as a doorman. When there is glucose traveling through the body via the bloodstream, insulin essentially opens doors in the cells' membranes — the insulin receptors — which allow the glucose in. Once inside, the glucose goes through a multistage metabolic process to produce energy so we can use our bodies to move and use our brains to think and generally get on with our day. If the glucose is not needed for immediate energy, it is stored in a form called glycogen in the muscles and liver for future use. But if the glycogen stores in these cells are already all topped up, the liver transforms the excess glucose into another kind of long-term storage unit: fat.

In a healthy body with normal fasting blood sugar, there are only about 5 grams of glucose, the equivalent of 1 teaspoon (5 mL), in the entire bloodstream. This comes as a bit of a shock to most people, but is very important to understand. Think about all the sugar that goes into your body each day. One 8-ounce (250 mL) glass of fresh orange juice, for instance, contains the equivalent of almost $6\frac{1}{2}$ teaspoons (32 mL) of sugar. What happens to all that sugar? When we drink the juice, the carbohydrates in the juice are broken down into individual glucose molecules and our blood sugar rises. In response to this rise in blood sugar, insulin is secreted from the beta cells in the pancreas and goes to work moving the glucose from the blood into the cells.

Although the pancreas is always secreting a low level of insulin, called basal insulin, the amount increases as blood glucose rises. Excess glucose in the blood is toxic and can damage the lining of our blood vessels, so it's important that insulin does its job well and moves glucose out of the bloodstream so it can't do any harm.

Insulin has an effect on a number of cells, including muscle cells, liver cells and fat cells, or adipose tissue.

DID YOU KNOW?

Glucose = Blood Sugar

Glucose is what we are referring to when we say "blood sugar." Virtually every cell of the body uses glucose for energy.

DID YOU KNOW?

The Energy-Storing Hormone

Insulin is our energy-storing hormone: it helps glucose move out of the blood and into the cell to be used as energy. If the cell has enough glucose for its immediate energy needs, it will store the excess first as glycogen in the muscle and liver cells, and then as fat in the liver and fat cells.

As the insulin goes to work, these cells take in glucose from the bloodstream, our blood sugar drops again to normal, and the beta cells reduce the amount of secreted insulin.

The Role of Glucagon

When we haven't eaten for a while and our blood sugar starts to drop, the pancreas secretes another hormone, called glucagon, this time from the alpha cells. Glucagon's job is to raise blood sugar so the body has access to enough energy to run properly. The release of glucagon signals the liver to release some of its glucose that was stored as glycogen into the bloodstream, to increase blood sugar levels. If needed, glucagon can also induce the liver to make glucose out of the building blocks of protein and fat.

Insulin Resistance: A State of Imbalance

The long-held insulin theory of type 2 diabetes brings us back to our food again. Remember that when we eat carbohydrates, they are broken down into individual glucose molecules that enter the bloodstream, increase our blood sugar and signal the release of insulin from the pancreas to move the sugar out of the bloodstream and into the cells. Glucose is the principle stimulus for insulin secretion. When we eat too much of the "fast" type of carbohydrates (refined sugar and grain products) too often, a lot of glucose ends up in the blood and a greater amount of insulin is released to deal with all that glucose. Over time, the insulin receptors on the cell membranes don't respond properly to insulin's signal to let glucose in. Essentially, the door no longer opens when the doorman knocks. If less glucose gets into the cells, more glucose stays in the blood — which, you will recall, is the signal for the pancreas to secrete even more insulin.

This is the state of insulin resistance. The cells are resistant to the action of insulin. For a time — years, even — the increased output of insulin by the pancreas does eventually force glucose into the cells, and blood sugar levels appear to stay normal (we'll talk about blood sugar testing soon). And for some people, this is as far as things progress. For others, however, eventually even hypersecretion of insulin can't do the job and their blood sugar numbers start to rise. At some point, the pancreas may become unable to make the amount of insulin required to move all of the glucose out of the bloodstream. Less insulin production means less glucose getting into the cells, and the net effect is rising blood sugar.

In either case, insulin is high. When we have high insulin as a result of excess carbohydrates, the liver ramps up a process called de novo lipogenesis, where it stores the excess carbohydrates as fat. As the liver gets fattier, it takes more and more insulin to store the excess sugar. Studies also suggest that a fatty liver creates a fatty pancreas, which can result in beta cell dysfunction and destruction, meaning less insulin production, which in turn leads to high blood sugar.

Research Spotlight

Genetic Factors in Blood Sugar Regulation

Nature or nurture? For type 2 diabetes, it appears to be a bit of both. There have been tremendous advances in gene research over the past decade, but a singular "diabetes gene" has not been uncovered. Instead, researchers have identified dozens of genes and gene variations that may each make small contributions to an increased risk for diabetes.

However, studies conducted on identical twins show that genes alone are not enough to determine whether someone might develop diabetes. Identical twins have been thought to have identical genes, yet research shows that when one twin has type 2 diabetes, the risk for the other twin is about 75% — not 100%. Something else is going on.

In an identical twin study conducted in 2014 at Lund University in Sweden, researchers found 1,400 sites on the twins' DNA where there was a difference in DNA methylation (which modifies the DNA's function) between the diabetic twin and the non-diabetic twin. According to Emma Nilsson, one of the researchers, "It is believed that these differences are due to differences in lifestyle and this confirms the theory that type 2 diabetes is strongly linked to lifestyle."

Human biology is complex, but to simplify what this means, our DNA contains our genes, which are inherited and cannot be altered. On the genes are things called methyl groups that can either turn a gene "on" or "off" — in other words, methyl groups affect the expression of a gene. The methyl groups are influenced in different ways by factors such as diet, exercise, stress and other lifestyle choices.

So while genetics does play a role in type 2 diabetes, the dramatic increase in the number of cases over the last generation has less to do with heredity than with the interaction between our genes, the world we live in and the lifestyle choices we make.

A helpful analogy is to think of your genetic risk for diabetes as a seed. On its own a seed won't grow into a tree, but if you give it the right environment (soil, water, sunlight), it will. Our modern food environment of processed and refined grains and sugar, combined with inadequate movement, high stress, lack of sleep and environmental toxins, can make those tiny genetic seeds flourish into type 2 diabetes. It has been said that genes load the gun, environment pulls the trigger.

Testing Blood Sugar and Insulin Levels

As you can see, the biological mechanisms of insulin resistance are intricate and incompletely understood. But whatever the precise combination of mechanisms is, a high insulin level is an early sign of a problem. Unfortunately, most doctors do not test insulin levels. The regular testing they perform is all about blood sugar, which, as we have seen, changes only *after* insulin has already been high, often for a long time.

Let's have a look at the tests that are typically used to determine the extent of our blood sugar imbalances, what they mean and how useful they are for helping us understand what is going on inside our bodies.

> A high insulin level is an early sign of a problem.

Fasting Plasma Glucose

The fasting plasma glucose (FPG) test, or fasting blood sugar test, is the one most commonly used by doctors. It measures the concentration of glucose in your blood after you refrain from eating for 8 to 12 hours. The important thing to understand here is that this test gives information only about how your blood sugar behaves in a fasting state, not about how your body responds to food or what your blood sugar levels are like in between meals, when your body is trying to deal with the incoming energy from your food.

Remember that, as we move along the spectrum from optimal blood sugar control to insulin resistance, insulin is what stays elevated between meals, because the cells are resistant to it. The insulin in the blood is high long before the fasting blood sugar. In fact, the fasting plasma glucose number is the *last* number to change when we have blood sugar dysfunction, yet it is the first and sometimes the only number tested.

In the United States, the normal reference range for fasting plasma glucose is 70 to 99 mg/dL (3.9 to 5.5 mmol/L) and the prediabetes range is 100 to 125 mg/dL (5.6 to 6.9 mmol/L). The Canadian Diabetes Association lists a smaller range for prediabetes of 110 to 125 mg/dL (6.1 to 6.9 mmol/L). In both countries, diabetes is diagnosed at 126 mg/dL (7.0 mmol/L) or above.

DID YOU KNOW?

Impaired Fasting Glucose

When your fasting plasma glucose numbers are in the prediabetes range, you are considered to have impaired fasting glucose.

Context Is Everything

When a client asks whether something is healthy to eat or healthy to do, our answer is always "It depends." We're not trying to be evasive — it's important to know the context. Is quinoa healthy? That depends on your ability to handle carbohydrates. Red wine is good for you, isn't it? That depends on your ability to detoxify alcohol (the state of your liver), what else you have had to eat and whether you are driving (okay, this one pertains to everyone: don't drink and drive).

This concept applies to blood sugar testing, too. The test results need to be examined within the context of your life, not just based on a chart of numbers from the government or a health organization. Measuring appropriately and understanding someone's whole blood sugar picture is like putting the pieces of a puzzle together. Having more than one test result helps us see the emerging picture of that puzzle: context is everything.

One more note about context. We need to look at the following tests in the context of modern medicine, the primary focus of which is identifying and treating disease, and not as much on promoting optimal health. In the lab blood tests we are all familiar with, there is a column called the normal reference range, which is where we think we want to be. The trouble is, we may be confusing "normal" with healthy. We believe that if we are in the normal range, we don't have a problem and are therefore healthy. Revisiting the North American diabetes and prediabetes statistics will tell you in a minute that "normal" is increasingly unhealthy. Your blood sugar may not be healthy even if the test says it is normal.

In the test descriptions in this section, we'll look at the current normal reference ranges for various blood sugar tests, but we're also going to examine the levels at which dysfunction of various systems in the body starts to happen. This will help us determine what the numbers might look like for optimal blood sugar health.

Hemoglobin A1c

The hemoglobin A1c (HbA1c) test has typically been used by doctors for people who have already been diagnosed with diabetes to track their blood sugar over time, and was formally accepted by the American Diabetes Association in 2010 as a diagnostic test. It is now increasingly being used before a diagnosis of diabetes in conjunction with the fasting plasma glucose test to get a better picture of someone's blood sugar story. This test is not a fasting test and can be done at any time of day, before or after eating.

The hemoglobin A1c test does not measure the concentration of sugar in your blood at a specific moment in time, like the fasting plasma glucose test. Instead, it measures glycated hemoglobin, the amount of the hemoglobin protein in your red blood cells that has glucose permanently stuck to it. As the average amount of glucose in the blood increases, so too does the amount of glycated hemoglobin. Since red blood cells have a lifespan of about 3 months, the idea is that the HbA1c test can be used to reflect the average blood glucose level over that time. In practice, however, approximately 50% of the value comes from the last 30 days, so the reading is weighted more heavily to the most recent month.

The HbA1c is expressed as a percentage because it reflects the percentage of red blood cells that have glucose bonded to them. The normal reference range for HbA1c is 4.0% to 5.6% in the United States and 4.0% to 5.9% in Canada. The American Diabetes Association lists the prediabetes range at 5.7% to 6.4%, while the Canadian Diabetes Association lists it at 6.0% to 6.4%. People with diabetes have HbA1cs ranging from 6.5% to as high as 15%.

Oral Glucose Tolerance Test

The oral glucose tolerance test (OGTT) is somewhat artificial because it doesn't measure how you respond to food. Instead, it measures how blood sugar responds after you consume a huge dose of pure glucose. Glucose doesn't need to be digested like food does, so it goes directly into the bloodstream. As a result, the OGTT causes intense blood sugar swings that can be more severe than those you would experience after eating the same amount of carbohydrate in the form of food.

Before the test, you fast for 8 hours and then have the first sample of blood taken to determine your fasting blood glucose. You are then asked to drink a mixture containing 75 grams of glucose. After this, more blood samples are taken at regular intervals, usually at 1 and 2 hours after drinking the glucose.

When the blood sugar reading at 2 hours is higher than or equal to 200 mg/dL (11.1 mmol/L), diabetes is diagnosed. If the reading is between 140 and 199 mg/dL (7.8 and 11.0 mmol/L), prediabetes is diagnosed. People whose blood glucose is 139 mg/dL (7.7 mmol/L) or lower at 2 hours after drinking the glucose are considered normal, although there is no functional difference between what is happening in the body of the "normal" person at 139 mg/dL and the "prediabetic" at 140 mg/dL, or between the "prediabetic" at 199 mg/dL and the "diabetic" at 200 mg/dL.

Blood Sugar Tests

Test	Normal	Prediabetes	Diabetes
FPG	ADA: 70–99 mg/dL (3.9–5.5 mmol/L) CDA: ≤109 mg/dL (6.0 mmol/L)	*Impaired Fasting Glucose* ADA: 100–125 mg/dL (5.6–6.9 mmol/L) CDA: 110–125 mg/dL (6.1–6.9 mmol/L)	≥126 mg/dL (7.0 mmol/L)
HbA1c	ADA: 4.0%–5.6% CDA: 4.0%–5.9%	ADA: 5.7%–6.4% CDA: 6.0%–6.4%	≥6.5%
OGTT	≤139 mg/dL (7.7 mmol/L)	*Impaired Glucose Tolerance* 140–199 mg/dL (7.8–11.0 mmol/L)	≥200 mg/dL (11.1 mmol/L)

Fasting Insulin

Fasting insulin is a test most people don't have done. A low level of insulin, our basal insulin, is always circulating, so our fasting insulin should never be 0, as it might be in a person with untreated type 1 diabetes. Chronically elevated insulin is a marker of metabolic dysfunction and a sure sign that you are moving along the continuum from normal blood sugar to insulin resistance to type 2 diabetes. Knowing your insulin number is like having another piece of your blood sugar puzzle.

In prediabetes it's possible to have significantly elevated levels of insulin and a completely normal fasting blood sugar — another reason fasting blood glucose is not a good measure of your blood sugar status. In this situation, your pancreas is pumping out high levels of insulin to keep glucose moving into the cells and out of the bloodstream, in order to protect the lining of the arteries, neurons and other tissues from the toxic effect of too much blood sugar. Elevated insulin levels are a definite sign of insulin resistance.

An optimal fasting insulin number is not mentioned by either the American Diabetes Association or the Canadian Diabetes Association; however, Stephan Guyenet, a neurobiologist and obesity researcher at the University of Washington, says that elevated fasting insulin is a hallmark of metabolic syndrome: "The average insulin level in the U.S., according to the NHANES III survey, is 8.8 mIU/mL for men and 8.4 mIU/mL for women. Given the degree of metabolic dysfunction in this country, I think it's safe

> Knowing your insulin number is like having another piece of your blood sugar puzzle.

Q *What is the difference between subcutaneous fat and visceral fat?*

A Excess insulin promotes weight gain by causing fat storage, specifically around the belly. The more often insulin levels rise, and the longer they remain high, the more excess belly fat we accumulate. Subcutaneous fat is the fat just beneath the skin, the kind you can see and pinch. Visceral fat, on the other hand, is the deep fat stored in the abdominal cavity around our internal organs. We do need a bit of visceral fat to cushion our organs, but storing more than we need is associated with an increased risk of insulin resistance, type 2 diabetes, heart disease and dementia.

Visceral fat is "active" fat that produces abnormally high levels of inflammatory hormones and chemical compounds that both ignite and promote inflammation within the fat itself, the nearby liver and throughout the entire body. At the same time, the inflammatory cytokines interfere with other hormones that regulate appetite, weight, mood and brain function. It becomes a nasty, vicious cycle.

There is no good way to determine how much of our belly fat is subcutaneous and how much is visceral except by CT scan, which is expensive and unnecessary. A good indicator is to measure the widest part of your belly. A big belly is not healthy. Women with a waist circumference of more than 35 inches (88 cm) and men with a waist circumference of more than 40 inches (100 cm) are at increased risk for heart disease, stroke, lipid problems, type 2 diabetes, cancer and dementia.

to say that the ideal level of fasting insulin is probably below 8.4 mIU/mL." Dr. Mark Hyman, bestselling author of *The Blood Sugar Solution*, believes a healthy fasting insulin should be below 5.0 mIU/mL (35.0 pmol/L).

Blood Sugar and Disease Risk

Many of us believe that if we get or keep our blood sugar numbers below the "diabetes range," we will be safe from the health problems associated with diabetes. Unfortunately, that isn't the case, as indicated by research published in *Diabetes Care* in 2003. The findings showed that by the time a diagnosis of diabetes was given, almost half of those diagnosed already had medical conditions, such as retinopathy and neuropathy, that are caused by having had high blood sugar for many years.

Let's have a closer look at some of the diseases associated with type 2 diabetes, and at when damage actually starts.

> Many of us believe that if we get or keep our blood sugar numbers below the "diabetes range," we will be safe from the health problems associated with diabetes. Unfortunately, that isn't the case.

Neuropathy

Exposure to high blood glucose levels over an extended period of time causes damage to the nerves in many parts of the body. The most common symptoms are noticed in the feet, including a burning sensation, tingling, throbbing, sharp pains and ultimately numbness. Although the nerves in the feet are what we are most aware of, it is likely that other nerves in the body are also affected, leading to problems with digestion, body temperature, sexual function and heart function.

Because neuropathy is seen as a long-term complication, we don't typically think of it as a problem in the early part of the blood sugar dysfunction continuum. However, a number of studies have shown that the prevalence of neuropathy rises significantly in those with blood sugar over 140 mg/dL (7.8 mmol/L) at 2 hours after a glucose tolerance test. This is early in the prediabetic range of our continuum, not over at the diabetic end.

Retinopathy

The retina is the light-sensitive layer at the back of the inner eye that converts the images coming through the lens into signals that are then carried by the optic nerve to the brain. Elevated blood sugar damages the tiny blood vessels in the retina, causing them to bleed or leak fluid, which distorts vision.

It had long been thought that diabetic retinopathy didn't develop until you'd had diabetes for a long time and your blood sugar levels on the oral glucose tolerance test went over 200 mg/dL (11.1 mmol/L). It was for this reason that the American Diabetes Association chose the 200 mg/dL cutoff as the blood sugar number used to actually diagnose diabetes. It appears that this number is also too high. In the Diabetes Prevention Program, a major multicenter research study in the United States with 3,234 participants, diabetic retinopathy was detected in 7.6% of those classified with prediabetes and almost 13% of those with early type 2 diabetes.

Another study, the French DESIR study, which followed people diagnosed with prediabetes, found after 10 years of tracking the participants that those with retinopathy had higher levels of fasting plasma glucose (130 mg/dL vs. 106 mg/dL) and higher HbA1c (6.4% vs. 5.7%) than they had when the study began.

We know that the longer a person has diabetes, the greater the risk of developing retinopathy, but these studies point to the fact that diabetic retinopathy can start in prediabetes, a fact many people who are early on the spectrum of blood sugar dysfunction are unaware of.

Cancer

Sugar feeds all the cells in our body, including cancer cells. This is not necessarily a cause-and-effect situation, but there are enough scientific studies to support the association between high blood glucose and increased cancer risk.

The Me-Can study (Metabolic syndrome and Cancer project) investigated this very association. The study followed 274,126 men and 275,818 women for at least 10 years. The researchers found that, overall, the higher the level of blood glucose, the higher the risk of both getting and dying from cancer. The data showed stronger associations for women than for men: with each additional 18 mg/dL (1.0 mmol/L) increase in blood glucose levels, the risk of getting cancer was increased by 5% for men and 11% for women.

Kidney Disease

Diabetes is the most common cause of kidney failure, accounting for almost 44% of new cases. High blood pressure comes in as the second primary cause, with 27% of new cases. Diabetic kidney disease takes many years to develop, but even when diabetes is "well controlled" it can lead to chronic kidney disease and then to kidney failure, where either dialysis or transplant is required.

At first, people who are developing kidney disease will have small amounts of the blood protein albumin leaking into their urine from the kidneys. This first stage of microalbuminuria progresses to macroalbuminuria, or proteinuria, as the functioning of the kidneys starts to drop and more albumin leaks out.

As kidney damage develops, the body is unable to get rid of various types of waste products, and blood pressure starts to rise. So high blood pressure becomes part of a vicious cycle as both a cause of and an effect of kidney disease.

Heart Disease

What improves the ratio of total cholesterol to HDL cholesterol? Reducing intake of dietary carbohydrates. Not reducing dietary fat, but reducing dietary carbohydrates.

Over the last few decades, most of us have been told and may have come to believe that high cholesterol is bad, low cholesterol is good and cholesterol levels predict heart attack risk. But it turns out that about 50% of people who have heart attacks have normal cholesterol.

The Framingham Heart Study was started in 1948 to identify the common factors or characteristics that contribute to cardiovascular disease. This study has now followed over three generations of participants. Analysis of data from this study shows that, for those who do have heart attacks and high cholesterol, it isn't LDL (low-density lipoprotein, or "bad") cholesterol or total cholesterol levels that predict heart attack; it is triglyceride levels and the ratio of total cholesterol to HDL (high-density lipoprotein, or "good") cholesterol. Guess what raises triglycerides? Dietary carbohydrates. And what improves the ratio of total cholesterol to HDL cholesterol? Reducing intake of dietary carbohydrates. Not reducing dietary fat, but reducing dietary carbohydrates.

Instead of looking only at cholesterol levels, we should also be looking at our HbA1c levels as a predictor of heart attack risk. A large study from England, called EPIC-Norfolk, found that in both men and women the relationship between

HbA1c and cardiovascular disease was continuous and significant in HbA1c concentrations between 5.0% and 6.9%. This relationship was independent of age, body mass index, waist-to-hip ratio, systolic blood pressure, serum cholesterol concentration, cigarette smoking and history of cardiovascular disease. In short, blood sugar levels alone predicted heart attack risk. The people with HbA1cs under 5.0% had the lowest rates of cardiovascular disease and death.

Research Spotlight

Blood Sugar and Carotid Artery Thickness

An insight into the relationship between heart attacks and blood sugar comes from a 2008 study published in *The Journal of Clinical Endocrinology & Metabolism*. For 5 years, the study followed a group of people who had type 2 diabetes and were measuring their blood sugar at home. The findings showed a direct correlation between how high their blood sugar rose after meals and the increase in thickness in the walls of their carotid arteries. Thickening carotid arterial walls indicates plaque buildup and represents an increased risk of heart attack.

Alzheimer's Disease and Age-Related Cognitive Decline

Alzheimer's disease is the most common form of dementia, and age is the greatest risk factor for Alzheimer's. An abnormal buildup of beta-amyloid and tau proteins between and within nerve cells in the brain is thought to play a key role in the loss of communication between neurons and the eventual death of brain cells. But beyond the trademark plaques and tangles, researchers are examining other factors that may play a role, including inflammatory, metabolic and vascular contributors.

The idea that Alzheimer's might be type 3 diabetes, or diabetes of the brain, has been around since 2005, when research was published in the *Journal of Alzheimer's Disease* showing that levels of both insulin and insulin receptors decline significantly in the brain in early Alzheimer's. The lead researcher, neuropathologist Suzanne de la Monte, suggested that many features of Alzheimer's appeared to be linked to abnormalities in insulin signaling within the brain. Multiple studies since then continue to strengthen the connection between diabetes and Alzheimer's disease.

Diabetes may also increase the risk of age-related cognitive decline. The Atherosclerosis Risk in Communities (ARIC) Study followed over 13,000 participants in the age range of 48 to 67 years for 20 years. The researchers found

DID YOU KNOW?

History of Alzheimer's

Dr. Alois Alzheimer first described what we now recognize as Alzheimer's disease in 1906, but it wasn't until the 1970s that researchers began to understand that the Alzheimer's type of dementia — then called senility — was not a normal part of aging.

that cognitive decline was 19% more severe in participants who had diabetes at the beginning of the study than in those who didn't. And people with blood sugar levels indicating prediabetes at the beginning of the study had greater cognitive decline than those with normal blood sugar levels.

Clinical trials have not yet demonstrated specifically that diabetes management will reduce the risk of cognitive decline or Alzheimer's, but let's not wait for these studies.

Non-Alcoholic Fatty Liver Disease

Non-alcoholic fatty liver disease (NAFLD) is characterized by an accumulation of fat in the liver that is not caused by alcohol use. The number of people affected by this condition is increasing alarmingly, and it is now the most common cause of chronic liver disease in both the United States and Canada. In the United States, studies report a 10% to 46% prevalence of the disease; however, that percentage increases to at least 70% in obese adults with type 2 diabetes.

The well-known causes of NAFLD include obesity, type 2 diabetes, dyslipidemia and insulin resistance. The precursor to these conditions is, of course, eating a diet high in sugar and refined grains, which switches on fat production (lipogenesis) in the liver.

In the first stage of NAFLD, triglycerides build up in the liver cells. As the fat accumulates, inflammation increases and NAFLD can progress to non-alcoholic steatohepatitis (NASH), a more serious condition that may cause fibrosis (scarring). As the fibrosis worsens, cirrhosis develops and the liver becomes irreversibly scarred, hardened and unable to function properly. A liver transplant is the only treatment available for severe liver cirrhosis.

The key to avoiding and reducing NAFLD is to stop eating sugar and refined grains — the usual suspects in unbalanced and dysfunctional blood sugar.

Keeping Track of Your Blood Sugar

What are we to make, then, of all this sobering information about blood sugar and disease risk? That blood sugar levels matter — a lot. High blood sugar has multiple effects, all over the body. And by high blood sugar, we mean anything that is farther along the spectrum than normal blood sugar values.

This is likely not the message you are used to hearing. And we know it's a tough message. Both the American Diabetes Association and Canadian Diabetes Association have recommended blood glucose targets for people with diabetes that they say will help you manage your diabetes and delay or prevent the complications of the disease. These are a HbA1c of 7.0% or less, a premeal blood sugar of 80 to 130 mg/dL (4.4 to 7.2 mmol/L) and a 2-hour postprandial (after eating) blood glucose of less than 180 mg/dL (10.0 mmol/L). We have just seen, however, that damage in various parts of the body begins at numbers lower than these.

If we are told it's okay to keep our blood sugars in the prediabetic range, we are being told it's okay to have early neuropathy or retinopathy, early kidney disease, the beginnings of heart disease and early dementia. Statistics show that almost 50% of those with prediabetes will go on to develop full-blown type 2 diabetes, so let's not get comfortable in the prediabetic range.

Now, before you panic or throw in the towel, thinking there's no way you can get your blood sugar levels low enough to prevent damage, remember what we said about context. Context is everything, and this applies to blood sugar numbers, too. We want to understand our numbers within the context of our own life and, more specifically, the food we eat. The best way to understand what happens to your blood sugar when you eat certain foods is to check your numbers with your own glucometer. When you do this, you will no longer have to wait for your doctor's appointment and blood test to know how you are doing. Plus, you'll learn the more important information about how you react to your food, not just what your blood sugar is like in the fasting state.

In chapter 4 we'll get into the ins and outs of using a glucometer, and in chapter 3 we'll discuss some factors other than food that affect our blood sugar numbers, but let's keep in mind that the most important factor for determining our blood sugar is what we put into our mouth.

> Statistics show that almost 50% of those with prediabetes will go on to develop full-blown type 2 diabetes, so let's not get comfortable in the prediabetic range.

CHAPTER 2
What Is Paleo?

We didn't have soda pop, cheese twists or candy bars in the Paleolithic era, and our bodies have not adapted to eating them now.

The term "paleo" refers to the Paleolithic era, a period in time that began about 2.5 million years ago and ended about 10,000 years ago when agriculture started to take hold. The Paleolithic era was the time of the cavemen: hunter-gatherers who ate the meat they hunted, the fish they caught and the green shoots, berries, roots, eggs and nuts they gathered as they roamed. The food they ate was diverse, nutrient-dense and most certainly unprocessed.

Archeologists and anthropologists who study the Stone Age suggest that, although the lifespan then was much shorter than it is today, it was accidents, violence and infection that killed our distant ancestors, rather than the chronic noncommunicable diseases that are the most common causes of mortality today and that are inextricably linked to our diet and lifestyle.

Why Paleo?

The rationale behind paleo eating is not to go blindly back 100,000 or 15,000 years to try to replicate the foods eaten by the caveman. It is, rather, a thesis that we are genetically adapted to the diet with which our Paleolithic forebears evolved, one of unprocessed whole foods, dense in nutrients and low in processed components and inflammation-provoking ingredients. The idea is that eating humankind's original diet optimizes our health.

Many of our modern foods are at odds with our ancient genetic makeup and lay the foundation for our modern diseases. The 10,000 years that agriculture has been around is just a blink of the eye in terms of the time it takes for genetic adaptation, which suggests we are not genetically suited to our processed, agriculture-based diet. According to Loren Cordain, who is considered the founder of the modern paleo movement, there is an evolutionary mismatch between what we eat now and what we should be eating. We didn't have soda pop, cheese twists or candy bars back then, and our bodies have not adapted to eating them now.

This doesn't mean we need to actually hunt and gather our own food (although some purists may think we should). What it does mean is that we should avoid refined, processed, nutrient-poor foods in favor of nutrient-dense whole foods.

The Diesel Fuel Analogy

Loren Cordain uses an analogy that is helpful when discussing the paleo approach. He likens the body to a car that is designed to run on gasoline. When we fill up the tank with gas, everything runs smoothly, but if we put diesel fuel in the tank, it's another story. The fuel injectors inject the diesel into the engine's cylinders, the spark plugs fire, but nothing happens after that. A gas engine works differently than a diesel engine. If you were to catch the fuel mistake early on, you would be able to fix it, but the longer diesel fuel sits in a car designed to run on gas, the more damage it does to the engine.

The same principle is true for our bodies. Our engines are designed to run on the plant and animal foods that we have eaten for millennia. Today's diet of processed cereal grains, refined sugars, industrial seed oils and other food-like products are like diesel fuel to our body's gas engines: they clog our metabolism, and the longer we continue to eat them, the more damage they do.

Dietary Diversity

You may point out that not all ancient hunter-gatherers ate the same thing; their diet depended on where in the world they had migrated. And indeed, when we look at examples of contemporary hunter-gatherers who follow a traditional diet and lifestyle, we see an incredible diversity in the types of food eaten.

The Inuit Diet

The Inuit from northern Canada, Greenland and Alaska eat fish, seal, caribou, walrus, whale and birds — a diet high in fat and protein, with up to 75% of their daily calories coming from fat. The rest of their food might be gathered from grasses, roots, berries and/or seaweed, depending on their location.

In the early 1920s, the anthropologist and arctic explorer Vilhjalmur Stefansson lived with and studied the Inuit. He noted that their low-carbohydrate diet had no adverse effects on their health and that they were able to get the nutrition they needed for robust health from their traditional winter diet. The positive effects of this diet on Stefansson's own health and his full recovery from typhoid during his time in the Arctic was documented in a 1926 edition of the *Journal of the American Medical Association*.

> When we look at examples of contemporary hunter-gatherers who follow a traditional diet and lifestyle, we see an incredible diversity in the types of food eaten.

The Indigenous Australian Diet

When Weston Price, a Cleveland dentist known as the "Isaac Newton of Nutrition," studied the diet of indigenous Australians in the 1930s, he found that it depended on whether they lived in the lush subtropical, coastal areas or the arid interior desert. Coastal groups had a diet higher in fish and seafood, while desert tribes hunted kangaroo, wallabies and small animals. Birds, insects and eggs rounded out the protein and fat component for both groups (although the game meat was incredibly lean), with tubers, fern roots, palm hearts, shoots, nuts, seeds, figs, berries and other fruit providing carbohydrates and fiber. According to Price, both groups experienced the same good health.

The Kitavan Diet

While studying the indigenous people of Kitava in 1989, Dr. Staffan Lindeberg found that the people of this island, off Papua New Guinea, did not have diabetes, hypertension, heart disease, obesity, strokes or dementia. Although the Kitavans are considered horticulturalists rather than true hunter-gatherers, until recently they were one of the last groups of people on earth still following a traditional diet similar to the diet of their ancestors. Their diet consisted exclusively of tubers and root vegetables, vegetables, tropical fruits, fish and coconuts.

Dr. Lindeberg estimated the diet to be very high in fiber, with a relatively low fat consumption of about 20%. Due to their high intake of coconut, however, the majority of the fat they did eat was saturated fat. But this saturated fat was mostly in the form of lauric acid, as opposed to palmitic acid, the predominant saturated fat in the standard North American diet.

The Kitavans were also found to have very low levels of insulin and leptin, hormones that regulate food intake and energy balance. Low levels of these hormones are associated with metabolic health and leanness.

The Macronutrients

The varied examples of traditional diets detailed above demonstrate that the human body can adapt to very different intake levels of the macronutrients: proteins, fats and carbohydrates. The body uses macronutrients for a variety of different functions, some of which provide structure and some of which provide energy for both immediate use and future use. Let's have a quick look at each macronutrient and how it works in the body.

The Power of Protein

Protein is the building block of all tissues in our body. When we eat and digest it, protein is broken down into its component parts — amino acids — which are then used by cells to repair DNA, grow new cells and make hemoglobin, hormones, enzymes, neurotransmitters and antibodies. Protein can also be converted by the body into glucose for fuel, if need be.

Most foods contain at least some protein. Animal sources, such as meat, fish, poultry, dairy and eggs, contain what are called complete proteins, meaning that all nine of the essential amino acids (see sidebar) are present in these foods. Plant sources, including grains, legumes, nuts, seeds, vegetables and even fruits, contain incomplete proteins, in that not all of the essential amino acids are present in each food. This is why vegans need to make sure they eat a good variety of plant foods to ensure they get all the essential amino acids in their diet.

Protein helps us feel full and satisfied. It also has a lower impact on our blood sugar than carbohydrate, as you can see in the diagram on page 32. After we eat protein, our blood sugar level rises more slowly than after we eat carbohydrates, and the level also peaks lower. When we have less of a blood sugar spike, we secrete less insulin, which can help reduce

in the diagram on page 32.

DID YOU KNOW?

Essential Amino Acids

We wouldn't survive without protein. In fact, there are a number of what are called essential amino acids, meaning that the body cannot synthesize them on its own and it is therefore *essential* that we get them in our diet. The nine essential amino acids are histidine, isoleucine, leucine, lysine, methionine, phenylalanine, threonine, tryptophan and valine.

Research Spotlight

Protein and Satiety

Protein affects our appetite and satisfies hunger far more effectively than either carbohydrates or fat. A study demonstrating this was conducted on healthy women in Stockholm, Sweden, who were each served a lunch with the same caloric value. The women ate either a high-protein casserole, where protein was 43% of the total calories, or a high-carbohydrate casserole, where carbohydrates were 69% of the total calories. At their next meal, 4 hours later, the women who had eaten the high-protein casserole ate 12% fewer calories than the women who had eaten the high-carbohydrate casserole, indicating that eating protein at one meal can affect our food choices at the next.

Another study, this time on men, was undertaken at the Rowett Research Institute in Aberdeen, Scotland. The men were fed a high-protein, high-fat or high-carbohydrate breakfast and then monitored for 24 hours. The high-protein breakfast was found to suppress hunger more over the full 24 hours than either the high-carbohydrate or the high-fat breakfasts.

the effects of insulin resistance. Slower and lower are good things when we're talking about blood sugar and insulin.

It seems, too, that ghrelin levels drop more after we eat protein than they do after we eat fat. Ghrelin is a hormone produced by the stomach and pancreas that is linked to hunger and our desire to eat. Making protein the foundation of each and every meal will reduce our hunger, keep us feeling satisfied longer and help control both blood sugar and insulin.

Fat: The Good, the Bad and the In-Between

There is a lot of confusion about fat. How many times have we been told that fat is bad for us and we need to cut back? This has been the overriding nutritional message of the last couple of decades — just look at the abundance of low-fat or fat-free food products on the grocery store shelves.

As with essential amino acids, there are essential fatty acids that we must get in our diet because the body can't make them on its own. Fat is needed to build cell membranes, absorb fat-soluble vitamins and form the myelin sheathes around our nerve fibers, among other important tasks. So fat is important; we just need to eat the right kinds.

In terms of the effect dietary fat has on blood sugar (and therefore insulin), as you can see in the diagram below, it has almost no effect.

> Fat is important; we just need to eat the right kinds.

Effects of the Macronutrients on Blood Sugar

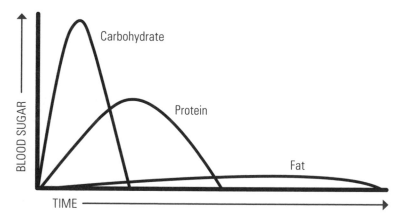

Trans Fats

The very worst kinds of fats for our health are industrial-made trans fats. These are created by pumping hydrogen molecules into liquid vegetable oil, thereby changing the chemical structure and causing the oil to become a solid fat.

FAQ

Q *Aren't there trans fats in meat and dairy products?*

A Technically this is true, as the digestion process in ruminant animals (cows, sheep, goats, buffalo, deer and elk) results in a small amount of natural trans fats in the meat and milk through the process of biohydrogenation. But don't confuse the man-made kind with the naturally occurring kind, which is called conjugated linoleic acid (CLA). They have a slightly different chemical structure that translates into much different effects in the human body. While research is ongoing, a number of scientific studies have demonstrated either no significant association or an actual inverse relationship between naturally occurring trans fats and heart disease, suggesting a beneficial health effect from naturally occurring trans fatty acids from animal products.

Trans fats increase the levels of low-density lipoprotein (LDL) cholesterol (often called "bad" cholesterol), especially the small, dense LDL particles that are damaging to our arteries. They also lower the levels of high-density lipoprotein (HDL) cholesterol ("good" cholesterol), create inflammation in the body and contribute to a redistribution of body fat to the belly area, all of which are linked to heart disease, stroke and diabetes.

Trans fats have been a mainstay in baked goods, crackers and snack foods for decades, because they don't spoil as easily as other fats and have a longer shelf life. As of 2006, laws in the United States and Canada have required trans fats to be listed in the Nutrition Facts panel of any packaged food. This would seem like a good thing for helping us to understand and identify what is in the foods we buy, so we can make the best decisions possible for our health. But there's a problem: thanks to convoluted labeling laws, a food may still contain a certain amount of trans fat without having to list it. In the United States, if the serving size of the food has less than 0.5 grams of trans fats, the label can say it has 0. In Canada, if the serving has less than 0.2 grams, the label can say 0. So truly the only way to know if there are trans fats in something is to read the ingredient list. Eating foods with even small amounts of trans fats can add up to a significant intake over time. If you see the words "hydrogenated vegetable oil," "partially hydrogenated vegetable oil" or "vegetable shortening" on a label, put it back on the shelf. (But a note of caution: just because something is free of trans fats doesn't mean it's healthy.)

DID YOU KNOW?

Identifying Trans Fats

You can identify trans fats in your foods by reading the ingredient list that is mandatory on any packaged food item. The terms "hydrogenated vegetable oil," "partially hydrogenated vegetable oil" and "vegetable shortening" mean that there are man-made trans fats in the food.

Saturated Fats and Cholesterol

The message to cut back on fat, especially saturated fats and cholesterol, because they're bad for us and promote heart disease really got its foothold in the 1950s and still haunts us today. Back then, Dr. Ancel Keys published a study known as the Seven Countries Study in which he linked coronary artery disease to the intake of dietary fat. Even if you have never heard of him, you know his theory, the diet–heart hypothesis: dietary saturated fat raises cholesterol in the blood, which causes heart attacks.

> There is not enough scientific evidence to conclude that saturated fat increases the risk of heart disease.

Despite some evidence to the contrary, Keys dug in hard and promoted any bit of data he could to support his theory. He ultimately won over the American Heart Association, the National Institutes of Health and, later, the U.S. government. For 50 years, this theory was vigorously promoted by the medical community, and we all came to believe that a diet high in saturated fat and cholesterol causes heart disease.

The evidence that contradicts this theory has always been there, but it's gaining speed. A meta-analysis (a statistical approach that combines the results of multiple studies) of 21 studies, published in *The American Journal of Clinical Nutrition* in 2010, evaluated the association of saturated fat with cardiovascular disease and determined that there was not enough scientific evidence to conclude that saturated fat increases the risk of heart disease. The meta-analysis also determined that replacing saturated fat with highly processed carbohydrates would likely increase heart disease.

A former president of the American College of Cardiology, Sylvan Lee Weinberg, voiced that concern a full 6 years earlier in an editorial in the *Journal of the American College of Cardiology*, where he stated, "A balanced appraisal of the diet–heart hypothesis must recognize the unintended and unanticipated role that the LF-HCarb [low-fat, high-carb] diet may well have played in the current epidemic of obesity, abnormal lipid patterns, type II diabetes and the metabolic syndrome. Defense of the LF-HCarb diet, because it conforms to current traditional dietary recommendations … is no longer tenable."

Monounsaturated and Polyunsaturated Fats

So-called good fats come mainly from fish and seafood, nuts, seeds and seed oils (vegetable oils). These foods contain both monounsaturated and polyunsaturated fats in varying proportions.

There are two main types of polyunsaturated fats, omega-3 fatty acids and omega-6 fatty acids, each with their own health benefits. Omega-3 fats are found predominantly in cold-water fish and seafood and, to a lesser extent, in grass-fed or pasture-raised meat. These fats help reduce blood pressure, lower triglycerides and raise HDL cholesterol, and may help with depression and other neurological conditions.

While omega-6 fats have also been linked to protection against heart disease, the ratio of omega-3 fats to omega-6 fats in the body is very important (see box, page 44). It's another area where we need to make some changes.

Carbohydrates

Remember from chapter 1 that dietary carbohydrates are the major contributors to increases in blood sugar and insulin. When we look at the breakdown of food categories eaten in North America today, it becomes apparent that the paleo way of eating is beneficial for anyone with diabetes, prediabetes, insulin resistance or blood sugar dysfunction. According to a report compiled by *National Geographic* entitled "What the World Eats," in North America today we get almost two-thirds (61%) of our calories from items not found in paleo-inspired eating. Of this 61%, sugar and sweeteners make up 16%, vegetable oils are 19%, grains account for 22%, and alcohol comes in at 4%. Compare that to the calories we get from meat (13%), fruit (3%) and, pulling up the rear, vegetables (2%). When we do the math, this means that we are getting almost half of our calories from carbohydrates.

Compare these figures to the anthropologic estimates that our average Paleolithic ancestor derived 30% to 40% of their calories from carbohydrates and between 35% and 65% from protein (meat and fish). Since they were not yet eating grains, all of their carbohydrates would have been from green plants, fruits, roots and nuts (as was seen in the more contemporary diets of the Kitavans and the indigenous Australians), rather than refined and processed grains. The Paleolithic carbohydrates would have contained a tremendous amount more fiber than our standard North American diet does, and would have been much more nutrient-dense.

Although there are essential amino acids (proteins) and essential fatty acids (fats), there are no essential carbohydrates. All of the carbohydrates we eat — whether simple or complex, low-glycemic or high-glycemic, nutritious or not — are eventually converted into glucose to provide energy. The more glucose we have in our blood, the higher our blood sugar. The higher our blood sugar, the greater the amount of insulin required to move it into the cells. The more often our insulin levels are high, the greater the chance that our pancreatic beta cells will lose function and be unable to produce enough insulin and/or that we will develop insulin resistance and our cells will fail to respond properly to insulin's message. In fact, we should think of insulin resistance and type 2 diabetes as states of carbohydrate intolerance.

> We should think of insulin resistance and type 2 diabetes as states of carbohydrate intolerance.

Data collected and analyzed from the National Health and Nutrition Examination Survey (NHANES 1998–2004) in the United States determined that insulin resistance is likely the most important contributor to coronary artery disease. So we need to produce less insulin. How do we do this? By reducing blood sugar. And how do we do that? First, by reducing the total amount of carbohydrates we eat; and second, by rethinking the type of carbohydrates we eat. The paleo approach to eating does both. We eliminate the big and fast carbohydrates, like sugar and grains, in favor of lower, slower carbohydrates that have more health benefits, like vegetables and fruit.

A look at the glycemic index and the glycemic load of foods will help explain what happens with this dietary shift.

Glycemic Index and Glycemic Load

You are probably familiar with the terms "simple carbohydrates" and "complex carbohydrates." This classification is based on the number of glucose molecules in a carbohydrate. The simplest carbohydrate is a monosaccharide, or single sugar. The two monosaccharides we are most familiar with are glucose and fructose. Then there are the disaccharides (two sugars), which are still classified as simple sugars. The best known disaccharide is sucrose, or white table sugar, which is made up of the two monosaccharides: glucose and fructose. Finally, we have the polysaccharides (many sugars), also called complex carbohydrates, which are composed of long chains of simple sugars. Complex carbohydrates are also known as fiber and starch.

In the past, we were advised to eat complex carbohydrates and avoid simple carbohydrates based on the assumption that the complex carbohydrates would result in smaller increases in blood sugar than the simple sugars. This was, however, too simplistic a thesis; our blood sugar response to complex carbohydrates varies considerably.

In the 1980s, researchers at the University of Toronto developed the glycemic index (GI). The Human Nutrition Unit, School of Molecular Bioscience at the University of Sydney, in Australia — the "home of the glycemic index" — defines the glycemic index as "a ranking of carbohydrates on a scale from 0 to 100 according to the extent to which they raise blood sugar levels after eating. Foods with a high GI are those which are rapidly digested and absorbed and result in marked fluctuations in blood sugar levels. Low-GI foods, by virtue of their slow digestion and absorption, produce gradual rises in blood sugar and insulin levels and have proven benefits for health. Low-GI diets have been shown to improve both glucose and lipid levels in people with diabetes (type 1 and type 2). They have benefits for weight control because they help control appetite and delay hunger. Low-GI diets also reduce insulin levels and insulin resistance."

When we eat high-GI foods, we have both higher and more rapid increases in our blood sugar levels. As we know, a fast increase in blood sugar is a powerful signal to the beta cells of the pancreas to secrete a lot of insulin. The high insulin levels can then cause a sharp decrease in blood sugar levels as the insulin moves glucose out of the bloodstream and into the cells, potentially causing hypoglycemia. It is when our blood sugar is falling quickly that we may feel shaky and irritable, with a craving for a fast hit of carbohydrates. This pattern of high-GI food, followed by a blood sugar crash, then more fast carbohydrates keeps us on the blood sugar roller coaster, taxes our pancreas and paves the way for insulin resistance.

Effects of High–GI and Low–GI Foods

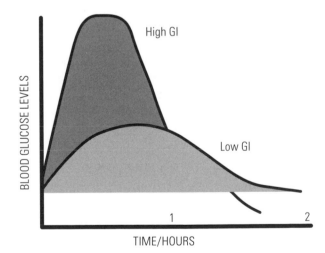

BLOOD GLUCOSE LEVELS

High GI

Low GI

1   2

TIME/HOURS

Eating low-GI foods, on the other hand, results in lower, slower increases in blood sugar and therefore lower insulin demands on the pancreatic beta cells.

It must be pointed out that the glycemic index tells us how foods react in someone with "normal" blood sugar 2 hours after they eat that food. If your blood sugar and insulin response are not normal, your blood sugar may rise

Glycemic Index versus Glycemic Load

	Glycemic index	Glycemic load
High	>70	>20
Medium	55–69	11–19
Low	54 or less	10 or less

higher than the GI indicates. The carbohydrates in a low-GI food will all still ultimately be digested into glucose, so in some of us the rise in blood sugar may be postponed but not eliminated.

The glycemic load (GL) is a newer way to assess the impact of dietary carbohydrates. The GI value of a food tells us how rapidly a particular carbohydrate turns into sugar, but it doesn't tell us how much carbohydrate per serving we are getting. The GL of a food takes into account both the quality and the quantity (portion size) of the carbohydrate. Let's look at a couple of examples.

Carrots have a high GI of 71. This is why a lot of people say carrots are high in sugar. But the GL of carrots is only 6, which is low. Because all GI measurements are based on 50 grams of available carbohydrate (total carbohydrate minus fiber) in the food being measured, there can be a huge variance in the actual amount of food the GI score represents. In the carrot example, you'd need about $1\frac{1}{2}$ pounds (750 g) to give you 50 grams of carbohydrates — that's why the GI is high and the GL is low. Most people don't eat that many carrots in one sitting.

Another example is watermelon. It has a high GI of 72, but a low GL of 7. The GI is based on 5 cups (1.25 L) of chopped watermelon, and the GL is based on the more modest serving size of 1 cup (250 mL). The low GL means that chopped watermelon doesn't contain too many carbohydrates because it is mostly water.

This may seem a bit confusing, but generally, foods with a lower GI and GL are more slowly broken down and their energy (glucose) is released more slowly into the bloodstream. That doesn't mean we need to know only the GI or GL of a food without considering anything else. Not all low-GI foods are good for you. For example, Peanut M&Ms have a low GI, but we don't recommend that you eat them. Your goal is still to eat nutrient-dense whole foods.

The GI and GL of Common Foods

Food	Serving size	GI per serving (with glucose as 100)	GL per serving
Grains			
Corn flakes cereal (Kellogg's)	1 cup (250 mL)	80	21
White bread	1 slice	71	11
White bagel	1 medium	69	24
Brown rice	1 cup (250 mL) cooked	66	21
White rice	1 cup (250 mL) cooked	72	30
Spaghetti	1 cup (250 mL) cooked	49	24
Fruits			
Apple	1 medium	39	6
Banana	1 medium	62	16
Blueberries	1 cup (250 mL)	53	5
Grapefruit	1/2 medium	25	3
Raisins	1 small box	64	28
Vegetables			
Avocado	1 medium	0	0
Broccoli	1 cup (250 mL)	0	0
Corn	1 cup (250 mL)	60	11
Mushrooms	1 cup (250 mL)	0	0
Russet potato, baked	1 small	111	33
Tomato	1 medium	38	1.5

The above chart of some common foods will help you better understand the GI and GL concepts. You will see that the foods included in the paleo approach to eating, as outlined in this book, are the ones with the least effect on blood sugar and insulin.

Nutrient Density

Our food supplies both nutrients and calories, which we can also call energy. All energy comes from the macronutrients — proteins, fats and carbohydrates. The micronutrients are the noncaloric vitamins, minerals, fiber and phytochemicals (plant chemicals). At present, we know that our bodies need about 40 different micronutrients for optimal function and good health, but nutritional science is expanding this list all the time. Less than adequate intake of any of these micronutrients means the body's functions are compromised, and we end up with dysfunction and ultimately disease.

Nutrient Synergism

Nutrients don't work alone in the body. These biologically active compounds are all interrelated in a complex system, and the more research is done, the more elaborate this system is revealed to be. When we take a supplement, like isolated vitamin C, we are taking in just a fragment of a web that has been separated from its other parts. It's just one piece of the larger puzzle; it isn't the whole picture. Compounds work together synergistically, and the benefit of fresh, whole foods is that they provide not only an abundance of individual nutrients but also the variety necessary for the optimal function of those nutrients.

An example was demonstrated by Cornell food scientist Dr. Rui Liu. He determined that while one medium apple contains only about 6 milligrams of vitamin C, a known antioxidant, it has the antioxidant power equivalent to 1,500 milligrams of vitamin C because of the synergistic action of all the phytonutrients it contains, including quercetin, procyanidins, catechins and epicatechins. It is the combination of phytochemicals in whole foods that is responsible for their health benefits.

In an article that appeared in the December 2004 issue of the *Journal of Nutrition*, Dr. Liu wrote: "The additive and synergistic effects of phytochemicals in fruits and vegetables are responsible for these potent antioxidant and anticancer activities and that the benefit of a diet rich in fruits and vegetables is attributed to the complex mixture of phytochemicals present in whole foods. This explains why no single antioxidant can replace the combination of natural phytochemicals in fruits and vegetables to achieve the health benefits. The evidence suggests that antioxidants or bioactive compounds are best acquired through whole-food consumption. We believe that a recommendation that consumers eat 5 to 10 servings of a wide variety of fruits and vegetables daily is an appropriate strategy for significantly reducing the risk of chronic diseases and to meet their nutrient requirements for optimum health."

The term "nutrient density" refers to the amount of nutrients in a food compared with the amount of energy it provides (nutrients versus calories). Naturally nutrient-dense foods have high levels of nutrients — vitamins, minerals, fiber and phytonutrients — compared with their calorie content. "Naturally" means the food is nutrient-dense as it is; nothing, such as fortification or enrichment, has been done to alter it.

Unfortunately, the current standard North American diet is calorie-dense and nutrient-poor. Industrial seed oils (vegetable oils) contribute 19% of the calories in a typical North American diet, while sugar and sweeteners add another 16%. Compare that to produce (fruits and vegetables), which supplies only 8% of our calories, and we can clearly see that our current diet is not providing the nutrients we need and is actually detrimental to our health.

Let's look at an example. One whole-grain, fruit-filled granola bar (which many of us might grab as a "healthy" snack) has the same number of calories as 2 cups (500 mL) of fresh strawberries. The strawberries, however, have more than twice as much magnesium, three times more fiber, seven times more potassium and a whopping 170 times more vitamin C. The most nutrient-dense foods are unprocessed whole foods — like those our Paleolithic ancestors ate.

> The most nutrient-dense foods are unprocessed whole foods — like those our Paleolithic ancestors ate.

Principles of the Modern Paleo Approach

The food we eat is the single most important influence on our health, especially in terms of blood sugar management. As such, the paleo approach provides us with a framework for diet as well as lifestyle. It is important to understand not only what is included in the diet, but also what is excluded, which may have even more of an impact on our blood sugar.

Interestingly, three categories of foods that weren't part of our ancestors' diet are the three categories from which we now get the majority of our calories: refined sugars and sweeteners, industrial seed oils and grains. This fact alone should alert us to the pitfalls of our modern standard North American diet and help us see the connection between what we put in our mouths and the state of our health. If we do nothing else in terms of eating paleo, eliminating these foods is the best step toward fixing blood sugar and insulin problems.

Avoid Refined Sugars and Sweeteners

In North America, sugar and sweeteners make up 16% of our daily caloric intake.

For our Paleolithic predecessors, sweetness meant calories, and that was always a good thing for the hunter-gatherers, who had to take advantage of whatever food they found, whenever they found it. The sweetness they encountered was part of a whole fruit or tuber, so it was always eaten with the accompanying fiber, minerals, vitamins and phytonutrients: it was nutrient-dense. With the exception of honey (which likely wasn't a daily occurrence), sugar was never eaten just as sugar. It wasn't added to their coffee, sprinkled on their oatmeal, added to their burger or eaten in condensed candy form, the way we eat it today.

Refined Sugar

Eating straight sugar will push up your blood sugar and insulin more than almost any other substance (except maybe refined grains). Yet in North America, sugar and sweeteners make up 16% of our daily caloric intake. In 2013, the pediatric endocrinologist Robert Lustig and his colleagues published research that examined sugar consumption and diabetes rates in 175 countries around the world. They found a strong link between sugar and type 2 diabetes. Here is what they had to say in the article abstract: "Duration and degree of sugar exposure correlated significantly with diabetes prevalence in a dose-dependent manner, while declines in sugar exposure correlated with significant subsequent declines in diabetes rates independently of other socioeconomic, dietary and obesity prevalence changes. Differences in sugar availability statistically explain variations in diabetes prevalence rates at a population level that are not explained by physical activity, overweight or obesity."

In other words, more sugar more often in the diet means more type 2 diabetes, and less sugar (no added sugar) means less type 2 diabetes. It's pretty clear-cut.

Artificial Sweeteners

Okay, but what about artificial sweeteners? Both the American Diabetes Association and the Canadian Diabetes Association consider daily intake of artificial sugars over a lifetime safe for people with diabetes. These nonnutritive sweeteners are noncaloric and don't contain any carbohydrates, so we think they can't possibly raise blood sugar.

One problem with sweeteners is that they are so much sweeter — up to hundreds of times sweeter — than regular

Research Spotlight

Artificial Sweeteners and Blood Sugar Dysfunction

In some animal studies, the sweet taste induced an insulin response in rats, but the human evidence is not nearly as clear-cut. A small study conducted by researchers at Washington University School of Medicine and published in 2013 by *Diabetes Care* looked at things from a different angle. The lead researcher is quoted as saying, "Our results indicate that this artificial sweetener [Splenda] is not inert — it does have an effect."

Subjects in the study were obese (BMIs of 42), but had not been diagnosed with diabetes. They were chosen specifically because artificial sweeteners are often recommended to help with weight loss. Each subject was given either water to drink or sucralose (Splenda) in an amount that mimicked a 12-ounce (341 mL) can of diet soda. They were then asked to drink 75 grams of glucose, and their blood was tested for their insulin and blood sugar response. Every participant was tested twice. Those who drank water followed by glucose in one visit drank sucralose followed by glucose in the next visit, 7 days later. When the participants drank sucralose before the glucose, their blood sugar peaked at a higher level than when they drank water first. Their insulin levels also rose about 20% higher when the sucralose came first.

These are important findings because, outside the lab in real life, people rarely consume only sweeteners, they have other sugars, too. People may use a sweetener in their coffee at breakfast while consuming sugar in their cereal or flavored yogurt. As the study demonstrated, the sweetener in the coffee may cause the blood sugar rise after the meal to peak higher than if sweetener had not been used. We know that higher blood sugar spikes promote more insulin release. This begins the downward spiral in which more insulin promotes more fat storage, inflammation, insulin resistance and progression of all the chronic diseases associated with blood sugar dysfunction.

table sugar. It is possible that these products change the way we taste food. Nonnutritive sweeteners are far more potent than table sugar. When we repeatedly eat sweet things, we train our flavor preferences. Overstimulation of our taste buds from frequent exposure to these intense sweeteners may reduce our tolerance for more bitter or complex tastes. In short, the more sweet we eat, the more we crave and expect it.

In addition, research suggests that artificial sweeteners may prevent us from associating sweetness with calories, which brings us back to our Paleolithic ancestors. We are hardwired to crave sweetness because it means calories, which, in the Paleolithic era, meant survival. But when the sweet taste has been engineered to eliminate calories, the body's natural mechanisms are short-circuited, with negative consequences.

DID YOU KNOW?

Natural Sugars

In their natural form, sugar-containing foods such as whole fruits are nutrient-dense, high in fiber and low in glycemic load.

The Omega-3 to Omega-6 Ratio

All vegetable oils contain a high proportion of polyunsaturated fatty acids (PUFAs), including a large amount of omega-6 fatty acids. Some omega-6 fat in our diet is essential, just not too much — and we need it in the proper ratio with another essential fat, omega-3.

It is estimated that the ratio of omega-3 fats to omega-6 fats in paleo diets was about 1:2. In our standard North American diet, this ratio is now somewhere between 1:10 and 1:20. Soybean oil consumption in the United States increased over a thousandfold between 1909 and 1999, and people now consume more than two and a half times more vegetable oil per day than they did 50 years ago. At the same time, our consumption of omega-3 fats has declined.

The problem is that these two fats compete for the same enzymes in the body, so if we are eating more omega-6s than omega-3s, fewer enzymes are available for the conversion of the omega-3s into beneficial anti-inflammatory compounds. The imbalance of these two important fats contributes to the development of systemic inflammation in the body, which, in turn, contributes to the progression of chronic disease, including insulin resistance and diabetes.

Avoid Industrial Seed Oils

In our haste to eliminate saturated fat from our diets following the work of Ancel Keys in the 1950s and the diet–heart hypothesis, the era of polyunsaturated vegetable oils and low fat was born (and we know where that got us).

Industrial seed oils, or vegetable oils, are made from plants such as soybean, corn, cotton, safflower and sunflower. As they are processed, these oils are bleached, defoamed and deodorized to make them blend more easily from a flavor perspective with virtually any food product.

As it does with whole grains, the refining process also removes a lot of the naturally occurring antioxidants in the oils, which would have protected them from becoming oxidized (rancid). These unsaturated oils are unstable when exposed to air, light and heat, and they react with oxygen to form free radicals. Again, balance is critical. Some free radicals help in biological functions, but too many can damage our cells and our DNA. When we cook with these oils and expose them to even more heat, light and air, we create even more free radicals. There is growing evidence that our increased use of these oils plays a significant role in the rise of inflammation-related conditions, including insulin resistance, prediabetes and type 2 diabetes.

DID YOU KNOW?

Industrial Seed Oils

Vegetable oils are called industrial seed oils because over time they have been used in the preparation and manufacturing of products ranging from soaps and lubricants to cosmetics and biodiesel fuel.

Avoid Grains — Even Whole Grains

Until about 10,000 years ago, we didn't eat grains. Now, grain products are the foundation of the U.S. MyPlate and Canada's Food Guide, with six to eight servings recommended per day.

From a blood sugar perspective, we must remember that grains are almost all carbohydrate and that these carbohydrates get digested into glucose molecules (very quickly when they have been refined). The glucose then raises our blood sugar, which forces our insulin up, which helps us store all that glucose from all those grain servings as, you guessed it, fat.

But what about whole grains? We are told they are healthy and are encouraged to eat more of them because they contain all sorts of fiber and other nutrients. The problem is that the official definition of "whole grain" refers to any mixture of bran, endosperm and germ in the proportions generally expected to be found in an intact grain. However, the grains are usually processed so that the three parts are separated and ground before being added back to foods. To make matters worse, in the United States, for a food product to be considered whole grain, it need only contain 51% whole grains by weight. This is a far cry from an actual intact grain, fresh from harvest in the field, which is what we are encouraged to think of when we hear "whole grain."

Even if we are talking about a real whole grain, once that grain kernel has been milled into flour, any blood sugar benefits that may have existed are lost. In 2008, a study was published in the journal *Diabetes Research and Clinical Practice* demonstrating just this. The study participants were all people with type 2 diabetes. They were fed whole wheat bread, wheat bran bread, rye bread or white bread, and both their blood glucose and insulin levels were measured

FAQ

Q *What foods are included in the grains category?*

A Grains are the seeds of plants in the grass family, including wheat, oats, barley, rye, millet, corn (maize), rice, wild rice, teff, triticale, spelt and Kamut. Quinoa, amaranth and buckwheat are considered pseudo-grains, but they act like grains in the body, so they are best included here. Grains have three parts: the outer fibrous bran, which protects the seeds; the germ, which contains the plant's reproductive information; and the endosperm, which is the concentrated starchy part. Most of our grains are refined, which means the germ and the bran have been removed, along with the minerals, vitamins, fats and fiber they contain.

before and at 2 hours after eating. No significant difference was found in either glycemic or insulinemic effects among the four types of bread. Let's not continue to be misled by "healthy whole grain" claims.

Evidence to Support Paleo for Diabetes

> Compared to the diabetes diet, the paleo diet resulted in lower mean levels of hemoglobin A1c, triglycerides, diastolic blood pressure, weight, body mass index (BMI) and waist circumference, and higher mean HDL cholesterol.

One of the early studies demonstrating the benefits of a modern paleo diet, done in 1984, was conducted with Australian Aboriginals who had become diabetic as a result of urbanization. The study participants were tested before and after living for 7 weeks as hunter-gatherers, as had been their traditional way before urbanization. The testing showed a large reduction of triglycerides and an improvement in both fasting glucose and postprandial (after-meal) glucose clearance from the blood. In addition, fasting glucose declined and the insulin response to glucose fell. Essentially, every marker of blood sugar dysfunction improved.

In a 2009 randomized crossover study, type 2 diabetic participants were placed on a paleo diet based on lean meat, fish, fruit, vegetables, root vegetables, eggs and nuts for 3 months. Following that phase and for another 3 months, the same participants followed the American Diabetes Association guidelines of evenly distributed meals with increased vegetables, root vegetables, fiber, whole-grain bread and other cereal products, fruits and berries, but decreased total fat, especially saturated fat. Compared to the diabetes diet, the paleo diet resulted in lower mean levels of hemoglobin A1c, triglycerides, diastolic blood pressure, weight, body mass index (BMI) and waist circumference, and higher mean HDL cholesterol. It doesn't get much clearer than that: this is no mere fad or gimmicky diet.

The Paleo Template

In this book, we approach the paleo diet as a template or framework on which to build a way of eating that controls blood sugar and insulin responses, reduces inflammation and allows the body to use food as fuel rather than storing it in inflammatory belly fat. There is considerable anecdotal evidence about paleo-inspired eating, but ultimately the best test subject is you. Our goal is to teach you the principles that will help you regulate blood sugar and insulin and thereby have a direct effect on the potentially devastating long-term consequences of blood sugar dysfunction. Even though the paleo diet can normalize things pretty quickly, it's a lifelong way of eating that optimizes both metabolism and weight.

CHAPTER 3

Beyond Food — Other Things to Consider

As the basketball coach John Wooden said, repetition is the key to learning. So, for the sake of repetition: The food we eat is the single most important influence on our health. With each bite, we have the opportunity to move in the direction of better health or in the direction of disease — it is our choice.

But as foundational as food is, it is not the only factor that affects our health. An abundance of research demonstrates that how we sleep, the chemicals we encounter, the way we move, the type of bacteria we have in our intestines and the stress we feel all affect our appetite hormones, how we process carbohydrates and, ultimately, our blood sugar and insulin levels. We must pay attention to these factors, too.

Get Enough Sleep

When our lives are busy and more demands are made on our time, sleep is often the first thing to go. We sacrifice it for work deadlines, laundry, our favorite TV program or a chance to finally have some "me" time. Then there is the "I'll sleep when I am dead" attitude, whose proponents pride themselves on how little sleep they get or think they need; these people see tiredness as a badge of honor and see sleep as a waste of time. But nothing could be further from the truth. Getting enough high-quality sleep is critically important for achieving and maintaining good health.

> Getting enough high-quality sleep is critically important for achieving and maintaining good health.

Sleep is actually a very active time inside the body, when our biological functions are focused on growth and repair. Lack of sleep not only makes us irritable, groggy and tired, but also wreaks havoc with our immune system, our learning and memory, the clearance of toxins from our brains and our insulin sensitivity.

Decades of research have shown us that sleeping between 7 and 9 hours per night has the best health benefits. So how are we doing with this? Not too well, apparently. Thirty-five percent of Americans report getting less than 7 hours of sleep per night, 63% say their sleep needs are not being met during a typical week, and 38% report unintentionally falling asleep during the day.

Compare that to 50 years ago, when just 2% of us averaged less than 6 hours of sleep per night. What's going on? Not only do we have the problem of busyness, mentioned earlier, but we are also using more and more electronic devices for both work and play — and more and more at night. Binge-watching our favorite shows, checking email or texting in bed may seem harmless enough — we are relaxing, after all — but the sleep disruption caused by those LED devices is significant and potentially harmful to our health.

The Harmful Effects of Artificial Light

Until we had artificial light, the sun, of course, was our major source of light. Essentially, we were awake when the sun was up and asleep when the sun was down. The sun gives off blue light as part of the visible light spectrum that, during the day, boosts alertness, heightens reaction times and elevates mood, but that seems to be disruptive at night, when it affects our circadian rhythm.

Dozens of studies have linked working the night shift and exposure to light at night to several types of cancer, including breast and prostate cancer. The mechanism is not entirely understood, but we do know that exposure to light at night suppresses the secretion of melatonin, a powerful hormone that influences our circadian rhythm and our sleep-wake cycles as well as many other biological functions, including decreasing cortisol and protecting us from the harmful effects of stress.

Blue light seems to be the worst for suppressing melatonin. Our TVs, computers, laptops, tablets and smartphones emit strong blue light waves. So our favorite devices (which we are now taking to bed with us) are decreasing our sleep duration and disrupting our sleep patterns for two reasons: the blue light they emit and the fact that we're using them well into the night, when we should be asleep.

So what are we to do? Let's start by seriously evaluating our evening activities. If we determine that we absolutely must use electronic devices throughout the evening and into the night, there are apps available that adapt the color temperature of the computer's display to the time of day in our particular time zone, thereby reducing the stimulating effects of blue light. There are also amber-colored glasses

> The sleep disruption caused by LED devices is significant and potentially harmful to our health.

Research Spotlight

The Effects of Too Little Sleep

Early evidence for the effects of short sleep duration came from a series of studies of partial sleep deprivation conducted in 1999 at the University of Chicago. The researchers found that restricting sleep to 4 hours per night for 6 nights resulted in a 40% decrease in the participants' ability to clear glucose from the blood. This effect was reversed with sleep recovery.

A restriction to 4 hours of sleep may be more severe than what happens in real life, but a 2009 study published in *The Journal of Clinical Endocrinology & Metabolism* examined the effects of sleeping 5.5 hours per night for 14 nights — a pattern closer to that experienced by many people in everyday life. These results supported the earlier study and showed a decrease in glucose tolerance due to decreased insulin sensitivity — hallmarks of insulin resistance.

Another study suggests that just one night of being deprived of 2 hours of sleep can result in unhealthy changes in appetite that, in turn, affect insulin sensitivity and metabolism. Lack of sleep seems to increase ghrelin, our appetite-stimulating hormone, and decrease leptin, our satiety and appetite-curbing hormone, which tells us we have had enough to eat. Unsurprisingly, this increases our hunger levels and steers us toward more high-sugar foods and refined carbohydrates for energy.

Outside the lab, epidemiological studies from different geographical areas have consistently indicated that short sleep and poor sleep are associated with an increased risk of type 2 diabetes. One of the largest and longest studies, the Nurses' Health Study, followed 70,000 nondiabetic women for 10 years. Compared to the nurses who slept 7 to 8 hours per 24-hour period, those who slept 5 hours or less had a higher rate of diabetes even after controlling for things that can also affect blood sugar like body mass index, shift work, high blood pressure, exercise and depression.

or goggles available that decrease the effects of blue light exposure from both electronic devices and bright room lighting.

Prioritizing Sleep

Over the long term, sleep deprivation increases our risk for obesity and type 2 diabetes, so we need to prioritize sleep. We can think of sleep loss as a chronic stressor. The body is constantly working to maintain a state of internal balance, or homeostasis, where it functions optimally. Sleep deprivation overloads the body's capacity to maintain this internal balance, resulting in changes within the body that lead to disease. This is why getting a good night's sleep is so crucial to maintaining or recovering health.

DID YOU KNOW?

Increased Sensitivity

The less sunlight we get during the day, the more sensitive we become to the negative effects of light at night.

Avoid Toxins

There's no doubt about it: we live in a chemical world. Every year, chemicals are manufactured that increase the toxic load in our environment. These chemicals end up in our air, food and water — and then in our bodies.

An early comprehensive look at the chemical burden we carry, published in 2002, was led by the Mount Sinai School of Medicine in New York, in collaboration with the Environmental Working Group. Researchers found 167 chemicals, pollutants and pesticides in the blood and urine of the study participants, none of whom worked with chemicals at their jobs.

A 2007 study by the Centers for Disease Control and Prevention found that 92% of the 2,500 subjects studied had detectable amounts of bisphenol A in their urine. And a 2013 report by Environmental Defence Canada described finding a total of 137 chemicals in the umbilical cord blood of a sampling of newborn babies.

This is the reality of the human body burden.

> The impact of our exposure to plastics is difficult to quantify because the effects are not easy to isolate.

Bisphenol A and Phthalates

Two chemicals used in plastics that have received a lot of attention over the past decade are bisphenol A (BPA) and phthalates. BPA is used in the production of polycarbonate plastics and epoxy resins, and is found in water bottles, the lining of metal food cans and some dental sealants. Phthalates are used to make plastics more flexible and harder to break and as solvents for other materials. They're found in everything from automotive plastics to children's toys, medical tubing, soaps, shampoos and nail polishes. Both are persistent organic pollutants (POPs) in that they are essentially nonbiodegradable compounds that stick around for a very, very long time. And both are the topic of scientific and public debate — figuring out how toxic plastics are to people at current levels of exposure is complex.

Chemicals like BPA pose a challenge for conventional toxicology because the way these hormone-mimicking chemicals work is different from that of typical toxins. They work by binding to receptors on our cells that the body's natural hormones use to regulate essentially all of our physiological functions. When these chemicals bind, they send different messages to the cells. The impact of our exposure to plastics is difficult to quantify because the effects are not easy to isolate. The time between exposure and the development of disease may be years or even decades. We may not know what chemicals we have been exposed to, and we are not exposed to chemicals in isolation.

With more scientific evidence emerging, what we do know is that the chemicals in our environment play a role in altering our biological processes.

> **DID YOU KNOW?**
>
> **Endocrine Disruptors**
>
> Bisphenol A (BPA) and phthalates are what are called endocrine disruptors, meaning they affect the way certain hormones work in the body.

Glyphosate

In February 2016, there was news that the U.S. Food and Drug Administration (FDA), the country's main food safety regulator, would start testing certain foods for the herbicide glyphosate. Glyphosate is the active ingredient in Roundup, which was patented by Monsanto in the 1970s. It is the most widely used herbicide in the world and was declared in 2015 by the World Health Organization to be a probable human carcinogen.

At the time of writing, there were no details about the

testing plans, but Lauren Sucher, an FDA spokeswoman, said the agency was considering measuring glyphosate in soybeans, corn, milk and eggs, among other potential foods.

The Toxin Puzzle

For many years, efforts to understand how environmental toxins affect human health focused on determining whether or not a substance produced cancer in lab animals. These efforts provided much insight into detoxification, metabolism and cell biology, but they didn't answer the questions about the capacity of these chemicals to alter the function of our biological systems or how they contribute to chronic illness. This is the puzzle that chemists, biologists, geneticists and toxicologists are endeavoring to piece together.

There is mounting evidence that environmental toxins interfere with glucose and cholesterol metabolism and induce insulin resistance through multiple mechanisms, including inflammation, oxidative stress, damage to the mitochondria, altered thyroid function and the impairment of our central appetite regulation. These chemicals are now even being called obesogenic, meaning that they cause obesity.

Reduce Your Exposure to Chemical Toxins

Although it is virtually impossible to steer clear of all potentially hazardous chemicals, we can limit and minimize our exposure by keeping some key principles in mind.

- Eat whole foods as close as possible to the way they were grown. This is the preeminent principle of this book. Processed and packaged foods — particularly cans — are a common source of BPA and phthalates. Choose grass-fed and pasture-raised animals, and follow the recommendations in this book about which organic fruits and vegetables to buy to reduce your pesticide load.
- Purchase and store your food and beverages in glass rather than plastic. There are lots of glass storage containers with easy-snap lids, so it's time to get rid of all the plastic stuff. If you microwave your food (we don't recommend it), heat tends to increase the release of chemicals from plastic, so be sure to use glass containers in the microwave. Unfortunately, even "BPA-free" plastics will likely leach other endocrine-disrupting chemicals that may be just as bad.
- Choose toys made from natural materials to avoid the phthalates and BPA found in plastic toys, especially for toys your child will be chewing!
- Phthalates are often used to help products hold their scent longer, so switch to fragrance-free toiletries and cosmetics, and always read the ingredients list.

Get Moving

If asked how much exercise we should be getting, we could likely all answer that it should be about 30 minutes per day of moderate to vigorous physical activity, for a total of at least 150 minutes per week, perhaps with some stretching and resistance training thrown in.

Increasing participation in leisure-time physical activity for both adult and child populations is a central tenet in government policy and health agency strategies for preventing major chronic diseases such as type 2 diabetes, cardiovascular disease and obesity. There are mass-media campaigns, public service announcements and community programs all focused on encouraging us to be more active. And some of us are. We go to the gym to lift weights or go to a spin class; we may even join a boot camp for a few weeks.

Evidence shows, however, that even if we do meet the current recommendations of 30 minutes of exercise per day (or more), our time spent sitting is turning out to be an important risk factor for the development of chronic disease.

The Risks of Being Sedentary

Many studies that examine levels of physical activity have the participants self-report their activity levels, and these levels are often over-reported, leading to inaccurate data. To get around this, a 2009 Australian study published in *Diabetes Care* measured physical activity by an accelerometer, a device worn during waking hours for 7 consecutive days that summarized sedentary time (primarily prolonged sitting), light physical activity (predominantly standing, with some walking) and moderate-to-vigorous activity. The researchers determined that, on average, adults spend more than half their waking time sitting. The remainder of the time is spent in light activity and only about 4% to 5% of the day is spent in moderate-to-vigorous activity.

During the study a glucose tolerance test was used to determine 2-hour blood sugar levels. The results showed that more sedentary time resulted in higher blood sugar after the glucose tolerance test, but that both light and moderate-to-vigorous activities were associated with lower blood sugar levels.

A meta-analysis of 47 studies, released in early 2015 in the *Annals of Internal Medicine*, looked at the health effects of sedentary behavior. Over the course of all the studies,

> **DID YOU KNOW?**
>
> **Metabolic Changes**
> When we are standing or walking, our leg muscles need to work to keep us upright and balanced, so we burn more calories than when we are sitting. But the effects of sitting go beyond fewer calories burned. Sedentary muscles release lower amounts of lipoprotein lipase, which is important for eliminating certain fats from the bloodstream. Reduced levels of lipoprotein lipase are associated with higher triglyceride levels.

> Time spent sitting is an important risk factor for the development of chronic disease.

people who sat for prolonged periods of time — even if they exercised regularly — had a higher risk of dying from all causes. The negative effects were even more pronounced in people who did little or no exercise.

Our bodies also become more resistant to insulin when we are constantly sitting, as was demonstrated in a 2011 study in the journal *Metabolism*. In this study, the participants completed three 24-hour conditions. In the first situation, they were active with no sitting; in the second, they were sitting, with no reduction in calorie intake to match the reduced expenditure; and in the third, they were sitting and had a reduced caloric intake. The results showed that insulin action was reduced by 39% in the second situation and 18% in the third. One day of sitting considerably reduces insulin action, even if fewer calories are ingested.

Just in case we need more compelling evidence that we need to sit less and stand more, the authors of a 2012 study published in the *British Journal of Sports Medicine* used actuarial tables and adjusted for smoking, waist circumference, dietary quality, exercise habits and other variables. They measured sitting time by the hours of television watched. The bottom line is that every single hour of television watched after the age of 25 reduces the viewer's life expectancy by 21.8 minutes. So an adult who spends an average of 6 hours a day watching TV over the course of a lifetime can expect to live 4.8 years less than a person who doesn't watch TV. Smoking one cigarette reduces life expectancy by about 11 minutes. Don't even think about watching TV while smoking!

Sit Less, Move More

Instead of giving you a prescription for an exercise routine, the take-home message here is to sit less. Sitting occurs in different contexts — commuting to work, at work, watching TV, studying, reading, etc. So let's be aware of how much we truly sit. There are lots of different wearable digital devices that will alert you when you haven't moved in 30 minutes (except when you are sleeping, of course). Many of the sitting studies also show that an increased number of breaks during sedentary time is beneficial.

Regular physical activity and lots of movement throughout the day are the best predictors of long-term health in large observational population studies. The bottom line? If we want to live longer, we need to move around more throughout the day and be physically active on a regular basis.

Improve Your Gut Health

You know the saying about Vegas: "What happens in Vegas, stays in Vegas"? Well, not so with your gut. What happens in your gut affects your whole body. The type of food you eat, the effectiveness of your digestion and the colonies of bacteria in your gut are important factors in determining your health.

When we digest proteins, carbohydrates and fats, they are all broken down by digestive enzymes into their individual building blocks: amino acids, glucose molecules, and fatty acids and glycerol, respectively. In a healthy gut, these component parts are absorbed through the lining of the small intestine into the blood, which goes to the liver and then on to the rest of the body.

Gut Permeability

The lining of the small intestine has a paradoxical function. It allows properly digested nutrients to pass through for assimilation, while also providing a barrier to keep out foreign substances, certain bacteria and large undigested molecules.

In between the cells of the lining of the small intestine are what are called tight junctions, which are, well, tight and don't allow large molecules through. When the area is irritated or inflamed, however, these junctions become loose, and larger molecules are able to pass through. This increased permeability is sometimes called leaky gut. Once these large molecules cross the intestinal wall, they are seen by our immune system as foreign objects, and an antibody reaction is activated. The immune system activates white blood cells to release their inflammatory cascade, resulting in widespread inflammation.

DID YOU KNOW?

Eliminating Disruptive Foods

What we eliminate from our diet is just as important as what we add to it. The paleo approach to eating addresses diet, alcohol and dysbiosis in that it removes alcohol and certain other elements of the diet that are the most problematic, including gluten, dairy and sugar. These food groups can promote dysbiosis, so by removing them, we are greatly reducing disruptions to the gut. At the same time, the paleo diet emphasizes foods that improve the health of our intestines.

Increased gut permeability is a problem because it means the body no longer has control over what is or is not allowed in. The inflammation that results is linked not only to intestinal conditions like irritable bowel syndrome (IBS), but also to chronic diseases such as autoimmune diseases and allergies, cardiovascular diseases, obesity and diabetes.

There isn't one single cause of increased gut permeability, but some of the most common causes are poor food choices, overuse of alcohol, dysbiosis (microbial imbalance in the gut), chronic stress and prolonged use of certain medications.

The Gut Microbiome

What happens in your gut affects your whole body.

The gut is home to a huge microbial ecosystem called the microbiome. Each of us has between 500 and 1,000 or more different types of bacteria in our digestive system; collectively, the total number of intestinal microbial cells is estimated to be 100 trillion — 10 times more than the number of human body cells. The average adult is carrying around 3 to 6 pounds (1.5 to 3 kg) of microbes in their intestine. There are more of "them" than there is of "you."

When these microbes are working in harmony, they produce certain vitamins and hormones, regulate our immune system and metabolism, and fend off disease-causing pathogens.

The study of the human microbiome is one of the newest and fastest-moving areas of biomedicine. Since the Human Genome Project was launched in 1990, new techniques in DNA sequencing, combined with the latest computer power,

Research Spotlight

Bacterial Imbalances in People with Diabetes

A 2012 study by researchers at the University of Copenhagen and the Beijing Genomics Institute, published in the journal *Nature*, found that people with type 2 diabetes have a unique gut bacteria profile. They suffer from bacterial imbalances in their gut, specifically showing a decrease in butyrate-producing bacteria. This is significant because butyrate is the preferred source of energy for repair and maintenance of healthy cells in the digestive system. The study also found that there were more opportunistic gut pathogens in people with type 2 diabetes and more oxidative stress, implying increased damage to the cells lining the gut.

The science doesn't necessarily show cause and effect yet, but it does show association: type 2 diabetes is associated with damage to the lining of our small intestine, promoting inflammation. This makes sense when you consider that insulin resistance is associated with chronic inflammation.

are giving us a glimpse of the diverse life within our guts. New research is emerging that suggests previously unknown links between our microbes and numerous diseases.

Promoting Microbial Balance

When our food choices lead to dysbiosis, we are contributing to the imbalance. The standard North American diet — high in refined grains, sugars and industrial seed oils and low in whole vegetables, fruits and fiber — causes unwelcome changes in the gut microbiome. Improving the quality of our diet with whole, fresh, high-fiber and minimally processed foods can significantly reduce dysbiosis and inflammation and support a healthy balance of gut bacteria that safeguards the integrity of the intestinal lining and improves our overall health.

Take Care of Your Microbiome

- Stop eating foods you are sensitive to or intolerant of that are loosening your tight junctions. The paleo way of eating eliminates the food groups that are the worst offenders. Once certain foods (like dairy) have been eliminated for a while, you may choose to reintroduce them in a controlled manner to see how they affect you and your microbiome. As you reintroduce foods, keep a close eye on your blood sugar.
- Eat more fruits and vegetables, especially non-starchy vegetables. The fiber in these foods feeds the good bacteria, helping them perform better and fight off the bad guys.
- Avoid being too clean. Yes, we should wash our hands (but not with antibacterial soap, with regular soap) before we eat, but we don't need to be dipped in antibacterial sanitizers. Overzealous cleanliness helps the bad guys.

Reduce Stress

Stress is the body's way of reacting to a challenge. When we talk about stress, we first need to understand something called homeostasis. The body is constantly working to keep critical physiological variables, like blood pressure, blood sugar and hormones, within the narrow range required for health and survival. This dynamic state of internal balance is homeostasis, and the body always strives to return to it.

When we perceive a threat, a cascade of physiological change is set in motion — our fight-or-flight response. It starts in the amygdala, an area of the brain that plays a key role in emotional processing, which, in turn, sends a distress signal to the hypothalamus. The hypothalamus activates our sympathetic nervous system, and epinephrine (adrenaline) and cortisol, the stress hormones from our adrenal glands, are circulated throughout the body.

The activation of the sympathetic nervous system is like pressing down on the gas pedal in a car. Almost instantaneously, our heart rate, breathing and blood pressure increase to supply more oxygen to the muscles and brain. Our hearing and sight become sharper, and our alertness is heightened. Blood flow is directed to the brain and skeletal muscles and away from processes that aren't needed for immediate survival, like digestion, immune function and reproduction. Natural painkillers are released into the bloodstream, and stored sugar and free fatty acids are mobilized as a ready source of energy, so we can run away (flight) or turn around and fight.

For our Paleolithic ancestors, a stressful situation was resolved by being victorious (hopefully) over the wild beast that was chasing them, allowing the gas pedal to be released, the brakes to be applied and all the hormone levels to return to homeostasis. In our hectic world today, however, we are not usually fighting or running away from wild beasts; instead, we are faced with work deadlines, commuting traffic and family and financial issues, all of which turns into chronic stress.

Chronic Stress

To understand how chronic stress contributes to blood sugar dysfunction, we need to revisit one of cortisol's jobs when the body is under acute stress: making sure the muscles and brain have access to immediate energy. To do this, the liver cells break down glycogen and crank out glucose, the muscle cells allow their amino acids to be converted into more glucose (via gluconeogenesis), and the fat cells move triglycerides into the bloodstream for even more energy.

At the same time, cortisol inhibits the action of insulin in an attempt to prevent glucose from being stored, so it can be used instead. In effect, the cells become insulin-resistant, at least in the short term, until the acute stress is resolved.

Chronic stress, however, is never resolved. Over the long term, elevated cortisol consistently produces glucose, leading to increased blood sugar levels. The body remains in a general insulin-resistant state, and over time, the pancreas begins to struggle to keep up with the high demand for insulin, glucose levels in the blood remain high, the cells cannot get the sugar they need, and the cycle continues.

Stress Management

Stress is unavoidable. And the very idea of stress management stresses some of us out. Stress management forces us to slow down and, for a brief time, step away from the hustle and bustle of our lives and the seemingly endless demands on our time. Prioritizing self-care in a culture that doesn't value it takes time, patience and practice — and we highly recommend it.

FAQ

Q *Does insufficient sleep affect stress levels?*

A There's no question about it: inadequate sleep is a chronic stressor. Sleep loss increases cortisol levels, and as we have seen, higher cortisol levels wreak havoc with our blood sugar and insulin. But it doesn't stop there. When we are tired, we reach for caffeine, specifically coffee, the most commonly used psychotropic drug in the world. It is estimated that North Americans drink over 450 million cups of coffee per day. Studies have shown that cortisol levels after caffeine consumption are similar to those experienced during acute stress. Drinking coffee, in other words, recreates stress conditions in the body, and we are adding stress to stress when we drink it as a way to keep ourselves going on inadequate sleep.

Reduce Your Stress Levels

- Evaluate your exposure to stress, both physical and psychological. Consider saying no to certain demands on your time, turn off the news, and reduce your exposure to online stress and the pressures of keeping up-to-date on social media.

- Mitigate the stress you cannot avoid with mindfulness-based stress reduction (MBSR). Research at the University of Massachusetts has shown that MBSR lowers blood pressure, reduces overall emotional reactivity and improves sleep. You can learn the basics of this program through in-person workshops, online courses or audio or video recordings.

- Spend time in nature. There is a lot of accumulated research that demonstrates nature's restorative effects on our health and our stress levels. Take your lunch to the local park, put a plant on your desk and go for a walk in the park after dinner.

DID YOU KNOW?

The Father of Stress

Stress has become such a pervasive part of our lives, it's difficult to imagine that the way we use the term today is relatively new: it was coined in 1936 by Hans Selye, "the Father of Stress."

CHAPTER 4
Getting Ready to Start the Paleo Diet

One of the most common complaints nutrition experts hear from their clients is that they don't have time to cook — they are just too busy. This feeling is certainly understandable. We are all busy, and many of us are working more hours than we used to. But when we consider that diet is one of the determinants of chronic disease risk, it becomes clear that we need to carve out time to cook real food.

One of the best ways to find more time for cooking is to be well prepared: have a plan and a well-stocked kitchen. We've provided meal plans in chapter 5, but for now, read on to learn what supplies you need to have on hand so you can cook for better blood sugar control.

Kitchen Tools and Equipment

You don't need a lot of fancy equipment to made great meals, just some basic tools and some good ingredients. Certain small appliances, such as a high-speed blender and a food processor, will come in handy from time to time, but more often than not, you'll likely find yourself preparing food with a cutting board and a very sharp chef's knife.

- **Bowls:** You'll need glass or ceramic bowls in several different sizes, from small to large.
- **Box grater:** This type of grater has four sides for slicing and fine, medium and coarse grating. It is the best choice for grating vegetables like cabbage, cauliflower and Brussels sprouts.
- **Casserole dishes and glass baking dishes:** It's a good idea to have baking dishes with lids in a couple of different sizes: 13- by 9-inch (33 by 23 cm) and 9-inch (23 cm) square.
- **Coffee grinder:** Instead of using this to grind coffee beans, you'll find yourself using it to grind nuts, seeds and spices — just make sure it's clean of any coffee residue. You can also use a mortar and pestle, for more of a workout.

FAQ

Q *When it comes to cutting boards, what material is best?*

A There are a lot of conflicting opinions on this subject. Many people believe that plastic cutting boards are the safest, especially if you can wash them in the dishwasher. However, a study conducted at the University of Michigan that examined various bacteria, including E. coli and salmonella, found that "more bacteria are recovered from a used plastic surface than from a used wooden surface."

Beyond the concerns over bacteria, professional testing shows that glass boards are the worst in terms of dulling your knives, some plastic boards slip around too much on the counter, and some wooden boards crack when washed in the dishwasher. Bamboo boards may be viewed as an environmental choice, but they are almost 20% harder than traditional maple and can be very tough on knives.

In the end, the choice of material is up to you and your personal preference. Just make sure to purchase at least two cutting boards — one for meat, chicken and fish, and one for fruits and vegetables — to avoid cross-contamination of bacteria.

- **Cutting boards:** Please stop cutting on plates and get some proper cutting boards in different sizes (you'll be glad to have a small one for small jobs, such as mincing garlic or chopping green onions). To avoid cross-contamination of bacteria, it's best to have one you use just for meat, chicken and fish and another one for fruits and vegetables. For tips on selecting cutting boards, see the FAQ above.
- **Food processor:** You likely won't use this on a daily basis, and you can probably get along without one, but it does make certain tasks, such as making Fried Cauliflower Rice (page 153), much easier.
- **High-power blender:** Like a food processor, a high-power blender isn't a necessity, but it does make Creamy Cashew Cheese (page 273) creamier and homemade nut milk (see box, page 68) easier.
- **Immersion blender:** This tool makes quick work of The Best Paleo Mayo (page 249) and Easy Hollandaise (page 251). It also simplifies the task of puréeing soups because you can use it (carefully) right in the saucepan.
- **Kitchen shears:** You'll be amazed by how many jobs there are for your kitchen shears. Plastic handles are a good idea so your hands won't slip as much when they are wet or greasy.

> Purchase at least two cutting boards — one for meat, chicken and fish, and one for fruits and vegetables — to avoid cross-contamination of bacteria.

Silicone Cookware

At this point there isn't a lot of safety information available about silicone muffin pans, cooking utensils, baking mats and oven mitts. It is considered "FDA approved as a food-safe substance," and Health Canada says, "Silicone rubber does not react with food or beverages, or produce any hazardous fumes." Food-grade silicone products are rated for temperatures from below freezing up to 428°F (220°C), but most testing of silicone has been done at body and room temperature. It is reputed to be stable and inert, and it does not affect the flavor of food or release any odor.

- **Knives:** At the very least, you'll need an 8-inch (20 cm) chef's knife and a 4-inch (10 cm) paring knife. Be sure to keep your knives very sharp. Good sharp knives make your life a lot easier, especially when you are preparing a ton of vegetables!
- **Large skillet:** An enameled cast-iron skillet is great for sautéing vegetables, while a regular cast-iron skillet works best for skillet burgers and steaks. Both types are ovenproof, meaning they can go from stovetop to oven or broiler. (Just be sure to use heavy-duty oven mitts when taking them out.) Skillets are also ideal for one-dish family meals. Health concerns have arisen regarding nonstick cookware; see the sidebar on page 63.
- **Mandoline slicer:** A mandoline makes thin, even slices quickly. It's certainly not a necessary tool — you can do the same job with a sharp knife and a cutting board — but it makes the task both faster and easier.
- **Measuring cups and spoons:** Make sure you have all the measuring spoons — $1/4$ tsp (1 mL), $1/2$ tsp (2 mL), 1 tsp (5 mL) and 1 tbsp (15 mL) — and measuring cups — $1/4$ cup (60 mL), $1/3$ cup (75 mL), $1/2$ cup (125 mL) and 1 cup (250 mL). Having a larger 2- or 4-cup (500 mL or 1 L) glass measuring cup is helpful for making larger batches of sauces and vinaigrettes.
- **Microplane grater:** This super-sharp fine grater makes grating ginger and citrus peel fast and easy. You just have to watch your knuckles!
- **Muffin pan:** On the paleo diet you won't be using a muffin pan for muffins or cupcakes full of grains and sugar, but you'll still need one if you plan to make Egg and Pancetta Muffins (page 178) or individual frittatas.

Research Spotlight

Aluminum Foil

Aluminum is all around us, in our soils, plants and water, and while our bodies are quite efficient at excreting small amounts of this potentially toxic metal, an accumulation in the body has been linked to osteoporosis and Alzheimer's disease. A 2012 study published in the *International Journal of Electrochemical Science* showed that there is considerable leaching of aluminum into food when aluminum foil is used in cooking. The higher the temperature and the more acidic the food, the higher the amount of leaching. The researchers determined that aluminum foil is not suitable for cooking or heating, but that it could be used for wrapping and storing cold food for a short time. We have made every effort to avoid the use of too much aluminum foil in this book, and where it is used in cooking, it is not in contact with the food.

- **Oven mitts:** A pair of heavy-duty oven mitts is a necessity for transferring foods to and from the oven and the barbecue.
- **Parchment paper:** Line your baking sheets with this heat-tolerant paper whenever you're roasting or baking: your food won't stick and cleanup will be a lot easier.
- **Peelers:** A julienne peeler turns zucchini, squash, cucumbers and carrots into wonderful "noodles" for salads, slaws and stir-fries. (You can also use a vegetable spiralizer for this task, if you happen to have one.) Regular vegetable peelers are for peeling, of course, but can also make lovely vegetable ribbons for salads and garnishes.
- **Pots and saucepans:** You want pots and pans in a number of different sizes, with heavy bottoms that distribute heat evenly. Aluminum pots are not recommended, as they are chemically reactive to acidic foods like tomatoes and lemons and can leach aluminum into the food, especially at high heat. The best options are enameled cast-iron and stainless steel. (See the sidebar on nonstick cookware.) Be sure to have a stockpot big enough (8- to 10-quart/L) for making stocks, such as Warming Chicken Stock (page 116). A Dutch oven — a large, heavy, lidded pot that can be used both on the stove and in the oven — is ideal for soups, stews and long-simmering, moist-heat cooking, such as braising.
- **Rimmed baking sheets:** These are great for roasting meats and vegetables, toasting nuts and making kale and zucchini chips. You'll need to use two baking sheets at the same time in some recipes, so make sure to have at least that many.
- **Salad spinner:** A salad spinner quickly spins dry salad greens, herbs and cooking greens like spinach and kale, but it's another tool that's not strictly necessary. Instead, you can roll the wet leaves up in two clean, dry kitchen towels and let stand for about 5 minutes.
- **Spoons, spatulas, tongs and flippers:** Everyone has their favorite utensils — wood, bamboo, silicone or metal. Find what works best for you.
- **Steamer basket:** Steaming vegetables helps preserve many of their nutrients, so a collapsible steamer basket is a must.
- **Strainer:** You'll need a strainer or colander for washing and draining vegetables and fruits.

> **DID YOU KNOW?**
>
> ### The Dark Side of Nonstick Cookware
>
> Nonstick cookware is very easy to use and clean, but convenience comes at a cost. The poly- and perfluoroalkyl substances (PFAS) used to create the slick surface are linked to decreased fertility, miscarriage, elevated cholesterol and certain cancers, among other health concerns. Older chemicals are being phased out, but many concerns remain about the safety of the replacements. Safer alternatives that still clean up easily include ceramic titanium and enameled cast-iron.

Kitchen Detox

Embarking on a healthier way of eating that promises to help you get your blood sugar and insulin under control requires a bit of preparation. Not too much, mind you — this isn't rocket science. But it is a reset of the way you approach eating, how you shop for food and how you stock your kitchen. A healthy kitchen makes it that much easier to have a healthy you.

So here's the first step: go look in your fridge, pantry and other food drawers and cupboards. Start with the three food groups we have already seen pose the biggest problems for blood sugar: sugars and sweeteners, grains and industrial seed oils. Get rid of all foods that contain any of these things. This is a terrific start. The Foods to Avoid lists on pages 86–88 will help you fine-tune the rest of your kitchen detox. This cleaning-out task can take a bit of time, so plan for that.

I suggest you also plan to go shopping right after you have done this kitchen cleanout, because until you fill your fridge and pantry again with the right foods, you may feel discouraged by the lack of food that remains.

What to Keep in the Fridge and Freezer

The daily meal plans at the end of chapter 5 will help you plan what specific groceries to purchase as you start eating a paleo diet. But there are a number of ingredients you should try to keep on hand all the time, so you can whip up a delicious blood-sugar-balancing, nutrient-dense paleo meal at a moment's notice.

Protein Foods

Protein is the first priority (see page 89). Meat, poultry, fish, seafood and eggs are concentrated protein sources. In chapter 5, you'll learn what to look for and how to read labels when shopping for protein foods. Watch for sales and specials on these items so you can fill up the freezer.

Non-Starchy Vegetables

These are the second priority. There are lots of different vegetables in the recipes in this book, but the following are staples, used in many recipes.

Leafy Greens

Mix and match leafy greens depending on what is on sale or in season. A handful of greens is always great added to scrambled eggs, tucked underneath a tuna salad or mixed with a great dressing beside a flank steak at dinner. You may find the bags of prewashed mixed greens easier to use, and they provide a lot of variety. Keep them at the front of the fridge, where you can grab a handful at every meal.

Fresh Herbs

No longer relegated to "garnish" status, parsley, cilantro, basil, dill and other herbs add an unmatched freshness to salads. When you get home from shopping, spend a little time preparing the herbs for optimal storage. Take the bunch of herbs apart, rinse them well under running water to wash away grit and sand, pinch off and discard the larger stems (which can be bitter), wrap the leaves in paper towels and store them in plastic bags in the fridge. Now they are ready to go, just like your other leafy greens.

Mushrooms

Mushrooms contain unique phytonutrients (glucans) that support a number of our immune system's actions. We don't often consider the tremendous nutrition lurking in the humble button or cremini mushroom, but they are a great source of at least 15 different vitamins, minerals and antioxidants.

Don't leave mushrooms on the countertop. For maximum retention of nutrients, store them in the fridge until use. Mushrooms need to breathe, so store them in a paper bag, not plastic. Use roasted portobello mushroom caps as "buns" for burgers or heart-warming Sloppy Joes (page 230). And you can't beat a simple sauté of onions and mushrooms in grass-fed butter (page 164)!

DID YOU KNOW?

The Genetics of Cilantro

Whether or not you like the flavor of cilantro may have a good deal to do with your genes. Researchers from the genetics company 23andMe analyzed the genomes of 30,000 people and discovered similarities in a group of smell receptor genes among those who thought cilantro tasted like soap. It appears that one gene in particular (OR6A2) is involved, but other genes that affect the taste of bitterness may also play a role.

Cleaning Mushrooms

Mushrooms are very porous and soak up water easily. If they get waterlogged, they will steam instead of browning and will taste rubbery. Instead of washing them, gently brush off excess dirt with a small mushroom brush, or use a damp paper towel to wipe the caps carefully (especially if the gills are exposed). It is best to clean mushrooms as close as possible to cooking them or slicing them (if using them raw).

Onions and Garlic

The allium family of vegetables, which also includes green onions, shallots, leeks and chives, is incredibly health-promoting. These vegetables provide high levels of flavonoids and sulfur-containing nutrients that are associated with heart and blood vessel health. Use them every day in eggs, salads or stir-fries, caramelized on top of burgers or crisped up and sprinkled on a warming soup.

Gingerroot

Fresh gingerroot is a must-have staple. Gingerol, the main active compound in ginger, is responsible for its anti-inflammatory and antioxidant properties. Keep gingerroot in the crisper or freezer and just break off a knob and peel it, grate it or slice it when you need it.

Fresh Fruit

Vegetables take center stage when we eat for blood sugar balance, but some antioxidant-rich fruits adds nice flavor to a salad, beside some eggs or after a protein-centered meal. Depending on the season, choose among berries, grapefruit, kiwifruits and pears. Two fruits I always have on hand are lemons and limes — not only for use in recipes, but also to add to tea and especially to enjoy freshly squeezed into a tall glass of sparkling water (along with a sprig of dill or a couple of fresh basil leaves).

What to Keep in the Pantry

Having a well-stocked pantry makes cooking and preparing blood sugar–balancing meals much easier. Now that you have gotten rid of all your sugars and grains, there's lots of room for the basics described below.

Some of the ingredients used in this book — and some of these pantry recommendations — are not found in a strict paleo diet, but keep in mind that we recommend the *principles* of the paleo diet, not the dogma. It is important to remember that paleo-inspired eating is simply a dietary framework for correcting blood sugar dysfunction.

DID YOU KNOW?

Avocados

Avocados are a great source of anti-inflammatory monounsaturated fats. As an added bonus, they are also rich in blood-sugar-friendly fiber. Buy several at different states of ripeness, so you always have at least one ready to go. If you find you have too many ripe avocados at the same time, put them in the fridge, where they'll keep for another 4 days or so, or whip up a batch of Classic Guacamole (page 247) and serve it with endive scoops.

Canned Tomatoes and Tomato Paste

It is so disappointing to cut into what appears to be a nice red tomato only to find it pulpy and tasteless. When tomatoes are out of season, they can be tricky. Many of the recipes in this book use canned tomatoes and tomato paste to add sweetness, thickness and depth of flavor. Make sure to have whole, diced and crushed tomatoes in the pantry at all times.

Yes, canned tomato products are processed, but if you read labels and purchase those that contain only tomatoes, you'll be fine. Be careful of added salt, sugar and gluten, and even added herbs and spices — not only will you pay more for the additions, but the results won't taste as good as if you added your own fresh herbs.

Most cans are lined with bisphenol A (BPA), which has a negative impact on hormone metabolism. Purchase BPA-free cans when you can or, better still, look for tomato products packed in glass jars.

> **DID YOU KNOW?**
>
> **Canned Tomatoes**
> Nothing beats ripe fresh produce, but if you've ever eaten tomatoes in February, you know how disappointing they can be. Canned tomatoes offer fresh summer ripeness with an added health benefit: heat-processing restructures lycopene, making it easier for the body to absorb. Tomatoes are one of the best sources of lycopene, a carotenoid linked to a decreased risk of prostate and breast cancers.

Canned Fish

Canned fish is nutrient-dense and protein-rich, with few additives except for the oil and salt it's packed in. According to the USDA's National Nutrient Database, canned and fresh fish have about the same amount of beneficial omega-3 fats, with certain types of canned salmon having even higher levels. Canned fish is generally also caught wild. While fresh sardines cooking on the grill are certainly delicious, so are Lemon and Herb Sardines (page 189) stuffed into half a perfectly ripe avocado. Skipjack tuna, salmon, sardines, anchovies and smoked mackerel are great options to have on hand.

Coconut Milk

Full-fat coconut milk adds creaminess and thickness to recipes without any dairy. When you place the can in the fridge overnight (without shaking it), the fat separates from the milk and rises to the top. To get at the rich, creamy coconut cream, turn the can over, open it at the bottom and pour off the milk, saving it for another use. The coconut cream is then ready to go for our Coconut Whip (page 275).

Nut and Seed Butters

Nut and seed butters offer a great-tasting way to enjoy nutrient-packed nuts and seeds in a different form. They can be a great addition to recipes, too. Almond butter, for example, adds thickness to dressings, sauces and dips, while cashew butter adds a wonderfully creamy sweetness to soups.

Be sure to read the ingredients list carefully and choose butters that are made from only ground nuts or seeds. Avoid those with sugar, salt or any other additives. Nut butters can be made with either raw or roasted nuts; let your taste be your guide. Refrigerate nut butters after opening.

Nut Milks

Nut milks are a great replacement for dairy milk in soups and sauces. When purchasing commercial nut milks, it is very important to read labels to make sure there is no added sugar or sweetener in any form. There *will* be things like carrageenan or guar gum; while these aren't great, they also aren't deal-breakers. But if you really want to make sure there are no unwanted additives in your nut milk, make your own — it may sound intimidating, but it is actually super-easy.

Making Your Own Nut Milk

To make your own almond, cashew or Brazil nut milk (or milk from any nut or seed, really), you will need a high-power blender and a nut milk bag or cheesecloth. The recipe below will make about 4 cups (1 L). If you like your nut milk a little thicker, use less water in step 3; in that case, your yield will also be a bit less.

1. Soak 1 cup (250 mL) raw nuts in a bowl of water overnight or for up to 24 hours. Use just enough water to cover the nuts.
2. Drain and rinse the nuts.
3. Add the nuts and 4 cups (1 L) filtered water to a high-power blender and blend for about 2 minutes or until smooth.
4. Strain the liquid through the nut milk bag or several layers of cheesecloth. Be sure to squeeze all the liquid out of the ground nuts.

That's it! Enjoy the milk immediately or store it in a covered jar in the fridge for up to 3 days.

Nut Flours and Coconut Flour

These flours are ideal for coating fish or chicken in place of panko or bread crumbs, and small amounts can be used as thickening agents. But don't use them in an attempt to recreate the sweet, carbohydrate-heavy foods from your old unbalanced-blood-sugar life. Please, no paleo muffins, cookies, waffles or anything that keeps you stuck in a rut of thinking about grain-like things. Shift your mindset — context is everything.

Tahini

Tahini is a paste made from ground sesame seeds. These tiny seeds are an excellent source of many minerals, especially calcium, as well as two unique substances called sesamin and sesamolin, which have been shown to have beneficial effects on blood pressure and cholesterol. Tahini is wonderful for thickening sauces and dressings, such as Creamy Lemon Tahini Dressing (page 255).

Mustards and Hot Pepper Sauces

You'll get a lot of use out of these two versatile condiments. There are commercial options out there that are fine, but read labels carefully and stay away from any ingredients on the Foods to Avoid lists (pages 86–88).

Vinegars

Each type of vinegar adds its own unique flavor to recipes. Keep several in your pantry, including white wine vinegar, red wine vinegar, balsamic vinegar, unseasoned rice vinegar and raw apple cider vinegar (keep that last one in the fridge).

DID YOU KNOW?

Ketchup

It is unlikely you'll find any commercial ketchup without sugar — in fact, about 25% of regular ketchup is sugar. A smarter choice is to use the Roasted Salsa (page 241) in place of ketchup. Once you try that, you won't go back to the commercial stuff, with almost 4 grams of sugar per tablespoon (15 mL).

Research Spotlight

Effects of Vinegar on Blood Sugar

You may have heard about the positive effects vinegar has on blood sugar. A 2004 study cited in *Diabetes Care* showed that taking vinegar before a meal significantly increased insulin sensitivity and reduced the glucose and insulin spikes that occurred after the meal. There are no large follow-up studies, but while we wait for more research, we can continue to enjoy all the great benefits of a daily salad with vinaigrette.

Pickles

As with mustards and hot pepper sauces, read the ingredients lists on commercial pickles carefully. Many brands include sugar. Your best bet here (other than making your own, but that's another book!) is to try the refrigerated section. Look for labels that list just water, salt and spices — these are fine. You might also like the Pickled Cucumber Salad (page 132).

Fish Sauce

Fish sauce adds a wonderful umami taste to recipes, but a little goes a long way, so start slowly and don't overdo it. Make sure the fish sauce has only three ingredients: fish, salt and water. Steer clear of non-paleo ingredients such as sugar and hydrolyzed wheat protein.

Tamari

Like soy sauce, tamari (also called Japanese soy sauce) is made from fermented soybeans, but tamari is made with little or no wheat. Look for organic gluten-free tamari to avoid any possibility of wheat or genetically modified soy. Strictly speaking, soy products are not included in the paleo diet, but for our purposes, tamari is an acceptable exception: it has a negligible effect on blood sugar and adds delicious flavor.

Cacao or 100% Cocoa

Cacao can add depth of taste to meat recipes and a deep, subtle chocolate taste if brewed with your regular ground coffee. Please don't use it to make sweetened desserts or drinks that will unbalance your blood sugar. Again, context is everything.

Nutritional Yeast

Nutritional yeast is the deactivated form of the *Saccharomyces cerevisiae* yeast, grown on cane sugar and molasses (no, there is no sugar in it). After it is harvested, it is dried into flakes. It is a great source of B vitamins and the mineral chromium, which is important for maintaining balanced blood sugar. It adds a wonderful cheesy taste to sauces, spreads and the Classic Kale Chips (page 266).

Salt

Strict paleo doesn't allow the use of salt, and we've heard for years that salt is bad for our blood pressure. Here's the thing, though: salt works in the body in partnership with potassium to regulate fluid balance and blood pressure. When we eat highly processed, refined foods, we are getting a lot of salt. And when we don't eat a lot of vegetables, we are not getting enough potassium. That's the double whammy that is the biggest part of the problem: the typical North American diet provides too much sodium and too little potassium. In this book, we recommend eating a lot of vegetables and eliminating highly processed, refined foods, a combination that will bring our sodium and potassium levels back into balance.

The recipes in this book call for sea salt. Celtic sea salt, a gray moist salt that has trace amounts of other minerals found in the sea, is our preferred choice. Himalayan rock salt is another good option.

> Salt works in the body in partnership with potassium to regulate fluid balance and blood pressure.

Spices

You can find most spices in both ground and whole forms. If you are in a hurry, it's just fine to use ground spices. But when you can, take the time to toast and grind whole spices — the added flavor is worth the effort! Toast whole spices in a dry skillet over medium heat just until you start to smell the spices. You can use either a clean coffee grinder or a mortar and pestle to grind the spices. (The grinder is easier!)

Shopping

We no longer live as hunter-gatherers, but we can "forage" in our grocery stores, big-box stores and farmers' markets. The paleo model allows us to copy the food groups of our ancient ancestors with the foods available to us today, while avoiding what have become the modern food groups of refined sugars, refined grains, industrial seed oils and trans fats.

When you enter most supermarkets, you find yourself in the produce section, which is where you will be doing a lot of shopping, since non-starchy vegetables will make up most of your plate at each meal. Always strive to eat the freshest food possible. In most cases, the order of preference is 1) fresh, 2) frozen and 3) canned or bottled. Having said that, frozen vegetables, fish and poultry can be a good, economical way to get top-notch protein and nutrient-dense carbohydrates when fresh options aren't available.

DID YOU KNOW?

The Outer Aisles
When we focus our shopping (foraging) on the outer aisles of the grocery store, we are able to avoid the processed foods lurking in the middle of the store.

Pantry Checklist

Keep these items on hand in your pantry. When they are called for in the recipes, it is often in small amounts, so you won't have to purchase them too often.

Canned or Bottled Goods

- ☐ full-fat coconut milk
- ☐ kalamata olives
- ☐ tomato paste
- ☐ crushed tomatoes
- ☐ diced tomatoes
- ☐ whole tomatoes
- ☐ chunk light tuna (skipjack)
- ☐ wild salmon
- ☐ sardines

Nuts and Seeds

- ☐ almonds
- ☐ almond butter
- ☐ almond flour
- ☐ cashews
- ☐ flax seeds
- ☐ hazelnuts
- ☐ pecans
- ☐ pine nuts
- ☐ psyllium husks
- ☐ green pumpkin seeds (pepitas)
- ☐ sesame seeds
- ☐ sunflower seeds
- ☐ walnuts

Fats and Oils

- ☐ avocado oil
- ☐ coconut oil
- ☐ extra virgin olive oil
- ☐ light-tasting olive oil

Vinegars

- ☐ apple cider vinegar
- ☐ balsamic vinegar
- ☐ red wine vinegar
- ☐ unseasoned rice vinegar
- ☐ white wine vinegar

Spices and Dried Herbs

- ☐ dried basil
- ☐ bay leaves
- ☐ ground cardamom
- ☐ cayenne pepper
- ☐ chili powder
- ☐ celery seeds
- ☐ ground cinnamon
- ☐ ground cloves
- ☐ ground coriander
- ☐ ground cumin
- ☐ fennel seeds
- ☐ garlic powder
- ☐ ground ginger
- ☐ ground nutmeg
- ☐ onion powder
- ☐ dried oregano
- ☐ paprika
- ☐ smoked paprika
- ☐ black peppercorns
- ☐ hot pepper flakes
- ☐ ground white pepper
- ☐ sea salt (Celtic)
- ☐ dried thyme
- ☐ ground turmeric
- ☐ wasabi powder

Seasonings and Flavorings

- ☐ ready-to-use organic chicken broth
- ☐ Dijon mustard
- ☐ fish sauce
- ☐ green curry paste
- ☐ hot pepper sauce
- ☐ nutritional yeast
- ☐ tahini
- ☐ organic gluten-free tamari or coconut amino acids
- ☐ vanilla extract

The Meat Label Maze

Processed foods won't be part of your shopping now, but there are still labels on meat, fish and eggs that you need to understand. When considering what type of meat or poultry to purchase, there are many options: organic, grass-fed, pasture-raised, free-range, raised without the use of antibiotics, grain-fed, grain-finished … the list goes on. With these terms, we enter the murky waters of certification and labeling. Here's a quick look at what some of these terms mean.

"Organic"

Animals that are certified organic cannot be treated with growth hormones or antibiotics and must be given feed that has been produced organically. If an animal becomes ill and requires antibiotics, it is isolated from the rest of the animals and treated, but its meat, milk or eggs cannot be claimed as organic. This label does not strictly define practices related to space per animal or outdoor access.

In Canada, the Canadian Food Inspection Agency (CFIA) is responsible for monitoring and enforcing the Organic Products Regulations; in the United States, these responsibilities fall to the United States Department of Agriculture (USDA). Both countries have a list of accredited certification bodies that carry out the actual certification.

> Animals that are certified organic cannot be treated with growth hormones or antibiotics and must be given feed that has been produced organically.

"Grass-Fed"

On January 12, 2016, the Agricultural Marketing Service of the USDA withdrew the labeling standard for grass-fed meat that had been in place, with apparent widespread farm and consumer support, since 2006. The original standard stated that grass and forage needed to be 99% or more of the energy source for the lifetime of a ruminant species after weaning in order for the meat to qualify as grass-fed with USDA's approval. Without this labeling standard, the fear now is that a multitude of nonuniform labels will enter the marketplace, creating confusion and lack of transparency in the food system.

In Canada in 2013, the CFIA approved the first Canadian certification label for grass-fed meat, which guarantees that the meat comes from an animal raised entirely outdoors in pasture and fed a 100% grass and forage diet after weaning. Despite this approval, the use of the term "grass-fed" on labels is not regulated in Canada. This is difficult for the consumer.

DID YOU KNOW?

Grass-Fed ≠ Organic
Many people think the terms "grass-fed" and "organic" are synonymous, but they aren't. Organic cattle are not necessarily grass-fed. They may still be in a feedlot of sorts but fed organic corn and soy and not exposed to antibiotic use.

Grain Finishing

There is another tricky part to the "grass-fed" label: unless it says 100% grass-fed, the animal may have been grain-fed for the last 90 to 160 days before harvest, a practice called grain finishing. This practice fattens the animal up quickly but generally negates the health benefits of grass-fed meat.

Because we do recommend choosing grass-fed meats whenever possible, we encourage you to shop at a reputable butcher where you can ask questions to understand where and how your food was raised. Frequenting farmers' markets and getting to know local farmers and their products is also a good idea.

Grass-Fed Meat and Antibiotics

Cows, just like goats, sheep, deer, buffalo and elk, are ruminants, meaning that they have stomachs with four compartments. They are designed to eat plants that will ultimately undergo microbial action, fermentation and the chewing of the cud. When we see beef that is labeled "100% grass-fed," it means the cow was raised in a pasture on the grasses and forage appropriate for its digestive system. If antibiotics are used on grass-fed cows, it is because they are sick; antibiotics are not used as a preventive precaution.

Cows raised in industrialized feedlots (also called conventionally raised meat), on the other hand, are fed mostly corn (a grain), soy (a legume) and other additives — foods that fatten them up quickly and efficiently but that their digestive system is not designed to eat. This practice often causes gastric distress and infections in the cattle,

Research Spotlight

Superbugs in Ground Beef

In December 2015, *Consumer Reports* published a study that analyzed 300 packages of ground beef from across the United States. The meat was purchased at grocery stores, big-box stores and natural-food stores. It included all types of ground beef, from conventionally raised beef to beef raised "in more sustainable ways" (which, at a minimum, meant raised without antibiotics).

The study analyzed the meat for five common types of bacteria found on beef. All of the samples contained at least some of these bacteria. However, three times as many of the conventional samples (18% versus 6%) contained superbugs — bacteria that have become resistant to the drugs normally used to treat or eradicate them — compared to the grass-fed samples.

The Centers for Disease Control and Prevention (CDC) estimates that, in the United States, more than 2 million people become ill each year with antibiotic-resistant infections, and at least 23,000 die as a result. According to data published by the FDA, there are more kilograms of antibiotics sold in the United States for food-producing animals than for people.

Even though some of the antibiotics used on animals are not used in human medicine, all uses of antibiotics have the potential to create drug-resistant bacteria and to reduce the effectiveness of antibiotics in people.

which necessitates the use of antibiotics in the herd to both prevent and treat disease. Unfortunately, antibiotics may also be used to fatten the animals more quickly so they can be brought to market sooner. This subtherapeutic use of antibiotics is problematic, as the routine use of antibiotics in farming can lead to the creation of drug-resistant bacteria, a serious and emerging threat.

Grass-Fed Meat Often Has a Better Fatty Acid Profile

The idea that "you are what you eat" applies as much to animals as it does to humans, and we can see differences in the meat depending on how the animal was raised and what it was fed. In 2014, researchers at Texas Tech University set out to determine the nutrient composition of grass-fed beef so that it could be included in the USDA's National Nutrient Database for Standard Reference. They compared grass-fed cows to conventionally fed cows and determined differences in the quantity and types of fat present, as well as the antioxidant status and the different levels of minerals in both types of meat.

Confirming the results of previous studies, the researchers found that, while the grass-fed meat was lower in total fat than the grain-fed meat, grass-fed meat had elevated levels of stearic acid, a saturated fat. It is widely acknowledged that stearic acid does not raise blood cholesterol levels, and having a higher proportion of stearic acid means that, proportionately, the grass-fed meat has lower levels of palmitic and myristic acids, the saturated fats that are more likely to raise blood cholesterol.

The grass-fed beef also had two times the concentration of conjugated linoleic acid (CLA), the naturally occurring trans fatty acid, which has been studied for its anticancer properties and its positive effects on the immune system and the maintenance of lean body mass. In addition, the grass-fed meat had significantly higher levels of omega-3 fats, which are associated with a decrease in cardiovascular disease and better neurological and immune function.

The study noted that there was a distinct difference in the color of the fat between the two types of meat. The fat on grass-fed meat was more of a yellowy-orange, indicating a higher level of antioxidant carotenoids, such as beta-carotene, which is present in much higher levels in the forage foods provided to the grass-fed cattle. As for mineral content, the grass-fed meat showed higher concentrations of zinc, iron, phosphorus, sodium and potassium.

DID YOU KNOW?

Increased Omega-6s

Over the past 50 years or so, the North American diet has increased in omega-6 fats — due mostly to the increase in industrial seed oils — at the expense of health-promoting omega-3 fats.

"Pasture-Raised" or "Pastured"

This label generally applies to pigs and chickens, but could be found on all types of meat. The label implies that the animals lived primarily in fields or wooded areas, where they ate grass and other plants, as well as bugs and insects. Grains might be added to the diet of pasture-raised animals during the winter, when pastures are covered with snow and the animals are brought inside. There is no legal or regulated definition of this term in the United States or Canada.

"Free-Range"

This label is used almost exclusively on poultry products, including eggs. The definition provided by the USDA states that producers must demonstrate that the poultry has been allowed access to the outside. While this sounds nice, it could just mean that there's a small door at one end of a very large barn that is open for a short amount of time each day and that very few birds, if any, actually make it outside. There are no standards as to how big the outdoor area is or whether it is concrete or pasture or bare ground.

"Free-Run"

"Free-run" is not the same as "free-range." While these birds are not in cages and are technically allowed to move around freely in the barns, the conditions are generally incredibly overcrowded. These birds do not have access to the outside.

Organic Fruits and Vegetables

Organic produce is those foods produced without conventional pesticides, herbicides, irradiation or genetic or synthetic engineering. Although people consider eating organic foods for various reasons, many do so with a view toward reducing their exposure to pesticides. But perhaps surprisingly, some organically grown produce does contain pesticide residues. There are a number of reasons why this might be so. For instance, when a field is sprayed with pesticide from an aircraft, not all of the pesticide makes it to the ground. The wind can carry the spray to organic farms that may be miles away. Despite the rigorous certification programs organic farms must go through to remain chemical-free, the soil may also contain residues of insecticides such as DDT and DDE, persistent organic pollutants (POPs) that remain in the environment even though they have been banned for years (or even decades). There are pesticide residues throughout our environment now, and some experts feel it is difficult to have a zero-pesticide residue in commercial food production.

Research Spotlight

The Benefits of Organic Produce

A 2014 review in the *British Journal of Nutrition* that used a very large database (343 studies) showed that organic crops were up to 60% higher in a number of key antioxidants, including polyphenols, than conventionally raised crops. The study also found that pesticide residues were four times more likely to be found in conventional crops than organic ones. As Dr. Carlo Leifert, one of the study's authors, states, "The organic vs non-organic debate has rumbled on for decades now but the evidence from this study is overwhelming — that organic food is high in antioxidants and lower in toxic metals and pesticides."

There is some good news, though. Although organic produce is not immune to pesticide residue, the quantity and incidence of the residues are consistently lower than those in conventional produce.

The Dirty Dozen and the Clean Fifteen

Each year the Environmental Working Group (EWG), an American nonprofit organization, puts together a "Shopper's Guide to Pesticides in Produce" aimed at giving consumers the information they need to reduce their exposure to overall concentrations of pesticide residues on common fruits and vegetables. The guide is based on laboratory tests done by the USDA's Pesticide Data Program and the FDA. From the thousands of food samples that are tested, the EWG determines the produce with the highest pesticide loads and calls this list the Dirty Dozen. It also publishes a list, called the Clean Fifteen, of the produce with the lowest pesticide residues.

Here are some of the highlights from the 2016 tests:

- A total of 146 different pesticides were found on the thousands of fruit and vegetable samples.
- Single samples of strawberries revealed 17 different pesticides.
- More than 98% of strawberries, peaches, nectarines and apples tested positive for at least one pesticide residue.
- The average potato had more pesticides by weight than any other produce.
- A single grape sample and a sweet bell pepper sample contained 15 pesticides.
- Avocados were the cleanest of the samples, with detectable pesticides found on only 1%.
- Only 5.5% of the Clean Fifteen samples had two or more pesticides.

DID YOU KNOW?

When to Buy Organic

For the most recent versions of the Dirty Dozen and the Clean Fifteen, visit the EWG's website, at www.ewg.org/foodnews. To reduce your exposure to pesticides, buy organic versions of the fruits and vegetables on the Dirty Dozen list. Because the produce on the Clean Fifteen list has substantially less pesticide residues, you may not need to buy organic versions of these fruits and vegetables.

Over the years that the EWG has been publishing the Dirty Dozen and Clean Fifteen lists, the particular items in each group have changed their order of appearance from time to time, but have overall remained relatively constant, with a few exceptions. Here's a list of the foods that appeared consistently in the Dirty Dozen from 2012 to 2016:

- apples
- celery
- cucumbers
- grapes
- nectarines
- peaches
- potatoes
- spinach
- strawberries
- sweet bell peppers

Cherries, collard greens, domestic blueberries, hot peppers, kale and snap peas popped in and out of the Dirty Dozen lists during that time frame.

These foods were consistently in the Clean Fifteen from 2012 to 2016:

- asparagus
- avocados
- cabbage
- cantaloupe
- cauliflower
- eggplants
- grapefruits
- kiwifruits
- mangos
- onions
- papayas
- pineapples
- sweet corn
- sweet peas (frozen)

Sweet potatoes, watermelon and mushrooms also made an appearance on the Clean Fifteen a couple of times during that time frame.

Self-Monitoring: Your Powerful Secret Weapon

The American Diabetes Association and Canadian Diabetes Association both state that self-management of diabetes is the cornerstone of diabetes care and recommend that self-monitoring blood glucose (SMBG) be considered as part of the self-management education that can help people with diabetes better understand their disease.

What they don't say is that self-monitoring your blood sugar with your own glucometer is your secret weapon against what we are (unfortunately) still told is a chronic and progressive disease.

Using a Glucometer

A glucometer puts the power of monitoring your health, quite literally, in your own hands. You prick your finger with something called a lancet, then you apply the drop of blood you get to a test strip that has been inserted into the glucometer, which then measures your blood sugar.

The spectrum of unbalanced blood sugar that we have discussed, from insulin resistance through type 2 diabetes, is at the same time both general and specific. Although everyone experiences a characteristic rise in blood glucose after eating straight sugar, individual situations and responses to other foods vary from person to person. Sweet potatoes may send one person's blood sugar sky-high, but may be fine for others. Unless you monitor your blood sugar with a glucometer after a meal, you will have a hard time understanding the relationship between what you just ate and your blood sugar response. The glucometer takes you beyond the grams of carbohydrates listed in nutrient databases and shows you *how* those specific carbohydrates act in your body.

The first step is to understand what happens to your blood sugar when you eat your usual diet — before you make the changes recommended in this book. We suggest you get a dedicated notebook in which to record everything, because you will be gathering a lot of interesting data. For a couple of days, use your glucometer to check your blood sugar at the following times:

- **Before you start your meal:** This is straightforward.
- **1 hour after your meal:** This means 1 hour after you start eating your meal. Record not only what you ate, but also the quantities of the food items you ate at each meal. This will help you start to understand your blood sugar responses to various foods. For people with normal blood sugar, blood sugar numbers peak about 1 hour after they finish eating. For people with insulin resistance, blood sugar levels usually peak later.
- **2 hours after your meal:** This is the typical time for testing. In people with normal blood sugar, the blood sugar value will be back down and close to the premeal reading. In those with blood sugar dysfunction, the blood sugar may not peak until this time.
- **3 hours after your meal:** Ensure that you haven't had a snack in the meantime. Typical self-monitoring guidelines have you test for the last time at 2 hours after

a meal, but this may not tell the whole story. You want to know how high *and* how long your blood sugar is outside the normal range, because, as we have seen, damage to the eyes, nerves, kidneys and heart becomes more likely the longer blood sugar remains high.

- **When you wake up in the morning:** This is your fasting blood sugar. It isn't first on the list because you don't necessarily have to start your self-monitoring at the beginning of the day. Whether you start checking your blood sugar before lunch or before dinner, the important thing is to start.

Assessing the Numbers

Once you've collected this information, really look at it and assess your numbers. And assess them compared to "normal" numbers, not just the "good for diabetics" numbers. As we have seen, these "good numbers for diabetics" will keep you within the range where neuropathy, retinopathy and cardiovascular disease are continuing to progress.

Here's the important fact to keep in mind: it is carbohydrates — the sugars and starches you eat — that cause your blood sugar to rise the most after meals. Every gram of carbohydrate, even if it's from "healthy whole grains," turns to glucose once it's digested. And that glucose will cause your blood sugar to rise when it enters your bloodstream.

If your blood sugar numbers are rising outside the normal range (more than 140 mg/dL, or 7.8 mmol/L) after a meal, you need to change both the amount and the type of carbohydrate in your meals. That is what this book is about. When you eliminate sugars, grains, alcohol and industrial seed oils and emphasize proteins and nutrient-dense non-starchy vegetables, you will lower your blood sugar dramatically.

People with diabetes must work closely with their health-care providers to ensure that the effects of their dietary changes are monitored and that any medications are adjusted properly. The accuracy of glucometers is quite good now, and is getting better with each meter generation that comes to market. But to know for sure how close your meter reading is to the numbers on your medical blood tests, take your meter to your next scheduled lab test. Test yourself right before the blood draw so you can compare your meter reading with the lab result.

> It is carbohydrates — the sugars and starches you eat — that cause your blood sugar to rise the most after meals.

Analyzing Patterns and Trends

Once you understand how your blood sugar responds to the way you typically eat, start following the principles of the Paleo Plan for Better Blood Sugar, outlined in chapter 5. Use your glucometer to monitor what happens. Test your blood sugar at the times listed on the previous pages and record the results in your notebook.

Each time you try one of the recipes in this book, check what your blood sugar does. After a while, you will know what happens with certain meals, and you may not have to record your blood sugar numbers for that meal every time.

If you try a recipe with sweet potatoes or beets and your blood sugar rises higher than the normal range, write down how much you ate. Then try the same meal again at another time, but eat less of the sweet potatoes or beets. If your numbers are still higher than normal, you are likely not yet able to handle the carbohydrates in sweet potatoes or beets.

Only by consistently recording your blood sugar numbers as measured by your glucometer, and analyzing them against both what and how much you ate, can you see the important patterns and trends. The patterns tell you what is working and what isn't, and can serve as motivation to stick with a specific routine or make a change. In contrast, one blood sugar measurement every now and then tells you very little and cannot be the basis of a treatment program — context is everything.

DID YOU KNOW?

A Treasure Trove

That tiny drop of blood you get when you prick your finger contains a wealth of information just waiting for you to use it.

CHAPTER 5

The Paleo Plan
for Better Blood Sugar

The food we eat is the most powerful medicine we can use to restore our blood sugar and therefore our overall health. There is overwhelming evidence that diet and disease are linked, and maybe nowhere quite so obviously and immediately as with diet and blood sugar dysfunction. Everything you eat — or don't eat — affects your blood sugar in one way or another, and moves you either closer to health or closer to disease. The best way to correct abnormal blood sugars is to cut down on carbohydrate intake, and the best way to do that is to cut consumption of sugars and grains. And the best way to start lowering your consumption of sugar is to remove all sugar-sweetened and artificially sweetened beverages and fruit juices from your diet. The elimination of just 1 cup (8 oz or 250 mL) of fresh fruit juice or soda will reduce your intake by about 25 fast-acting carbohydrates.

The paleo approach to eating is backed by solid scientific research and provides us with a blueprint of how to eat for health and well-being. It is about eating real whole food and understanding that what we put in our mouth has a direct effect on our health.

> Choosing to eat whole, unprocessed, nutrient-dense food and exclude processed, industrial foods is the most important decision you can make to improve your health.

Jumping In

Change can be hard. We know that. But we also know that if you have insulin resistance, prediabetes or type 2 diabetes and you don't change how you are eating to better manage your blood sugar dysfunction, all of the effects and conditions associated with the dysfunction will continue to progress and accelerate.

From our own personal experience with eating paleo and working with our nutrition clients, we have found that jumping right in is generally the best way. Eliminating sugars, sweeteners, grains, alcohol and dairy all at once is a little like ripping the adhesive bandage off a cut: it hurts for a short time, but then you feel much better. It's much easier than a slow, agonizing pull, where you are tempted to just stop and leave everything the way it was. The most important step in the transition is making up your mind to change and then getting started. Choosing to eat whole, unprocessed, nutrient-dense food and exclude processed, industrial foods is the most important decision you can make to improve your health.

We challenge you to make the paleo way of eating a priority for the next 30 days. Set aside any preconceived notions you have about cutting out a food group or not getting enough calcium without dairy, and make eating lean meat, poultry, fish and seafood, vegetables, fruit, natural fats and nuts and seeds your number one goal for each of the next 30 days.

Here's what we expect will happen when you do this: your blood sugar numbers will fall, so be prepared for this and work with your doctor and health-care professionals to monitor the drop and adjust any medication you are on. You will also likely have more energy overall, fewer energy crashes (if any!), less brain fog and better sleep.

We are confident that you will quickly begin to see that cooking and eating real food for three meals a day, every day, is what is needed to improve your health and move away from disease. The power is in the doing, so let's get started.

DID YOU KNOW?

Just Do It

As a friend always says, the best way to get started is to get started. Don't let anxiety about making changes cause you to give up before you have even begun.

FAQ

Q *Is the paleo diet a high-protein, low-carb diet?*

A Contrary to what you may read, this is not a high-protein diet. It is an *adequate*-protein diet — adequate to provide the tools the body needs for repair and growth, as well as for sustained energy between meals. The protein this diet provides is spaced throughout the day at each of three meals instead of being concentrated in the evening hours as is typical in the standard North American diet.

This is also not a low-carb diet, per se, although it is probably a lot lower in carbs than what you are eating now. It is an *adequate*-carbohydrate diet that gives you the nutrient-dense carbohydrates needed for sustained and even energy.

The Paleo Plan for Better Blood Sugar at a Glance

Enjoy Whole Foods

Meat, poultry, seafood, eggs: These concentrated protein foods should be the foundation of every meal. Proteins provide the amino acid building blocks for repair and growth in the body. Adequate protein does a great job of making us feel satisfied for a longer period of time. Ensuring that you have the right amount of protein at three meals per day helps regulate blood sugar and insulin levels and can help you move away from snacking on fast carbohydrate foods between meals.

Non-starchy vegetables: These will make up the majority of your plate. They are powerhouses of antioxidants and phytonutrients, which offer protective health benefits beyond those offered by vitamins and minerals. These high-quality non-starchy carbohydrates also contain both soluble and insoluble fibers to help normalize blood sugar and insulin levels.

Fruits: Fruits are chock-full of antioxidants, phytonutrients, minerals and vitamins. They should be somewhat limited in quantity, in order to prevent blood sugar spikes and maximize blood sugar control. You will determine your own personal tolerance for fruit when you self-monitor your blood sugar.

Nuts and seeds: Nuts and seeds contain at least twice as much fat (in grams) as they do protein and carbohydrates, with many of these fats being healthful monounsaturated fats. Nuts and seeds also have a good balance of carbohydrates and proteins and help keep blood sugar stable. We just have to be careful not to eat too many!

Fats and oils: Using oils and fats with the right nutritional qualities is important. We need healthful dietary fats to make important things like cell walls, hormones and the myelin sheaths around our nerves. Fat also improves mood and brain function, and can help prevent impaired cognitive function and dementia. The outdated low-fat message is being replaced by scientific evidence showing that people who eat fatty nuts have a lower risk of developing type 2 diabetes, and those who add olive oil to their diet and consume nuts on a regular basis have a lower risk of heart attack.

Avoid Refined Foods

Sugars and sweeteners: Added sugar in our food is the easiest way to provoke an unhealthy hormonal response. Sugar hits your bloodstream fast and hard and keeps you on the blood sugar roller coaster. But don't think noncaloric sweeteners are any better. Artificial sweeteners keep us craving the sweet taste, slow our metabolism, increase hunger and alter gut flora, and can contribute to the insulin response.

Refined and whole grains: Both refined and whole grains act like sugar in the body. When grains, even whole grains, are milled into flour, the blood sugar and insulin response can be as fast and high as it is when you eat sugar. There are no nutrients in grains that you cannot get in vegetables.

Industrial seed oils: The increasing imbalance of omega-3 and omega-6 fatty acids in the standard North American diet can trigger inflammation, which is at the root of all chronic diseases. The use of industrial seed oils is one of the biggest reasons for this imbalance.

Alcohol: On its own, alcohol interferes with the regulatory actions of insulin and glucagon, and when you mix it with sugar (cola, tonic, fruit juice), the effects are compounded, leaving people with diabetes at risk for hypoglycemia for up to 24 hours.

Dairy products: Most people are genetically unable to digest dairy properly (even if they aren't aware of it), leading to increased intestinal permeability, inflammation, sensitivities and intolerances. Many dairy products are sweetened with sugar, processed fruit or sweeteners and, as a result, contribute to unbalanced blood sugar. Certain people may be able to add unsweetened full-fat dairy back into their diet once their blood sugar is normalized.

Legumes: Despite being touted as high in protein, legumes are still, on average, over 65% carbohydrates and can be problematic when blood sugar is unbalanced. As with dairy, for certain individuals, there may be a place for legumes in the diet once blood sugar is normalized.

Foods to Avoid

Just so we're clear and there is no misunderstanding, here's a list of foods to avoid in each of the categories. We have tried to be as complete as possible, but if you don't see a food you know contains something in one of the broad categories of Foods to Avoid, please don't try to sneak it in because it wasn't on the list. We hope these lists help you understand how far blood sugar–disrupting foods reach into our lives, especially in processed foods.

Sugars

- agave syrup/ nectar
- barley malt
- beet sugar
- brown rice syrup
- brown sugar (light or dark)
- candy
- cane juice
- cane sugar
- caramel
- coconut sugar/ nectar
- corn syrup
- corn syrup solids
- date sugar
- demerara sugar
- dextrose
- evaporated cane juice
- fructose
- fruit juice
- fruit juice concentrate
- glucose
- glucose solids
- golden sugar
- golden syrup
- granulated sugar
- grape sugar
- high-fructose corn syrup
- invert sugar
- lactose
- malt syrup
- maltitol
- maltodextrin
- maltose
- mannitol
- maple syrup
- molasses
- palm sugar
- panela
- rapadura sugar
- refiners syrup
- sorbitol
- sorghum syrup
- sucrose
- table sugar
- treacle
- turbinado sugar
- white sugar
- yacón syrup
- yellow sugar
- xylitol

Noncaloric Sweeteners

- acesulfame K (Sweet One)
- aspartame (Equal, NutraSweet)
- saccharin (Sweet'N Low)
- stevia (Truvia, Sun Crystals)
- sucralose (Splenda)
- tagatose

Grains and Flours

- amaranth
- barley
- buckwheat
- bulgur
- corn
- couscous
- durum wheat
- farro
- graham flour
- Kamut
- malt
- millet
- oats
- quinoa
- rice (all kinds)
- rye
- semolina
- spelt
- tapioca
- teff
- triticale
- wheat
- wild rice

Grain Products

- bagels
- biscuits
- breading
- breads
- brownies
- cake
- cereal
- challah
- chapatti
- cookies
- crackers
- croissants
- croutons
- doughnuts
- granola bars
- meatballs and meatloaf made with bread
- muffins
- naan
- nachos
- oatmeal
- orzo
- pancakes
- panko
- pasta
- pie
- pitas
- pizza
- power bars
- rice cakes
- rice noodles
- rolls
- roti
- sandwiches
- scones
- snack bars
- soup bases
- soy sauce
- stuffing
- thickeners
- toast
- tortillas

Industrial Seed Oils

- canola oil
- corn oil
- cottonseed oil
- hydrogenated vegetable oil
- partially hydrogenated vegetable oil
- peanut oil
- rice bran oil
- safflower oil
- soybean oil
- sunflower oil
- vegetable oil
- vegetable shortening

Beverages

- alcohol (all types)
- commercial smoothies
- diet soda
- energy drinks
- fresh fruit juice
- fruit drinks
- fruit juice from concentrate
- nonalcoholic beer
- shakes
- soda
- sweetened coffees
- sweetened teas

Dairy Products

- buttermilk
- cheese (all types)
- condensed milk
- cottage cheese
- cow's milk (all types)
- cream
- cream cheese
- curds
- evaporated milk
- frozen yogurt
- gelato
- goat's milk
- half-and-half (10%) cream
- ice cream
- kefir
- lassi
- milk solids
- powdered milk
- quark
- sheep's milk
- sour cream
- whey
- whipping cream
- yogurt

Legumes

- adzuki beans
- black beans
- black-eyed peas
- broad beans
- cannellini beans
- chickpeas (garbanzo beans)
- fava beans
- Great Northern beans
- kidney beans
- lentils
- lima beans
- mung beans
- navy beans
- peanuts
- pinto beans
- red beans
- split peas
- soybeans (tofu, tempeh, edamame)
- white beans

Foods to Enjoy

Now that you know what you are not going to eat with the Paleo Plan for Better Blood Sugar, let's take a look at what you *are* going to eat, along with some principles of eating for blood sugar control and how to approach each meal in order to ensure the best possible blood sugar outcome. Just as an architect creates blueprints as a plan to follow when constructing buildings, the following four questions are your plan to follow for better blood sugar. Ask yourself these questions each time you are planning or eating a meal.

Question 1: What Is My Protein?

Every meal should be built around a protein. Protein provides the anchor for blood sugar and helps us stay satisfied until our next meal. It keeps us from taking a ride on the blood sugar roller coaster.

So how much protein should you eat? This program is not about weighing and measuring food down to the last ounce or gram. When we do that, we stay stuck in a relationship with food where it is something we are working against instead of our biggest ally in our quest for health. The classic "size (and thickness) of the palm of your hand" is the amount of protein you want to have at each meal. If your piece of protein is irregularly shaped or seems thinner than your hand, don't worry. Eyeballing the amount is okay.

If you are a big person or are very active all day (like someone who works in construction, for example), you may need a bit more protein at each meal. If you are small or quite inactive during the day, you may need a little less.

Think of protein as the foundation of every meal, the place to start. The rule of thumb is for protein to make up about one-quarter of your plate at each meal.

> Protein provides the anchor for blood sugar and helps us stay satisfied until our next meal.

Protein Portion of Plate

Protein should make up about one-quarter of your plate at every meal.

FAQ

Q *Isn't red meat a carcinogen?*

A Some of you may be wondering whether you should continue to eat red meat after the announcement in 2015 that the International Agency for Research on Cancer (part of the World Health Organization) classified processed meat as a group 1 carcinogen and red meat as a "probable carcinogen." First, don't panic, and second, put it in perspective. Even though processed meat and cigarettes are in the same category, it cannot be said that eating salami is comparable to smoking cigarettes, which contain many known carcinogens and increase the risk of lung cancer by almost 20 times.

In addition, no context was considered in this classification; it was based solely on observational studies, which, in scientific analysis, don't determine causation. Context includes other dietary factors (such as high sugar and processed carbohydrate intake, alcohol consumption, low intake of fruits and vegetables), behavioral factors (smoking, physical activity and total sitting time) and how the meat was raised (grass-fed or a concentrated animal feeding operation).

Context should also take into account one of the newest and fastest-growing areas of scientific research: the gut microbiome. The health of your gut may be more important for cancer risk than how much bacon you eat.

Meat and Poultry

Meat and poultry, along with fish and other seafood, are the biggest, most concentrated protein sources. Along with bioavailable protein, these foods are good sources of important minerals, such as iron and zinc, as well as vitamin B_{12} and omega-3 fatty acids.

Grass-fed or free-range beef, bison, lamb, pork and poultry are preferable if you have the choice. Conventionally raised meats are, however, less expensive and would still be a nutritious foundation for your blood-sugar-balancing program. Farmers' markets enable you to buy directly from the farmer in many cases, which can not only save a few dollars, but can also give you valuable information about where your meat came from and how it was cared for. Buying in bulk can help make grass-fed meat more affordable, and freezing it does not significantly change its nutritional qualities (and means there is always a satisfying piece of protein around!).

A note about pork and turkey bacon. While technically an "okay" paleo food, bacon is not as dense a source of protein as other meats, and it can be easy to overeat. Treat it like a condiment (and not one you use at every meal), and really try to find a grass-fed source.

What to Eat: Meat and Poultry
Including but not limited to:

- beef
- bison
- boar
- buffalo
- chicken
- duck
- emu
- game meats
- goat
- goose
- kangaroo
- lamb
- mutton
- organ meats
- ostrich
- pork
- quail
- rabbit
- squab
- turkey
- venison

Fish and Seafood

Fish and other seafood are a perfect combination of high-quality protein, high omega-3 fatty acids and low total fat. The omega-3 fats help to correct the inflammation promoted by overconsumption of omega-6 fats in the standard North American diet. Fish and shellfish are also good sources of the fat-soluble vitamins A and D and the mineral iodine, which is crucial for our thyroid health.

One of the sad realities of our oceans and waterways is their contamination with mercury. Fish accumulate mercury in their muscle and fat tissue, primarily as a result of eating other fish. As larger predatory fish eat smaller ones, the mercury bioaccumulates up through the food chain. The result is that the largest predatory fish contain the highest amounts of mercury. Fish consumption advisories vary among countries, but it is generally agreed that shark, swordfish, king mackerel and tilefish should not be eaten because of their mercury content.

Tuna is also a large predator, and consumption advisories have a recommended limit on fresh and frozen tuna, as well as canned albacore (white) tuna. Canned tuna described as "light tuna" contains other types of tuna, such as skipjack, yellowfin and tongol, all of which have lower mercury levels.

There are lots of other fish and seafood options that have low or negligible levels of mercury, so don't let fear of mercury exposure deter you from eating fish.

> **DID YOU KNOW?**
>
> **Choose Wild When Possible**
>
> Look for the "wild" label when purchasing fish. Wild fish have a higher omega-3 content than their industrial farm-raised counterparts. Having said that, if only farmed fish are available, don't let that be a deal-breaker. From a blood sugar perspective, it is better to eat farmed salmon than to opt for a pizza instead.

What to Eat: Fish and Seafood
Including but not limited to:

- bass
- catfish
- clams
- cod
- crab
- haddock
- halibut
- herring
- lobster
- mackerel
- mussels
- oysters
- perch
- prawns
- salmon
- sardines
- scallops
- shrimp
- snails
- snapper
- trout
- tuna

FAQ

Q *Shouldn't I avoid eating egg yolks because they are high in cholesterol?*

A We have been told for the past 50 years that the cholesterol in egg yolks is bad for our hearts. Many studies, however, do not support this position, including an analysis of the data from the National Health and Nutrition Examination Study (NHANES) in the United States, where the researchers stated in their conclusion, "We did not find a significant positive association between egg consumption and increased risk of mortality from cardiovascular disease or stroke in the U.S. population. These results corroborate the findings of previous studies."

Even the 2015 U.S. government-issued dietary guidelines (released in 2016) removed the limit on dietary cholesterol, stating, "Cholesterol is not considered a nutrient of concern for overconsumption."

It is estimated that only about 20% of our blood cholesterol comes from our diet, with the rest produced by our liver. If we need to address our cholesterol levels, we need to look to other factors, including what is going on in our liver and how much fiber we are eating. Eliminating sugar and refined carbohydrates from the diet is one of the best ways to restore overall liver health.

Eggs

Eggs are an incredibly nutrient-dense food. They are an excellent source of all the B vitamins, the fat-soluble vitamins A, E and D (which is important for bone growth and immunity) and the minerals zinc, phosphorus, iron, calcium, iodine, potassium and selenium. Eggs also contain lutein and zeaxanthin, both of which protect against cataracts and macular degeneration. To top it off, egg yolks are a concentrated source of essential choline, which is vital for the formation of cell membranes, cell signaling and neurotransmitter synthesis.

We do want to make sure we get eggs from free-range or pasture-raised hens that scavenged bugs and shoots outdoors. These eggs are much lower in omega-6 fats, which can become inflammatory when out of balance with our omega-3 intake. Hens that are fed flax seeds produce the omega-3 eggs we see on the shelves.

> **DID YOU KNOW?**
>
> **Eating Enough Eggs**
>
> Remember that you should be eating the whole egg, not just the egg white. And keep in mind that one egg is not enough protein for most of us to make it to the next meal. Most people will need two eggs at a meal, and some will need three.

Question 2: What Are My Non-Starchy Vegetables?

Vegetables, with their dense supply of vitamins, minerals, fiber and phytonutrients, play a starring role in paleo-inspired eating. Almost all of the vegetables featured in the recipes in this book are non-starchy, low-glycemic, nutrient-dense carbohydrates that help stabilize blood sugar and insulin concentrations in the blood. These slow-release carbohydrates normalize your energy levels throughout the day by preventing blood sugar surges and crashes.

After you have chosen your protein to fill one-quarter of your plate, fill up the other three-quarters with non-starchy vegetables. Try to include at least two vegetables with each meal. You'll notice that many of the egg, seafood, poultry and meat recipes in the book already include a vegetable component, so adding another one or two to fill up your plate is easy, and there are lots to choose from.

Non–Starchy Vegetable Portion of Plate

Non-starchy Vegetables

Fill up the other three-quarters of your plate with non-starchy vegetables.

DID YOU KNOW?

Before You Shop

Before shopping trips, take a look in the fridge and see what still needs to be used up. In many of the recipes in this book, you can substitute a different vegetable and/or protein, so you can use up what you have on hand.

You can basically eat as many of the vegetables listed on pages 94–95 as much as you like at meals, with one caveat: you need to know how they affect your own personal blood sugar levels. When you monitor your blood sugar with a glucometer, you will come to know if there are any vegetables that raise your blood sugar too much. You may find that it rises too high after you eat sweet potatoes, squash or beets. In that case, avoid recipes with these ingredients (or replace them in the recipe with another vegetable, such as zucchini). Try them again when your blood sugar and insulin are better balanced; you may be able to reintroduce them into your diet. But never simply assume a vegetable is okay for you to eat just because it is a vegetable. Test yourself. It's the only way to know for sure.

While we prefer to eat organic versions of foods that have appeared on the Dirty Dozen list (see page 77), it's not essential. Don't walk away from any vegetable or fruit just because it isn't organic. It is better to eat conventionally grown produce than not to eat produce at all.

DID YOU KNOW?

Cooked or Raw?

How you eat your vegetables, cooked or raw, is really up to you. The recipes provide you with both options. Although most foods can generally be found in stores year-round these days, you may find certain vegetables suit different seasons better, depending on where you live. So mix it up — chop, sauté, grill or bake — just be sure to fill up your plate with vegetables.

Potatoes

White potatoes are not included in the recipes or vegetable list in this book, not because they aren't a whole, nutrient-dense food, but because they generally act like grains and sugar in the body and have unfavorable effects on blood sugar and insulin.

Corn

While many people consider corn a vegetable, it is actually a grain. As such, it can have an adverse effect on your blood sugar levels, and we have not included it in the recipes.

Green Beans and Peas

Although green beans, sweet peas, snow peas and snap peas are actually legumes, and therefore not strictly paleo, we have included them in this diet. Because we are eating mostly the big green seed pod that contains the small amount of legumes inside, these foods generally don't affect blood sugar much — but test yourself when you eat them to make sure.

Tomatoes and Avocados

Yes, tomatoes and avocados are technically fruits. But we're including them in the vegetable section because we tend to use them as vegetables and they act like vegetables in the body — with very little blood sugar effect.

You will also notice that some of the recipes use canned tomatoes and tomato paste. While these are processed, they are still just tomatoes and provide a delicious, rich tomato flavor, especially in the Sloppy Joes (page 230).

DID YOU KNOW?

Purchasing Canned Tomatoes

Be sure to read the ingredient list carefully when buying canned tomatoes and tomato paste, to avoid added salt and other surprising ingredients, like sugar and gluten. Purchase BPA-free cans when you can or, better still, look for tomato products packed in glass jars.

What to Eat: Vegetables
Including but not limited to:

- artichokes
- arugula
- asparagus
- bamboo shoots
- basil
- beet greens
- beets
- bell peppers
- bok choy
- broccoli
- Brussels sprouts
- cabbage
- carrots
- cauliflower
- celery
- chives
- cilantro
- collard greens
- cucumbers
- daikon radish
- dandelion greens
- dill
- eggplant
- endive
- fennel
- garlic
- green beans
- green onions
- horseradish
- jicama
- kale
- kohlrabi
- leeks
- lettuce
- mint
- mushrooms
- mustard greens
- olives
- onions
- parsley
- peppers (all kinds)
- purslane
- radicchio
- radishes
- rapini

- rutabaga
- seaweed
- shallots
- snap peas
- snow peas
- spinach
- squash
- sweet potato
- Swiss chard
- tomatillos
- tomatoes
- turnip greens
- turnips
- watercress

Question 3:
What About Fruit (If Any)?

Sweet, delicious fruit. It has always been lumped into the "fruits and vegetables" category, and because we have always been told to eat more of these, we feel healthy when we eat fruit, even a lot of it, and even to the exclusion of vegetables, because, you know, we had our "fruits-n-vegetables."

Certainly fruits are full of vitamins, antioxidants, phytonutrients and fiber, but they also have their fair share of sugar — fructose and glucose, to be exact — and they have varying effects on different people's blood sugar.

We already know that virtually all cells in the body use glucose, but fructose is a different story. After fructose is absorbed, it goes to the liver, where it is metabolized and then either stored as glycogen or converted into that long-term energy storage unit: fat. High fructose intake has been shown to play a role in insulin resistance and blood sugar dysfunction.

The biggest culprit in blood sugar dysregulation is not usually fruit, but it does need to be emphasized that the priority is vegetables. Fruit should not take their place.

> **DID YOU KNOW?**
>
> **High-Fructose Corn Syrup**
> Much of the sugar in the standard North American diet comes from high-fructose corn syrup, which averages around 55% fructose — not that different from some types of fruit.

What to Eat: Fresh Fruits

Including but not limited to:

- apples
- apricots
- bananas
- blackberries
- blueberries
- cantaloupe
- cherries
- cranberries
- elderberries
- figs
- grapefruit (red and white)
- grapes
- guavas
- honeydew melon
- jackfruits
- kiwifruits
- lemons
- limes
- lychees
- mangos
- melons
- nectarines
- oranges
- papayas
- passionfruit
- peaches
- pears
- persimmons
- pineapple
- plums
- pomegranates
- raspberries
- rhubarb
- star fruits
- strawberries
- tangerines
- watermelon

Guidelines for Eating Fruit

1. **Eat fresh fruit.** Dried fruits, such as dates, are nature's candy, and they can have negative effects on blood sugar. Commercially prepared dried fruits are generally made with sucrose syrup or concentrated fruit juice, both of which are problematic for blood sugar and insulin levels. If you dry your own fruit (see Oven-Baked Apple Chews with Cinnamon Nut Butter, page 272) and know there isn't any added sugar, that's okay. But you should still be aware of how much you eat. When fruit is dried, it is pretty easy to eat what would amount to two to three servings of fresh fruit, so measure it out and only eat the number of apple slices that there would be in a fresh apple, for example. And then monitor your blood sugar to make sure you can handle the fruit.

2. **Don't eat fruit by itself.** Eat fruit with a protein and/or a fat — and preferably with a food that offers both, like nuts and seeds. Fat and protein slow the release of food from the stomach, which means the sugar from the fruit hits your bloodstream more slowly, blunting the impact of the blood sugar response.

3. **Limit the amount of fruit you eat.** Take care not to eat more than one or two whole fruits (or 1 to 2 cups/250 to 500 mL of fruit) per day. Yes, fruits are good for you, but only if your blood sugar doesn't spike into dangerous territory when you eat them. Context is everything. When you include a fruit in your meals or snacks, use your glucometer to measure your blood sugar at 2 and 3 hours afterward, to really understand whether that fruit is improving your health or not. You may find that, for the time being, you need to be quite limited in the amount of fruit you eat, because of its effects on your blood sugar.

4. **Don't drink fruit juice.** When we remove all of fruit's pulp and fiber and turn it into a juice, yes, some vitamins and phytonutrients remain, but we are left with mostly water and sugar, which hits your system quickly, driving up blood sugar and insulin as if it was soda. Just eat the whole fruit.

Question 4: What Is My Good Fat?

For the past few decades, fat has been a problem. All types of fat were lumped together and painted with the same unhealthy label. As we have seen, we need a certain amount of the right kinds of fat to support our metabolism and help us make cell walls and hormones and important things like that.

Most of the recipes in the book include one or more nutritious fats, so we've got you covered there. And don't worry if you end up with a meal of Cauliflower Garlic Mash (page 152), which includes grass-fed butter, with Almond-Crusted Salmon (page 185), which is full of omega-3 fats, and a green salad with dressing made from extra virgin olive oil. You won't need to add another fat, but you also don't need to worry that there is too much.

Nuts and Seeds

Nuts and seeds are a rich source of monounsaturated fats (MUFAs). MUFAs help lower both total cholesterol and low-density lipoprotein (LDL) cholesterol ("bad" cholesterol) while maintaining high-density lipoprotein (HDL) cholesterol ("good" cholesterol), all of which helps to lower the risk of heart disease and stroke.

A downside to nuts and seeds is that they have a higher level of omega-6 fatty acids than omega-3 fatty acids. This can tilt the scale toward inflammation, so we want to make sure we are not overeating nuts and seeds, which is easy to do. As you get started with this program, outside of any called for in the recipes, limit yourself to about $1/2$ cup (125 mL) total of nuts and seeds per day.

Purchase nuts and seeds raw and double-check the label to make sure they have not been coated in industrial seed oils to increase shelf life. Roasted nuts or seeds are delicious, but when you buy them that way, you don't know what oils were used or at what temperature they were cooked (high temperatures damage the natural oils in nuts and seeds). Roasting or toasting your own is the best way to go.

DID YOU KNOW?

Storing Nuts and Seeds

Store nuts and seeds in the fridge or freezer if you have the room. The cold will help preserve the beneficial oils and prevent them from going rancid.

What to Eat: Nuts and Seeds

- almonds
- Brazil nuts
- cashews
- chestnuts
- chia seeds
- flax seeds
- hazelnuts (filberts)
- hemp seeds
- macadamia nuts
- pecans
- pine nuts
- pistachios
- green pumpkin seeds (pepitas)
- sesame seeds
- sunflower seeds
- walnuts

Roasting and Toasting Nuts

- **Oven method for roasting nuts**: Spread nuts or seeds in a single layer on a rimmed baking sheet and place in a 225°F to 250°F (110°C to 120°C) oven. (The low temperature helps prevent damage to the oils in the nuts and seeds.) Start checking on them and stirring after the first 10 to 15 minutes. Some varieties (almonds) can take up to 60 minutes or more; others are done much sooner. Be sure to set a timer to remind you to keep checking on them, as it is easy to forget. When the nuts or seeds are golden brown, transfer them to a plate and spread them out to cool.
- **Skillet method for toasting nuts**: Spread nuts or seeds in a single layer in a dry skillet and place over medium heat. Stir often and watch for the browning to start. Once they start to brown, turn the heat down a bit and continue to toast and stir until the nuts or seeds are golden brown. Be sure to remove them from the heat source when they are done; don't just turn off the burner, or they will be overcooked. Transfer them to a plate and spread them out to cool.

Fats and Oils

We know that industrial seed oils are on our avoid list, so what do we use instead? Olive oil, avocado oil, coconut oil and butter are the mainstays for many of the recipes in this book. They have favorable fat profiles and are relatively stable with heat. Be sure to purchase oils in dark glass bottles to protect them from light damage and the chemicals that leach from plastics.

Olive oil quality varies widely. We recommend extra virgin olive oil in many of our recipes, especially those that are eaten raw. Look for a label that says "first cold pressed" to indicate that no chemicals were used to extract the oil. Avoid using extra virgin olive oil in recipes cooked at high temperatures; instead, use regular olive oil, avocado oil, coconut oil or butter.

Avocado oil is a relative newcomer to the cooking oil category. It is pressed from the pulp of the avocado, rather than the seed, and its bright green color is due to its chlorophyll content. It has a similar omega fatty acid profile to olive oil — mostly oleic acid, an omega-9 monounsaturated fat. Avocado oil has quite a high smoke point of about 480°F (250°C), making it a good choice for sautéing and for marinades that will be subject to high grilling heat.

Grass-fed butter (or, rather, butter from grass-fed cows) is one of our favorites. But butter is dairy, isn't it? Yes, so it is not technically paleo. We include it in the book because the fatty acid profile of grass-fed butter (lower palmitic acid, higher conjugated linoleic acid) is so much better than that of regular butter. Plus, you can't beat the taste. Many paleo books recommend ghee (a form of clarified butter) instead. If you are sensitive to dairy, any amount of butter can disrupt your gut and increase intestinal permeability; in that case, you may find ghee easier to digest.

DID YOU KNOW?

Coconut Oil

Coconut oil is a highly saturated fat and is therefore very stable when heated, making it a good choice for all-around cooking. Coconut oil is about 50% lauric acid — a medium-chain triglyceride shown to have antiviral, antifungal and antimicrobial properties. Look for raw, unrefined, virgin coconut oil, which will have a mild coconut flavor and scent. More heat used during the extraction of the oil means more coconut flavor in the oil.

What to Eat: Fats and Oils

- avocado oil
- bacon fat/lard (from pasture-raised pigs)
- coconut oil
- duck fat
- extra virgin olive oil
- flaxseed oil*
- ghee
- grass-fed butter
- hempseed oil*
- macadamia nut oil
- palm oil (unprocessed)
- schmaltz (chicken fat)
- sesame oil
- tallow (beef, lamb)
- walnut oil*

* These oils should not be heated at all; use them only for cold or room-temperature dishes.

Q *What should I drink while following the paleo plan?*

A There are no two ways about it: water is your best option. Adequate hydration helps nutrients move into tissues and cells better and helps move waste products out. Drinking enough water also supports kidney health and helps prevent constipation. Here are some ways to meet the recommended eight glasses per day:

- Drink water with freshly squeezed lemon or lime juice — hot or cold, no sweeteners.
- Drink water infused with herbs. Put some crushed fresh mint or basil leaves in a jug of water and let the herbs infuse the water as you drink it over about 2 days. Try a combination of basil and lime slices.
- Drink sparkling water or mineral water (not soda water).
- Drink Warming Chicken Stock (page 116) or Beef Bone Broth (page 114).
- Drink green tea, herbal tea or coffee (no dairy or sweeteners), but make sure the caffeinated versions are not interfering with your sleep.

Eating Away from Home

When you are first starting the Paleo Plan for Better Blood Sugar, eating out can be a bit stressful. The best way to ensure you are successful in sticking to the plan is to remember the four questions:

1. What is my protein?
2. What are my non-starchy vegetables?
3. What about fruit (if any)?
4. What is my good fat?

Commit them to memory: protein, vegetable, fruit and fat. Armed with the answers, you'll know how to approach any situation, especially those where you didn't prepare the food.

At Work

When it comes to bringing your lunch to work, the absolute easiest thing to do is to take leftovers from dinner the night before. Instead of worrying about it in the morning, when you might be tempted not to take the time to pack it, put the lunch helping into a glass or stainless steel container while you are cleaning up after dinner, so all you need to do is grab it out of the fridge in the morning.

DID YOU KNOW?

Cook Extra for Dinner

Making lunch in the morning works for some, but if you find you are too rushed, plan to cook extra at dinner so you are covered.

There are a lot of options at the grocery store when it comes to premade salads and precut vegetables. Or toss together some cooked shrimp, chicken or salmon, mixed greens, cherry tomatoes, chopped cucumber and a splash of homemade vinaigrette, and you have a great lunch.

At Restaurants

At any restaurant, the first thing we are asked is usually what we would like to drink. Ask for sparkling or still water with lemon or lime. This puts something in your hand, gives you something to do and relaxes your server.

Next, say no to the bread basket. (In our experience, most people are happy not to have the temptation, but check with your dinner companions first.) Some restaurants will bring olives, celery, carrots or cucumber instead; you just have to ask.

Once you have the menu in hand, remember that your meals revolve around a protein, so start there. Do you want beef, chicken or fish? Look for grilled, broiled or baked options, which are less likely to be breaded. Don't even look at the pasta section.

Next come the vegetables. Many restaurants won't make you a special vegetable dish, but if you see good non-starchy vegetable options for another entrée, ask if they could be substituted for the rice or mashed potatoes that your meal would have come with. If, for some reason, absolutely no substitutions are possible, simply ask for the meat to be brought on the plate by itself, then order a green salad with vinaigrette. You have your protein, your vegetables and your fat (in the meat and vinaigrette). Problem solved: plan followed, blood sugar balanced.

While Traveling

If you are traveling by car, stocking a small cooler is a great way to stay on plan and know that you have your protein and vegetables. It also takes the guesswork out of what may or may not be available on the road. Hard-cooked eggs or individual serving–sized cans of tuna or salmon are great to have on hand.

When you are flying, packing your own food can be more difficult, what with airline regulations (not to mention the fact that the people sitting around you may not want you to eat a can of sardines on the flight). Cut vegetables like zucchini, jicama, radishes and olives travel well and could be combined with some nuts and seeds to keep blood sugar stable.

Q *What's the best way to deal with questions about my food choices?*

A If you feel like explaining your new diet plan to your tablemates, and you think they are truly interested, then tell them about all the delicious things you *can* eat instead of emphasizing what you can't eat. There can be a lot of adult peer pressure around food and alcohol, with some people calling you a party pooper or telling you to "live a little." (That's the whole point — you want to live a lot!) Those comments are more likely a reflection of how they are feeling about what they are doing or not doing with their diet and health; they are not really about you at all. The dining experience is about being social with the company you are with, not about whether or not you had rice.

At Other People's Homes

It's the end of a long week and you've been invited to a friend's place for dinner. You don't know what they will be serving, and you don't know what to do. Best-case scenario, they'll have made a protein-based meal with vegetables and potatoes (which you can avoid). Worst case, it'll be pasta with a super-decadent dessert.

There will be times when staying exactly on plan is not possible. But just because lasagna is being served, that doesn't mean you go back for seconds. Try to fill your plate up as much as you can with salad, make the best of it and be gracious.

The flip side is to examine what you serve when others come to your place. You don't need to serve crackers and cheese and cheesecake. Prepare some of the recipes in this book, and you and your guests will end the evening full and happy — and with balanced blood sugar.

> If you have high-carbohydrate breakfasts, cheat days and desserts, you will not achieve the desired metabolic changes, nor will you enjoy any of the resulting health benefits.

Food Traps to Avoid

There are a number of particularly tricky areas to navigate when it comes to eating for blood sugar control: grain-filled breakfasts, cheat days, the 80/20 rule, desserts and snacks. Some of these are touted as a way to boost metabolism or feel less deprived. We see them as a good way to maintain high insulin and unbalanced blood sugar.

When you change your diet as outlined in this book, certain metabolic changes take place that improve your health. If you have high-carbohydrate breakfasts, cheat days and desserts, you will not achieve the desired metabolic changes, nor will you enjoy any of the resulting health benefits.

There is plenty of discussion in the nutrition world about food addiction. If you keep having something you are addicted to, you keep the addiction going. We wouldn't think of using the "everything in moderation" approach with people addicted to other substances that harm the body and destroy health, and we shouldn't be using it when it comes to sugar or grains. Plus, we shouldn't be eating nutrient-dense non-starchy vegetables in moderation — we need to pile our plates high! So let's stop using this tired phrase.

Traditional Grain-Laden Breakfasts

In part 2 of this book, you will note that there isn't a specific breakfast chapter. This is on purpose. We are paralyzed by grains at breakfast in North America. If it's not cereal, bread, muffins, waffles, bagels, granola bars, pancakes or a breakfast sandwich of some sort, we don't know what to eat.

The body needs nutrient-dense whole foods at every meal, not just lunch and dinner. When we start the day with processed grains and sugar (which are in all of the items mentioned above), we start the engine of the blood sugar roller coaster. Our blood sugar and insulin increase quickly after a toasted bagel with "lite" cream cheese and then, 2 hours later, they come crashing down, sending us for that mid-morning skinny latte and low-fat muffin.

Breakfast really does set you up for the day, so give yourself the right start. Your breakfast plate should look no different than your other meals. What is your protein? What are your non-starchy vegetables?

In the 30-Day Paleo Meal Plan (pages 105–109), you will find an egg recipe for almost every breakfast, because this is what most of you will be comfortable with at the start. Having said that, we encourage you to eat other proteins at your morning meal. Leftover dinner is fantastic. Salmon and chicken aren't on many breakfast menus in North America, which is too bad. Go ahead and try dinner for breakfast — you'll see the results in your blood sugar numbers.

> We are paralyzed by grains at breakfast in North America. If it's not cereal, bread, muffin, waffles, bagels, granola bars, pancakes or a breakfast sandwich of some sort, we don't know what to eat.

Cheat Meals and the 80/20 Rule

When we talk about a "cheat meal," we are perpetuating the self-destructive vocabulary of dieting. This term implies that you are getting away with something that won't be a problem unless you get caught. You might cheat on the weekly crossword, but you can't cheat on your blood sugar. Planning a cheat meal means you are purposefully making a food choice that will have negative ramifications in your body beyond just that meal. If it's a really bad cheat, your blood sugar and insulin may stay elevated until your next meal, potentially pushing you to higher blood sugar levels than you've had before.

Following the 80/20 rule is essentially the same thing as having a cheat meal. If you have 21 meals per week, 20% is about four meals in which you are not eating for health. Or does 80/20 mean that 20% of *every* meal is off-plan? (Okay, we're pushing the envelope here, but you understand where we're coming from.)

For those of us with blood sugar dysfunction, cheat meals and the 80/20 rule and the "everything in moderation" approach don't apply. Break out of the dieting mindset and understand that you are in control of what you eat — and what you eat immediately affects your blood sugar and insulin levels. These, in turn, directly affect whether you are moving toward disease (end-stage diabetes) or toward improved blood sugar and improved health. Eating as outlined in this book will help you stabilize your physiology while you work on your psychology. As low-carb eater Jenny Ruhl says, "Blood sugar control is a marathon, not a sprint."

> You might cheat on the weekly crossword, but you can't cheat on your blood sugar.

Desserts

Does following the paleo plan mean no dessert? Well, other than fruit, yes. You see, the "normal" rules don't apply to those of us with blood sugar issues (which is really the majority of the North American population). Typical desserts will raise your blood sugar into territory where there is physiological damage, and none of us wants that. So try a bit of fruit after your meal and see what happens to your blood sugar. When you test, you will know. A few fresh berries or a bit of pineapple with some Coconut Whip (page 275) are nice, but only if you can handle them.

Snack Attacks

Snacking has become ubiquitous. The traditional purpose of snacking — something small to tide you over between meals — has morphed into something else. It's big business, with big dollars being spent to convince you that you need that new type of chewy "good-for-you" thing in the shiny new package. Nielsen retail sales data puts North American snack sales at $124 billion per year. That's a lot of money vying for your attention.

Snacking now replaces whole meals, or promises to give you added nutrients (like extra protein after a workout), or answers the 3 p.m. craving that has been created by unbalanced food choices — maybe even from other snack foods. We have come to rely on commercial snacks, mostly to the detriment of our blood sugar.

Snacking is not something we recommend. It means that you are really grazing all day, going only a couple of hours at most without putting something in your mouth. This pattern keeps your blood sugar and insulin at elevated levels, setting you up for insulin resistance. That is why snacks aren't built into the meal plan (pages 105–109).

In part 2, you will see a chapter called Extras, in which the recipes might look like snack food. These foods are intended to be additions to your meals. The Crispy Baked Zucchini Chips (page 268) and Seed Crackers (page 269) are nice with soup or when you want something crunchy as part of your meal. And the Grilled Pineapple (page 274) can be your fruit for dessert.

Although most people find themselves less hungry with the Paleo Plan for Better Blood Sugar, you may feel hungry between meals as your metabolism and appetite adjust to more balanced blood sugar. Feeling hungry isn't necessarily a problem, but if you do need to eat in between meals in the short turn, do so wisely with the guidance of the four questions: What is my protein? What are my non-starchy vegetables? What about fruit (if any)? What is my good fat? Any eating you do should replicate the fundamentals of a meal, on a much smaller scale. That is what will keep your blood sugar stable.

The 30-Day Paleo Meal Plan

The meal plan that follows is a guide. Would we like you to follow it exactly and reap all the blood sugar benefits of these delicious recipes? Absolutely. But we also know that life happens, and schedules get changed at the last minute. Maybe your grocery store was out of red peppers or ginger or chicken thighs. Or maybe you think you won't like the Rainbow Roots Slaw with Tahini Parsley Dressing (page 130) — but we bet you will.

This is why the four questions posed by the Paleo Plan for Better Blood Sugar are so important: they provide the guidelines and structure for you to follow when, despite your good intentions, life throws you a curveball. Don't get thrown off. Remember that the food we eat is the single most important influence on our health. There is power in the structure provided by these questions. Learn them and apply them even if you are not making one of the recipes. As we have said many times throughout the book, context is everything. Figure out how to make the principles of the four questions work in your life.

As you work your way through the recipes, you will no doubt have favorites, which you may want to put into rotation more frequently. This is absolutely fine, but we do encourage you to try all of the recipes and move beyond the 10 to 15 dishes the average North American has in their repertoire.

> The four questions posed by the Paleo Plan for Better Blood Sugar provide the guidelines and structure for you to follow when, despite your good intentions, life throws you a curveball.

Day 1
Breakfast: Basic Vegetable Frittata (page 175) and Baked Bacon (page 221)
Lunch: Modern Tuna Salad with Avocado and Ginger (page 191)
Dinner: Butter Chicken with Cilantro Cauliflower Rice (page 204) and cucumber slices

Day 2
Breakfast: leftover Basic Vegetable Frittata and All Fruit Chop (page 142)
Lunch: leftover Butter Chicken with Cilantro Cauliflower Rice
Dinner: Taco Salad (page 231)

Day 3
Breakfast: Nori Egg Rolls (page 177) and leftover All Fruit Chop
Lunch: Classic Turkey Burger (page 215) and a green salad with Ranch Dressing (page 252)
Dinner: Skillet-Grilled Lamb with Avocado Mint Sauce (page 236) and
Green Beans with Shiitakes, Shallots and Toasted Almonds (page 144)

Day 4
Breakfast: Basic Scrambled Eggs with Roasted Salsa (page 173)
Lunch: Cooked Shrimp Ceviche (page 196) and Seed Crackers (page 269)
Dinner: Flattened Roast Chicken (page 198) and Easy Sautéed Greens (page 160)

Day 5
Breakfast: Egg and Pancetta Muffins (page 178) and a sliced pear
Lunch: Creamy Broccoli Soup (page 121) with Leek Chips (page 267) and cubes
of leftover Flattened Roast Chicken
Dinner: Spaghetti Squash Bolognese (page 232) and a green salad with
Classic Vinaigrette (page 258)

Day 6
Breakfast: leftover Egg and Pancetta Muffins and half an avocado
Lunch: leftover Spaghetti Squash Bolognese and a green salad with leftover
Classic Vinaigrette
Dinner: Almond-Crusted Salmon (page 185) with Kale and Sweet Potato Sauté (page 161)

Day 7
Breakfast: Scrambled Eggs Florentine (page 174) with Easy Hollandaise (page 251)
Lunch: Seafood Gazpacho (page 124) with leftover Seed Crackers (from day 4)
Dinner: Ginger Beef with Broccoli and Shiitakes (page 224) and a green salad with
Creamy Lemon Tahini Dressing (page 255)

Day 8
Breakfast: Peppers Stuffed with Eggs, Mushrooms and Broccoli (page 176)
Lunch: Lemon and Herb Sardines (page 189) and Roasted Asparagus Salad
with Arugula and Hazelnuts (page 126)
Dinner: Sweet Potato Shepherd's Pie (page 227) and Light and Breezy Coleslaw (page 129)

Day 9

Breakfast: Eggs in a Hole (page 172) and half a sliced pear
Lunch: leftover Sweet Potato Shepherd's Pie and leftover Light and Breezy Coleslaw
Dinner: Asian Chicken Lettuce Cups (page 208)

Day 10

Breakfast: Basic Vegetable Frittata (page 175)
Lunch: Turkey-Stuffed Peppers (page 214)
Dinner: Classic Fish Sticks (page 186) and a green salad with Strawberry Balsamic Vinaigrette (page 259)

Day 11

Breakfast: leftover Turkey-Stuffed Peppers with ½ cup (125 mL) Summer Salsa (page 243)
Lunch: Thai Coconut Shrimp Soup (page 123) with Crispy Baked Zucchini Chips (page 268)
Dinner: Chicken Chili (page 205) and a green salad with Green Goddess Dressing (page 253)

Day 12

Breakfast: leftover Chicken Chili with ½ cup (125 mL) leftover Summer Salsa
Lunch: Modern Tuna Salad with Avocado and Ginger (page 191)
Dinner: Barbecue-Rubbed Chicken Wings (page 213) and Classic Coleslaw (page 128)

Day 13

Breakfast: Smoked Salmon Nori Rolls (page 188)
Lunch: leftover Barbecue-Rubbed Chicken Wings and a green salad with Ranch Dressing (page 252)
Dinner: Sloppy Joes (page 230) on a Portobello Mushroom Cap Bun (page 163) and a green salad with leftover Ranch Dressing

Day 14

Breakfast: Basic Scrambled Eggs with Roasted Salsa (page 173) and Cauliflower Zucchini Hash Browns (page 158)
Lunch: Modern Cobb Salad (page 139)
Dinner: Baked Haddock with Peppers and Tomatoes (page 184) and Cauliflower Garlic Mash (page 152)

Day 15

Breakfast: Egg and Pancetta Muffins (page 178) and half an avocado
Lunch: leftover Baked Haddock with Peppers and Tomatoes and leftover Cauliflower Garlic Mash
Dinner: Chicken Thighs with Artichokes and Capers (page 199) and Garlicky Roasted Broccoli (page 148)

Day 16

Breakfast: leftover Egg and Pancetta Muffins and half an avocado
Lunch: Rich Mushroom Soup (page 122) and leftover Chicken Thighs with Artichokes and Capers
Dinner: Paleo Cabbage Rolls (page 228) and Shredded Kale Salad with Pecan Parmesan (page 136)

Day 17

Breakfast:	Peppers Stuffed with Eggs, Mushrooms and Broccoli (page 176) and a sliced pear
Lunch:	leftover Paleo Cabbage Rolls and a green salad with Green Goddess Dressing (page 253)
Dinner:	Chicken Fajita Wraps (page 206)

Day 18

Breakfast:	Nori Egg Rolls (page 177)
Lunch:	Greek Chicken Salad (page 210) with Rosemary Pecans (page 265)
Dinner:	Thai Basil Beef (page 226) and Garlicky Roasted Broccoli (page 148)

Day 19

Breakfast:	Eggs in a Hole (page 172)
Lunch:	Detox Vegetable Soup (page 117) and Lemon and Herb Sardines (page 189)
Dinner:	Skillet-Grilled Flank Steak (page 222), Rustic Sautéed Onions and Mushrooms (page 164) and a green salad with Caesar Dressing (page 254)

Day 20

Breakfast:	eggs any way you like them, Baked Bacon (page 221) and Easy Sautéed Greens (page 160)
Lunch:	Buffalo-Inspired Chicken Lettuce Wraps (page 207)
Dinner:	Pan-Seared Sea Scallops (page 192) and Fennel, Grapefruit and Mint Salad (page 140)

Day 21

Breakfast:	Scrambled Eggs Florentine (page 174) with Easy Hollandaise (page 251)
Lunch:	Curried Chicken Salad (page 211) on a bed of mixed greens
Dinner:	Classic Skillet Burger (page 234) on a Portobello Mushroom Cap Bun (page 163) with Caramelized Onions (page 165) and Beet and Carrot Salad with Toasted Cashews (page 127)

Day 22

Breakfast:	Egg and Pancetta Muffins (page 178) and leftover Beet and Carrot Salad with Toasted Cashews
Lunch:	Salmon Cakes (page 187) and Cauliflower Couscous with Lemon and Pine Nuts (page 155)
Dinner:	New Classic Meatballs (page 220) and Zucchini Noodles (page 167) with Basic Marinara Sauce (page 239)

Day 23

Breakfast:	leftover Egg and Pancetta Muffins
Lunch:	leftover New Classic Meatballs and Asian Cabbage Crunch (page 131)
Dinner:	Fish Tacos (page 180)

Day 24

Breakfast:	Turkey-Stuffed Peppers (page 214)
Lunch:	Warm Spinach Salad with Eggs and Bacon (page 138) and Watermelon Salad (page 141)
Dinner:	Chicken with Almond Satay Sauce (page 200) and Jicama, Avocado, Radish and Orange Salad with Cilantro (page 134)

Day 25

Breakfast: Eggs in a Hole (page 172) and leftover Watermelon Salad
Lunch: Mexican Chicken Soup (page 118) with Seed Crackers (page 269)
Dinner: Classic Rack of Lamb (page 235), Cauliflower Steaks (page 150) and Brown Butter Green Beans with Pine Nuts (page 145)

Day 26

Breakfast: Nori Egg Rolls (page 177) and leftover Watermelon Salad
Lunch: Mediterranean Shrimp with Wilted Spinach (page 193)
Dinner: Dry-Rubbed Baby Back Ribs (page 218), Beets in Mustard Sauce (page 146) and a green salad with Classic Vinaigrette (page 258)

Day 27

Breakfast: Basic Scrambled Eggs with Roasted Salsa (page 173)
Lunch: roasted chicken breast, Rainbow Roots Slaw with Tahini Parsley Dressing (page 130)
Dinner: Stuffed Mushrooms (page 219) and Balsamic Roasted Vegetables (page 169)

Day 28

Breakfast: Basic Vegetable Frittata (page 175) and a kiwifruit
Lunch: Modern Tuna Salad with Avocado and Ginger (page 191)
Dinner: Jerk Chicken Kebabs (page 202), Fried Cauliflower Rice (page 153) and cucumber slices

Day 29

Breakfast: leftover Basic Vegetable Frittata
Lunch: Lemon Pepper Chicken Wings (page 212) and Beet and Carrot Salad with Toasted Cashews (page 127)
Dinner: Roasted Black Cod with Warm Tomato Vinaigrette on Seared Rapini (page 182)

Day 30

Breakfast: Scrambled Eggs Florentine (page 174) with Easy Hollandaise (page 251)
Lunch: Sautéed Shrimp with Zucchini Noodles and Creamy Avocado Pesto (page 194)
Dinner: Flattened Roast Chicken (page 198) and Roasted Broccolini with Creamy Lemon Tahini Dressing (page 149)

The Last Word

This book has provided you with a 30-day meal plan, but that doesn't mean you should go back to the way you used to eat once those 30 days are up. The paleo approach is a lifetime way of eating — one that, when followed, will result in rapidly improved blood sugar and insulin levels.

> The paleo approach is a lifetime way of eating — one that, when followed, will result in rapidly improved blood sugar and insulin levels.

There are nutrient breakdowns with each recipe, so those of you who want to can calculate your carbohydrate intake for your meal. Keep in mind, however, that these carbohydrates, because they don't come from refined grains or sugars, will affect your blood sugar levels differently than the same number of carbohydrates from a bagel, for instance.

Improving your health is a process that gets easier and more effective with practice — and practice means asking yourself those four questions every day, at every meal. This program is not a diet in the popularly accepted definition of the word. It is, rather, a strategy you can use to build a way of eating that will correct your blood sugar dysfunction and help reverse many, if not all, of the physiological consequences of high blood sugar. It's a plan for health. It's a plan for life.

Part 2

Paleo Recipes for Healthy Blood Sugar

About the Nutrient Analysis

The nutrient analysis done on the recipes in this book was performed using the USDA National Nutrient Database for Standard Reference, Release #28 (2016), retrieved January 2016 from the USDA Agricultural Research Service website: www.nal.usda.gov/fnic/foodcomp/search.

Recipes were evaluated as follows:

- The larger number of servings was used where there is a range.
- Where alternatives are given, the first ingredient and amount listed were used.
- The smaller quantity of an ingredient was used where a range is provided.
- Optional ingredients and ingredients that are not quantified were not included.
- Calculations were based on imperial measures and weights.
- Nutrient values were rounded to the nearest whole number for calories, fat, carbohydrate, fiber and protein.
- Olive oil was used where the type of fat was not specified.
- Recipes were analyzed prior to cooking.

It is important to note that the cooking method used to prepare the recipe may alter the nutrient content per serving, as may ingredient substitutions and differences among brand-name products.

Soups

Beef Bone Broth

Makes about 6 cups (1.5 L)

For the best possible health benefits of this wonderful broth, ensure that you are using bones from grass-fed meat. The best broth has a 1:1:1 ratio of bones (marrow bones) to joints (and necks) to feet (chicken feet). Don't forgo the chicken feet if you can find them. They provide a tremendous amount of collagen, one of the most important nutrients in the broth. The vegetables listed in this recipe add flavor as well as some vitamins and minerals, but they are entirely optional — the broth is delicious either way.

- Preheat oven to 350°F (180°C)
- Rimmed baking sheet or shallow roasting pan, lined with parchment paper

3 lbs	grass-fed beef bones	1.5 kg
3	free-range chicken feet (optional)	3
2 tbsp	apple cider vinegar	30 mL
14 cups	filtered water	3.5 L
6	cloves garlic, peeled (optional)	6
2	onions, peeled and quartered (optional)	2
2	carrots, chopped (optional)	2
2	stalks celery, chopped (optional)	2

1. Place beef bones and chicken feet (if using) on prepared baking sheet and roast in preheated oven for 45 minutes.

2. Transfer roasted bones and feet to a large stockpot and add vinegar and water. Bring to a boil over high heat. Skim off the foam that rises to the top. Cover, reduce heat to low and simmer for 18 hours.

3. If desired, add garlic, onions, carrots and/or celery; cover and simmer for 6 hours (if not adding vegetables, simply continue to simmer for 6 hours).

4. Place a colander or large-mesh strainer over a large heatproof bowl in the sink. Carefully pour broth through the colander to strain. Discard bones and vegetables (if using). Let cool, then skim off any fat that rises to the surface (you can keep this fat in the freezer and use it for cooking).

5. Transfer broth to airtight containers and refrigerate for up to 4 days or freeze for up to 6 months.

NUTRIENTS PER 1 CUP (250 ML)	
Calories	1
Fat	0 g
Carbohydrate	0 g
Fiber	0 g
Protein	0 g

Tips

To make this broth in a 6-quart slow cooker, in step 2, place the bones in the slow cooker and add the vinegar and water, making sure the bones are covered. Cover and cook on Low for 48 hours. Continue with step 3.

Be sure to wait until about 6 hours before the broth will be done to add the vegetables if you are using them. Cooking the vegetables in the broth for the entire time can impart a bitter taste. If adding leafy greens, such as parsley or celery leaves, add them only in the last hour of cooking.

Freeze some of the broth in ice cube trays. Once frozen, pop out the cubes and store them in a freezer bag in the freezer. These are very useful for sautéing vegetables instead of using oil, or for adding small amounts of rich-tasting concentrate to sauces and gravies.

Nutrition Tip

Bone broth is a rich source of minerals, such as calcium, magnesium, potassium and phosphorus, all of which play important roles in healthy bones. The gelatin that is formed from the breakdown of the collagen in the bones contains amino acids like glycine and glutamine that soothe the lining of the digestive tract and contribute to the broth's healing qualities.

Warming Chicken Stock

**Makes about
10 cups (2.5 L)**

The best parts of the
chicken to use for
the most delicious
broth are the necks,
wings and backs.
When Jill makes the
Flattened Roast Chicken
(page 198), she freezes
all the backs for just
this purpose. The roast
chicken is a staple in
her house, so there
are always bones for
making stock.

- **Fine-mesh sieve**

3 lbs	bone-in skin-on free-range chicken parts	1.5 kg
4	cloves garlic, cut in half	4
3	carrots, coarsely chopped	3
3	stalks celery, coarsely chopped	3
2	onions, peeled and quartered	2
8	whole peppercorns (black, green or pink)	8
3	bay leaves	3
1 tsp	dried thyme	5 mL
1 tsp	sea salt	5 mL
10 cups	filtered water	2.5 L

1. In a large stockpot, combine chicken, garlic, carrots, celery, onions, peppercorns, bay leaves, thyme, salt and water. Cover and bring to a boil over high heat. Reduce heat to low and simmer for 2 hours, skimming foam occasionally.

2. Strain stock through a fine-mesh sieve into a large bowl. Press liquid out of bones and vegetables and discard solids.

3. Taste the stock; if you would like it stronger and more concentrated, return it to the pot, bring to a boil over high heat and boil for about 15 minutes or until reduced.

4. Let cool, then transfer to airtight containers and refrigerate for up to 4 days or freeze for up to 6 months.

Nutrition Tip

Chicken soup has long been used to nourish the sick, and some scientific evidence supports that use. The *American Journal of Therapeutics* published research showing that the carnosine in chicken broth helped bolster the body's immune system in the early stages of the flu. Earlier research by Dr. Stephen Rennard found that chicken soup has an anti-inflammatory effect that helps to reduce upper respiratory cold symptoms. Other studies have shown that hot soup (more so than hot water) helps increase the movement of nasal mucus and relieve cold symptoms. Whatever the mechanism, chicken soup is good for the soul and soothes from the inside out.

NUTRIENTS PER 1 CUP (250 ML)	
Calories	2
Fat	0 g
Carbohydrate	0 g
Fiber	0 g
Protein	0 g

Detox Vegetable Soup

This is the kind of soup you're looking for when you want to feel full and satisfied but not weighed down by anything too rich.

Tip

If you don't have homemade stock or broth on hand, you can use ready-to-use organic chicken or beef broth.

Nutrition Tip

If you flip through the Nutrition Tips in this book, you will find nutrition facts about all of the vegetables in this soup, and even some of the spices. Each vegetable has its own strengths, and nutrients work synergistically with each other, so imagine the nutrition synergy going on when they are all combined here!

2 tsp	extra virgin olive oil	10 mL
1	onion, finely chopped	1
2	small cloves garlic, minced	2
3 cups	sliced cremini or button mushrooms	750 mL
2 cups	chopped broccoli	500 mL
1 cup	chopped carrots	250 mL
$\frac{1}{2}$ cup	chopped celery	125 mL
1 tsp	grated gingerroot (or to taste)	5 mL
1 tsp	sea salt (approx.)	5 mL
$\frac{1}{2}$ tsp	ground turmeric	2 mL
$\frac{1}{2}$ tsp	ground cumin	2 mL
$\frac{1}{4}$ tsp	freshly ground black pepper (approx.)	1 mL
$\frac{1}{8}$ tsp	ground cinnamon	0.5 mL
5 cups	Warming Chicken Stock (page 116) or Beef Bone Broth (page 114)	1.25 L
2	sheets nori, cut into $\frac{1}{2}$-inch (1 cm) strips (optional)	2
2 cups	torn kale or Swiss chard leaves (tough stems removed)	500 mL
6	lemon wedges (optional)	6

1. In a large pot or Dutch oven, heat oil over medium heat. Add onion and cook, stirring, for 3 to 4 minutes or until translucent. Add garlic and cook, stirring, for 1 minute. Add mushrooms, broccoli, carrots and celery; cook, stirring, for 5 minutes. Add ginger, salt, turmeric, cumin, pepper and cinnamon; cook, stirring, for 2 minutes.

2. Stir in stock and bring to a boil. Reduce heat and simmer, stirring occasionally, for 15 minutes or until vegetables are tender. Stir in nori (if using) and kale; simmer for 2 minutes or until wilted. Taste and adjust seasoning with salt and pepper as desired.

3. Ladle soup into serving bowls and, if desired, serve each bowl with a lemon wedge on the side, for diners to squeeze over their soup.

NUTRIENTS PER SERVING	
Calories	113
Fat	4 g
Carbohydrate	15 g
Fiber	2 g
Protein	7 g

Mexican Chicken Soup

This is a lot like Mexican tortilla soup, but without the soggy tortilla chips. If you want a crunch, serve it with Crispy Baked Zucchini Chips (page 268).

Tip

If you don't have homemade stock or broth on hand, you can use ready-to-use organic chicken broth.

2 tbsp	extra virgin olive oil	30 mL
1 cup	finely chopped onion	250 mL
½ cup	chopped carrot	125 mL
½ cup	chopped celery	125 mL
1 tsp	diced seeded jalapeño pepper (optional)	5 mL
½ tsp	sea salt (approx.), divided	2 mL
2	small cloves garlic, minced	2
¼ tsp	ground cumin	1 mL
¼ tsp	dried oregano	1 mL
1	can (14 oz/398 mL) diced tomatoes, with juice	1
6 cups	Warming Chicken Stock (page 116)	1.5 L
1½ cups	thinly sliced cooked free-range chicken (see tip, opposite)	375 mL
2 tbsp	freshly squeezed lime juice (approx.)	30 mL
½	avocado, diced	½
2 tbsp	chopped fresh cilantro	30 mL

1. In a Dutch oven or stockpot, heat oil over medium heat. Add onion, carrot, celery, jalapeño (if using) and ¼ tsp (1 mL) salt; cook, stirring, for 3 to 5 minutes or until vegetables start to soften. Stir in garlic, cumin and oregano, then add tomatoes and cook, stirring, for 1 minute.

2. Stir in stock and bring to a boil. Reduce heat to low, cover and simmer for 15 minutes or until vegetables are tender.

NUTRIENTS PER SERVING	
Calories	378
Fat	28 g
Carbohydrate	14 g
Fiber	5 g
Protein	19 g

Tips

Use leftover Flattened Roast Chicken (page 198) or a store-bought free-range roast chicken.

To make this soup even heartier, add 2 cups (500 mL) cauliflower rice with the chicken. It becomes almost like a stew. To make cauliflower rice, follow step 1 in the recipe for Cilantro Cauliflower Rice (page 154).

3. Stir in chicken, lime juice and the remaining salt; simmer, uncovered, for 5 minutes. Remove from heat. Taste and adjust seasoning with salt and lime juice as desired.

4. Divide soup among serving bowls and top with avocado and cilantro.

Nutrition Tip

Bisphenol A (BPA), which is used in the vinyl liner of food cans, is a known endocrine disruptor that can contribute to hormonal imbalance in our bodies. Whenever possible, therefore, it is best to buy food packed in glass containers, as glass is inert. It is possible, but not common, to find tomatoes packed in glass jars. A 2010 study determined that the BPA concentration in canned vegetables is relatively low, with canned tomato paste coming in lower than other canned tomato products. This is a small consolation, so try to find glass, if you can.

Chilled Avocado and Cucumber Soup

Makes 4 servings

You may not need to seed your cucumbers, depending on what cucumbers are available when you make this soup. If we are using English cucumbers, we don't seed them — and we don't peel them when they are organic and the skin is thin and tender. For field cucumbers, we prefer to seed and peel them, as the skin can be bitter.

Tips

For a zesty alternative to the lemon juice, use an equal amount of freshly squeezed lime juice.

This soup is also nice topped with crispy Leek Chips (page 267).

- **Food processor or blender**

2	large avocados, cut into chunks	2
1	small clove garlic, finely chopped	1
3 cups	diced seeded peeled cucumber	750 mL
1/4 cup	firmly packed arugula	60 mL
1/4 cup	finely chopped fresh cilantro	60 mL
1 tbsp	finely chopped green onion	15 mL
1/2 tsp	sea salt (approx.)	2 mL
Pinch	cayenne pepper (optional)	Pinch
1 1/2 cups	filtered water	375 mL
2 tbsp	extra virgin olive oil	30 mL
4 tsp	freshly squeezed lemon juice (approx.)	20 mL
1	avocado, sliced	1
	Additional diced seeded peeled cucumber	

1. In food processor, combine avocado chunks, garlic, cucumber, arugula, cilantro, green onion, salt, cayenne (if using), water, oil and lemon juice; process until smooth and creamy.

2. Transfer soup to a bowl, taste and adjust seasoning with salt and lemon juice as desired. Cover and refrigerate for at least 1 hour, until chilled, or for up to 6 hours.

3. Divide soup among serving bowls and top with sliced avocado and diced cucumber.

Nutrition Tip

Cucumbers are like celery in that people think they are just water with a bit of fiber thrown in. Yes, they do contain quite a bit of water, but they provide a lot of nutrients, too. The top vitamins and minerals in cucumber are vitamin K (which supports heart and bone health), potassium (which protects against heart disease) and vitamin B_5 (which is essential for metabolism). The top phytonutrients are lignans, cucurbitacins and flavonoids, all of which provide valuable anti-inflammatory, antioxidant and anticancer benefits.

NUTRIENTS PER SERVING	
Calories	316
Fat	29 g
Carbohydrate	16 g
Fiber	11 g
Protein	4 g

Creamy Broccoli Soup

Makes 4 servings

This super-creamy soup hasn't come anywhere near any cream. The secret ingredient is the cashews that give the soup its richness.

Tips

If you don't have homemade stock or broth on hand, you can use ready-to-use organic chicken or beef broth.

If you're pressed for time, in step 1 you can cover the cashews with boiling water and let soak for 15 minutes.

If you don't have an immersion blender, let the soup cool slightly while you proceed with step 4. At the end of step 4, transfer the cashew cream to a bowl. Working in batches, transfer the soup to the blender and purée until smooth. Return soup to the pan and continue with step 5.

NUTRIENTS PER SERVING	
Calories	267
Fat	15 g
Carbohydrate	25 g
Fiber	4 g
Protein	13 g

- **Immersion blender (see tip, at left)**
- **Blender**

1/2 cup	raw cashews	125 mL
	Water (or boiling water)	
1 tbsp	grass-fed butter	15 mL
1	large onion, finely chopped	1
1	stalk celery, chopped	1
2	cloves garlic, minced	2
4 cups	chopped broccoli	1 L
4 cups	Warming Chicken Stock (page 116) or Beef Bone Broth (page 114), divided	1 L
3/4 tsp	sea salt (approx.)	3 mL
1/4 tsp	freshly ground black pepper (approx.)	1 mL

1. Place cashews in a small bowl, cover with water and let soak for at least 30 minutes or up to 5 hours.

2. In a large saucepan, melt butter over medium heat. Add onion and cook, stirring, for 3 minutes. Add celery and cook, stirring, for 3 minutes. Add garlic and broccoli; cook, stirring, for 5 minutes.

3. Stir in $3^{1}/_{2}$ cups (875 mL) stock, salt and pepper; bring to a boil. Reduce heat to low, cover and simmer for 15 minutes or until vegetables are very tender. Remove from heat and, using an immersion blender, purée soup until smooth.

4. Drain cashews and add to blender with the remaining stock. Blend until very smooth and creamy, with no lumps.

5. Stir cashew cream into soup. Taste and adjust seasoning with salt and pepper as desired. If necessary, reheat over medium heat until steaming.

Nutrition Tip
Broccoli provides tremendous benefit for our detoxification system. Most of the toxins we encounter are detoxified in our livers in a two-step process: phase I and phase II. The isothiocyanates made from the glucosinolates in broccoli are able to modify and impact both phases. The combination of the glucosinolates and their action is unique to broccoli and is extraordinarily healthful for us.

Rich Mushroom Soup

Makes 4 servings

The variety of mushrooms in this soup adds a wonderful depth of flavor. There's nothing like a mug of rich soup to take the chill out of a fall or winter afternoon or evening.

Tips

To clean mushrooms, wipe them with a damp cloth.

If you don't have homemade stock or broth on hand, you can use ready-to-use organic chicken or beef broth.

If you don't have an immersion blender, let the soup cool slightly after it has simmered, then, working in batches, transfer it to a blender or food processor and purée until smooth. Return soup to the pan and season to taste with salt and pepper. Reheat over medium heat until steaming.

- **Immersion blender (see tip, at left)**

5 tbsp	grass-fed butter, divided	75 mL
1	onion, chopped	1
1	clove garlic, minced	1
4 cups	chopped cremini mushrooms (about 10 oz/300 g)	1 L
1 cup	chopped assorted mushrooms (oyster, shiitake caps, button)	250 mL
4 cups	Warming Chicken Stock (page 116) or Beef Bone Broth (page 114)	1 L
¼ tsp	sea salt	1 mL
¼ tsp	freshly ground black pepper	1 mL

1. In a Dutch oven or large saucepan, melt 2 tbsp (30 mL) butter over medium heat. Add onion and cook, stirring, for about 4 minutes or until soft and translucent. Add garlic and cook, stirring, for 1 minute. Add cremini mushrooms, assorted mushrooms and the remaining butter; cook, stirring occasionally, for about 8 minutes or until mushrooms are soft.

2. Stir in stock and bring to a boil. Reduce heat and simmer, stirring occasionally, for 30 minutes. Remove from heat and, using an immersion blender, purée soup to desired consistency. Season with salt and pepper.

Nutrition Tip

Making your own soup does take a bit longer than opening a can, but when you know exactly what you're eating, it's worth it in more ways than just the taste. Here's what's in a typical can of mushroom soup: water, mushrooms, corn, cottonseed, canola and/or soybean oil, modified food starch, wheat flour, salt, monosodium glutamate, soy protein concentrate, dehydrated cream, yeast extract, flavoring and dehydrated garlic. Compare that to the all-natural, wholesome ingredients in your homemade soup.

NUTRIENTS PER SERVING	
Calories	254
Fat	17 g
Carbohydrate	17 g
Fiber	1 g
Protein	9 g

Thai Coconut Shrimp Soup

Jill used to get takeout when she craved the wonderful Thai flavors of coconut, lemongrass, basil and curry. No more expensive takeout now!

Tip
Make sure the fish sauce has only three ingredients: fish, salt and water. Steer clear of non-paleo ingredients such as sugar and hydrolyzed wheat protein.

8	quarter-size slices gingerroot	8
1	red bell pepper, finely chopped	1
1	stalk lemongrass, woody parts removed, cut into 1-inch (2.5 cm) pieces	1
1½ cups	mushrooms, quartered	375 mL
2	bottles (each 8 oz/227 mL) clam juice	2
1 cup	filtered water	250 mL
1 tbsp	fish sauce (see tip, at left)	15 mL
1 tbsp	Thai green curry paste	15 mL
1	can (14 oz/398 mL) unsweetened full-fat coconut milk	1
1 lb	medium wild shrimp, peeled and deveined	500 g
16	fresh basil leaves	16
2	green onions, sliced on the diagonal	2
1 tbsp	freshly squeezed lime juice	15 mL

1. In a large saucepan, combine ginger, red pepper, lemongrass, mushrooms, clam juice, water, fish sauce and curry paste. Bring to a boil over medium-high heat. Reduce heat to medium-low, cover and simmer for 15 minutes.

2. Stir in coconut milk and simmer until heated through, about 5 minutes. Increase heat to medium, stir in shrimp and cook for about 3 minutes or until shrimp are pink, firm and opaque. Remove from heat and stir in basil, green onions and lime juice. Serve immediately.

Nutrition Tip
We all want to get the best value for the money we pay for our food, and storing our vegetables the right way ensures that we get the most nutritional value, too. The longer mushrooms are kept at room temperature, the more quickly they lose phytonutrient content and therefore their beneficial immune and cardiovascular benefits. Be sure to store your mushrooms in the fridge as soon as you get home from the store and use them within 3 to 4 days.

NUTRIENTS PER SERVING	
Calories	366
Fat	19 g
Carbohydrate	13 g
Fiber	2 g
Protein	28 g

Seafood Gazpacho

The addition of crab-meat to this otherwise traditional gazpacho means this soup really does eat like a meal!

Tips

To protect your fingers from burning, wear gloves when seeding and chopping the jalapeño.

To make your own tomato juice, mix 1½ cups (375 mL) filtered water with ¼ cup (60 mL) tomato paste.

Nutrition Tip

In this gazpacho, the carbohydrates are nicely balanced with good lean protein from the crab or shrimp and monounsaturated fats from the avocado. The avocado also provides a good amount of fiber, to help keep blood sugar nice and stable. All in all, it's a great meal in a bowl.

NUTRIENTS PER SERVING	
Calories	270
Fat	7 g
Carbohydrate	20 g
Fiber	6 g
Protein	34 g

- **Blender**

1½ lbs	plum (Roma) tomatoes, seeded and chopped	750 g
1	seedless cucumber, peeled and finely chopped	1
1	red bell pepper, finely chopped	1
1	clove garlic, minced	1
1	small red onion, finely chopped	1
1	jalapeño pepper, seeded and finely chopped	1
1½ cups	tomato juice (see tip, at left)	375 mL
½ cup	ice water	125 mL
1 tbsp	freshly squeezed lime juice	15 mL
3 tbsp	chopped fresh basil	45 mL
1 tbsp	chopped fresh cilantro	15 mL
1 tbsp	extra virgin olive oil or avocado oil	15 mL
2 tsp	balsamic vinegar	10 mL
	Sea salt and freshly ground black pepper	
½	avocado, cut into ¼-inch (0.5 cm) dice	½
1 lb	cooked backfin (lump) crabmeat or cooked deveined peeled shrimp, cooled	500 g
	Additional diced avocado	

1. In a large bowl, combine tomatoes, cucumber, red pepper, garlic, onion, jalapeño, tomato juice, ice water and lime juice, stirring well.

2. Transfer 3 cups (750 mL) of the mixture to a blender and purée until smooth.

3. Return the puréed soup to the bowl and stir in basil, cilantro, oil and vinegar. Season to taste with salt and pepper. Cover and refrigerate for at least 2 hours, until chilled, or overnight.

4. When ready to serve, stir in avocado. Divide soup among serving bowls, top with crab and garnish with additional avocado. Serve immediately.

Salads

Roasted Asparagus Salad with Arugula and Hazelnuts

This is a definite favorite during asparagus season. Roasting the asparagus gives it an altogether different flavor than steaming, and the roasted hazelnuts are a perfect combination with the peppery arugula.

Tips

The woody tough end of the asparagus isn't tasty, so snap off the last 2 to 3 inches (5 to 7.5 cm). If the stalks are very small, cutting off just the last inch (2.5 cm) is enough. Use a vegetable peeler to gently shave the stringy bits off the bottom 2 inches (5 cm) of larger stalks.

You can leave the skins on the nuts, but if you prefer to remove them, wrap the hot nuts in a clean tea towel and rub vigorously. The majority of the skins will come off in the towel.

You can substitute walnut halves, pistachios or pine nuts for the hazelnuts.

NUTRIENTS PER SERVING	
Calories	198
Fat	16 g
Carbohydrate	11 g
Fiber	6 g
Protein	6 g

- Preheat oven to 375°F (190°C)
- Rimmed baking sheet

⅓ cup	hazelnuts	75 mL
2 lbs	asparagus, ends snapped off (see tip, at left)	1 kg
3 tbsp	extra virgin olive oil, divided	45 mL
¼ tsp	sea salt	1 mL
¼ tsp	freshly ground black pepper	1 mL
1 tsp	grated lemon zest (optional)	5 mL
2 tbsp	freshly squeezed lemon juice	30 mL
5 cups	loosely packed arugula	1.25 L

1. Spread hazelnuts on baking sheet and roast in preheated oven for 7 to 10 minutes or until lightly browned. Transfer to a plate and remove skins, if desired (see tip, at left), then let cool. Coarsely chop hazelnuts.

2. Increase oven temperature to 400°F (200°C). Place asparagus on baking sheet, drizzle with 1 tbsp (15 mL) oil and season with salt and pepper. Toss well to coat, then spread in a single layer. Roast for 8 minutes or until asparagus is just tender and lightly browned.

3. In a small bowl, whisk together lemon zest (if using), lemon juice and the remaining oil.

4. Place arugula in a large bowl, drizzle with half the lemon dressing and toss until evenly coated. Divide among serving plates or arrange on a platter. Arrange asparagus on top, drizzle with the remaining dressing and top with hazelnuts.

Nutrition Tip

Asparagus contains significant amounts of a unique type of carbohydrate called inulin (a polyfructan). Unlike most carbohydrates, inulin doesn't get broken down in the small intestine but makes it all the way to the colon, where it becomes a food source for the favorable bacteria living there. As a prebiotic, inulin supports our digestive health and therefore the health of our entire body.

Beet and Carrot Salad with Toasted Cashews

Makes 4 servings

Raw beets — really? You bet! This delicious salad is so colorful and crunchy, you'd never know it also offers nutritious detox support for your liver.

Tips

To toast nuts or seeds, place them in a dry skillet over medium heat and stir occasionally until aromatic (about 2 to 4 minutes, depending on the nut or seed). At this point, reduce the heat to medium-low and cook, stirring constantly to ensure even browning, until nuts or seeds are evenly golden brown (about 2 to 5 minutes, depending on the nut or seed). Transfer to a plate or cutting board to cool. (If you leave them in the pan, they will continue to cook and may burn.)

You can make this salad a couple of hours ahead, but wait to add the cashews until just before serving so they don't get soggy.

NUTRIENTS PER SERVING	
Calories	282
Fat	19 g
Carbohydrate	24 g
Fiber	3 g
Protein	8 g

1 lb	beets (2 large or 3 small)	500 g
1 lb	carrots (5 medium)	500 g
½ tsp	sea salt	2 mL
	Juice of 2 limes (about ¼ cup/60 mL)	
2 tbsp	sesame oil	30 mL
3	green onions, thinly sliced	3
1 cup	raw cashews, toasted (see tip, at left)	250 mL

1. Wash, trim and peel beets and carrots. Using a box grater (or a food processor with a grating disk), grate beets and carrots into a large bowl. Sprinkle with salt.

2. In a small bowl, whisk together lime juice and sesame oil.

3. Pour dressing over beets and carrots and toss until well coated. Add green onions and cashews and toss again.

Nutrition Tip

A study from the Netherlands followed people for 10 years and tracked their intake of fruits and vegetables by dividing the produce into four color groups: green, orange/yellow, red/purple and white. The orange/yellow group proved to be most protective against cardiovascular disease, and carrots appeared as the most prominent member of this group. Who said carrots were just good for your eyes?

Classic Coleslaw

Coleslaw is the perfect timesaver. Try shredding a whole cabbage and leaving half of it undressed in a bag in the fridge. Then you can use different dressings for an entirely new taste.

Tips

To make shredding cabbage fast and easy, first cut the cabbage into quarters and remove the thick white core from each section. Place each quarter on a flat side and cut it crosswise with a sharp knife, working from top to bottom.

Use the side of your box grater with the largest holes to shred carrots.

NUTRIENTS PER SERVING OF SALAD WITHOUT DRESSING	
Calories	27
Fat	0 g
Carbohydrate	6 g
Fiber	2 g
Protein	1 g

NUTRIENTS PER 1 TBSP (15 ML) DRESSING	
Calories	108
Fat	11 g
Carbohydrate	1 g
Fiber	0 g
Protein	0 g

Dressing

¼ cup	The Best Paleo Mayo (page 249)	60 mL
3 tbsp	Dijon mustard	45 mL
2 tbsp	apple cider vinegar	30 mL
½ tsp	celery seeds or poppy seeds	2 mL

Slaw

2	green onions, thinly sliced on the diagonal	2
3 cups	shredded green or red cabbage (see tip, at left)	750 mL
1 cup	shredded carrots (see tip, at left)	250 mL

1. *Dressing:* In a small bowl, whisk together mayo, mustard, vinegar and celery seeds until well combined.

2. *Slaw:* In a large bowl, combine green onions, cabbage and carrots. Add half the dressing, tossing well. Taste and add more dressing as desired.

3. Serve slaw immediately or cover and refrigerate for up to 3 days. Store any remaining dressing in the refrigerator for up to 3 days.

Variation

Add ¼ cup (60 mL) pomegranate seeds for more color and a sweet pop of flavor.

Nutrition Tip

Reach for red or purple cabbage instead of the green. Although they are all great, red cabbage has four times as many anthocyanin polyphenols as green. Anthocyanin polyphenols offer both antioxidant and anti-inflammatory benefits, making them protective (and possibly preventive) against chronic diseases.

Detox Vegetable Soup (page 117)

Mexican Chicken Soup (page 118)

Roasted Asparagus Salad with Arugula and Hazelnuts (page 126)

Jicama, Avocado, Radish and
Orange Salad with Cilantro (page 134)

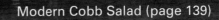

Modern Cobb Salad (page 139)

Green Beans with Shiitakes,
Shallots and Toasted Almonds (page 144)

Kale and Sweet Potato Sauté (page 161)

Scrambled Eggs Florentine (page 174)
with Easy Hollandaise (page 251)

Light and Breezy Coleslaw

This coleslaw is much lighter than the classic version thanks to the dressing and the type of cabbage. It goes well with any protein choice, especially Flattened Roast Chicken (page 198) and Almond-Crusted Salmon (page 185). Because it keeps in the fridge for a few days, you can pair it with whatever leftover protein you have — chicken, meat, fish or seafood.

Dressing

¼ cup	freshly squeezed lemon juice	60 mL
⅓ cup	extra virgin olive oil	75 mL
1 tsp	Dijon mustard	5 mL
¼ tsp	sea salt	1 mL
¼ tsp	freshly ground black pepper	1 mL

Slaw

1 lb	savoy or napa cabbage, finely shredded (about 4 cups/1 L)	500 mL
1 cup	shredded carrots (see tip, page 128)	250 mL
2 tbsp	basil chiffonade (see tip, page 140)	30 mL
¼ cup	toasted sesame seeds (see tip, page 127)	60 mL

1. *Dressing:* In a small bowl, whisk together lemon juice, oil, mustard, salt and pepper until well blended.

2. *Slaw:* In a large bowl, combine cabbage, carrots and basil. Add dressing a little bit at a time, tossing well, until salad is dressed as desired.

3. Serve slaw immediately or cover and refrigerate for up to 3 days. Store any remaining dressing in the refrigerator for up to 2 weeks. Top with sesame seeds just before serving.

Variation

Substitute shredded fennel for the carrot, for a bright refreshing taste.

Nutrition Tip

Different types of cabbage contain different phytonutrients. Savoy cabbage is rich in a compound called sinigrin, which is being studied for its effects in cancer prevention, specifically with regard to bladder, colon and prostate cancers. Using all of the different types of cabbage featured in these coleslaw recipes will help you get the benefits of all the different phytonutrients the cabbage family has to offer.

NUTRIENTS PER SERVING OF SALAD WITHOUT DRESSING	
Calories	83
Fat	5 g
Carbohydrate	9 g
Fiber	4 g
Protein	3 g

NUTRIENTS PER 1 TBSP (15 ML) DRESSING	
Calories	68
Fat	7 g
Carbohydrate	1 g
Fiber	0 g
Protein	0 g

Rainbow Roots Slaw with Tahini Parsley Dressing

This colorful salad brightens up any meal and it's like a detox in a bowl. Antioxidants and liver-supporting nutrients never tasted so good!

Tips

Yes, the beets are eaten raw in this recipe. Beets stain everything, so you may want to wear rubber gloves when you peel and grate them.

The beets are added last so they don't turn the whole salad red.

This salad can be stored in an airtight container in the refrigerator for up to 3 days.

NUTRIENTS PER SERVING OF SALAD WITHOUT DRESSING	
Calories	64
Fat	0 g
Carbohydrate	15 g
Fiber	4 g
Protein	1 g

NUTRIENTS PER 1 TBSP (15 ML) DRESSING	
Calories	88
Fat	8 g
Carbohydrate	3 g
Fiber	1 g
Protein	2 g

Tahini Parsley Dressing

1	small clove garlic, minced	1
¼ cup	minced fresh flat-leaf (Italian) parsley	60 mL
1 tsp	ground cumin	5 mL
¼ tsp	sea salt	1 mL
¼ cup	tahini	60 mL
2 tbsp	freshly squeezed lime juice	30 mL
1 tbsp	extra virgin olive oil	15 mL
2 tbsp	filtered water (approx.)	30 mL

Rainbow Roots Slaw

2 cups	shredded green cabbage	500 mL
2	large carrots, grated	2
1	firm pear (such as Bosc), grated	1
2	medium red beets, peeled and grated (see tip, at left)	2

1. *Dressing:* In a small bowl, whisk together garlic, parsley, cumin, salt, tahini, lime juice and oil. Whisk in 1 tbsp (15 mL) water. If the dressing is too thick, add the remaining water (or more, as needed).

2. *Slaw:* In a large bowl, toss together cabbage, carrots and pear. Add dressing and toss until vegetables are well coated. Add beets and toss to coat.

Variations

Substitute golden beets for the red beets.

Substitute a Granny Smith apple (or any firm apple) for the pear.

Nutrition Tip

Beets contain phytonutrients called betalains, which, like all phytonutrients, offer both antioxidant and anti-inflammatory benefits. Betalains also provide support for the detoxification systems in our liver, specifically the phase II detoxification steps that involve our major antioxidant, glutathione. This raw salad helps you maximize betalain intake, as betalains are lost from food at a steady rate when it is cooked.

Asian Cabbage Crunch

Makes 6 servings

The multitude of reds and greens in this crunchy salad makes it a visual feast. Not only does it look great, but this twist on a classic slaw provides antioxidant and liver-loving nutrients that will help balance your hormones and your blood sugar levels.

Tip

When toasting sesame seeds, it's worth it to do a cup (250 mL) or more at a time so you always have some on hand. Pay attention when toasting nuts and seeds, as they can change from perfectly toasted to burnt very quickly. Store any extra seeds in a sealed glass container.

3	green onions, thinly sliced on the diagonal	3
1	red bell pepper, thinly sliced	1
3 cups	shredded red cabbage	750 mL
3 cups	shredded napa cabbage	750 mL
¼ cup	finely chopped fresh cilantro or basil	60 mL
2 tbsp	finely chopped fresh mint	30 mL
½ cup	Creamy Sesame Dressing (page 256)	125 mL
1 tbsp	toasted sesame seeds (see tip, page 127)	15 mL

1. In a large bowl, combine green onions, red pepper, red cabbage, napa cabbage, cilantro and mint. Drizzle with dressing and toss to coat. Let stand for a few minutes to allow the dressing to penetrate the cabbage. Sprinkle with sesame seeds just before serving.

Nutrition Tip

Sesame seeds are rich in many nutrients, including two that are unique to sesame seeds: sesamin and sesamolin. These compounds are both lignans, which are the building blocks of plant cell walls. In humans, lignans have been shown to have cholesterol-lowering effects, making them valuable for heart health.

NUTRIENTS PER SERVING	
Calories	90
Fat	5 g
Carbohydrate	9 g
Fiber	2 g
Protein	4 g

Pickled Cucumber Salad

Makes 4 servings

This delicious cross between a pickle and a salad has its roots in a previous era. It's the perfect refresher on a hot summer day.

Tip

Most of the oil and vinegar is left over after you eat this salad, and the nutritional analysis can't reflect this. A more accurate take on the analysis would be that, when you eat this salad, you are eating the carbohydrates, fiber and protein and very little of the fat.

¼ cup	extra virgin olive oil	60 mL
¼ cup	unseasoned rice vinegar	60 mL
2 tbsp	apple cider vinegar	30 mL
1	English cucumber, very thinly sliced (about 4 cups/l L)	1
½ cup	very thinly sliced red onion	125 mL
¼ cup	chopped fresh dill (optional)	60 mL
	Sea salt and freshly ground black pepper	

1. In a large bowl, whisk together oil, rice vinegar and cider vinegar until emulsified. Add cucumber, onion and dill (if using), tossing to coat. Let stand for 30 minutes, then mix well. Season to taste with salt and pepper.

Nutrition Tip

Dill has a long history as a culinary spice and as a treatment for digestive disorders like gas and bloating, thanks to its carminative properties. The health benefits of dill come from its vitamins, minerals and flavonoids, but also from compounds called monoterpenes, which help activate and support one of the strongest antioxidants in the human body, glutathione.

NUTRIENTS PER SERVING	
Calories	145
Fat	14 g
Carbohydrate	5 g
Fiber	1 g
Protein	1 g

Thai Zucchini Noodle Salad

Makes 2 servings

Make this salad a complete meal by serving it with grilled or sautéed shrimp, sliced chicken or leftover Marinated Flank Steak (page 223).

Tip

If you have a vegetable spiralizer, you can use it instead of the julienne peeler to create the vegetable noodles.

• Julienne peeler

2	small zucchini	2
1	small cucumber	1
1	medium carrot	1
$\frac{1}{2}$	red bell pepper, cut into thin strips	$\frac{1}{2}$
$\frac{1}{2}$	yellow bell pepper, cut into thin strips	$\frac{1}{2}$
$\frac{1}{2}$ cup	chopped fresh cilantro	125 mL
2 tbsp	Thai Almond Sauce (page 238)	30 mL
1 tsp	cold water (if needed)	5 mL
$\frac{1}{2}$ cup	chopped dry-roasted cashews	125 mL
	Additional chopped fresh cilantro	

1. Using the julienne peeler, make long slices along one side of a zucchini until you get to the seeded core. Rotate the zucchini and peel another side in the same way. Continue until you have done all four sides. Discard the seeded core. Do the same with the remaining zucchini and the cucumber, then use the julienne peeler to peel the carrot into long strips.

2. In a large bowl, combine zucchini, cucumber, carrot, red pepper, yellow pepper and cilantro.

3. Thin the Thai Almond Sauce with 1 tsp (5 mL) cold water if it is too thick. Add to the salad and toss well to combine. Garnish with cashews and additional cilantro.

Nutrition Tip

Contrary to popular belief, cashews are lower in fat than other nuts, including almonds and walnuts. Plus, more than half of the fat they do contain is monounsaturated, similar to that found in olive oil. In many scientific studies, regular consumption of nuts and seeds is associated with a reduced risk of heart disease.

NUTRIENTS PER SERVING	
Calories	259
Fat	17 g
Carbohydrate	23 g
Fiber	5 g
Protein	9 g

Jicama, Avocado, Radish and Orange Salad with Cilantro

Jicama and radish give this salad a crispy crunch — the jicama a sweet crunch and the radish a peppery one. Remember to purchase organic fruit when you plan to use the zest.

Tip

White or red grapefruit can be substituted for or combined with the oranges.

3	oranges	3
1	clove garlic, very finely minced (almost to a paste)	1
1 tsp	ground cumin	5 mL
¼ tsp	sea salt (approx.)	1 mL
¼ tsp	chili powder	1 mL
¼ cup	freshly squeezed lime juice (approx.)	60 mL
¼ cup	extra virgin olive oil	60 mL
1	small jicama (about 1 lb/500 g)	1
6	radishes, cut into very thin round slices	6
4	green onions, cut diagonally into thin slices	4
½ cup	fresh cilantro leaves	125 mL
	Freshly ground black pepper (optional)	
1	ripe but firm avocado, sliced	1

1. Using a grater or a zester, grate 2 tsp (10 mL) orange zest; set aside. Slice off enough of both ends of the oranges that you see the ends of the fruit segments. Set each orange on a cut end and slice off the remaining peel and pith, one section at a time, following the curve of the fruit from top to bottom. Trim away any remaining white bits. Set a colander or strainer over a bowl. Hold each orange over the colander and carefully cut along both sides of each membrane, freeing the segments and letting them fall into the colander. Once all segments are done, squeeze as much juice as possible from the membranes. Measure out 2 tbsp (30 mL) juice and reserve any extra for another use.

2. In a small bowl, combine orange zest, orange juice, garlic, cumin, salt, chili powder and lime juice. Let stand for 5 to 10 minutes to blend the flavors. Whisk in oil.

3. Peel jicama and cut into ⅛-inch (3 mm) thick sticks about 2 to 3 inches (5 to 7.5 cm) long.

NUTRIENTS PER SERVING	
Calories	194
Fat	13 g
Carbohydrate	21 g
Fiber	8 g
Protein	1 g

Tip

Different types of oranges will lend different flavors to this salad. A blood orange will add a beautiful hit of color, not to mention health-promoting anthocyanins.

4. In a large bowl, combine orange segments, jicama, radishes, green onions and cilantro. Add three-quarters of the dressing and toss to coat. Taste and adjust seasoning with salt, pepper (if using) and lime juice as desired.

5. Line a serving bowl with avocado slices, reserving 3 slices, and arrange jicama salad on top. Arrange the remaining avocado on top of the salad and drizzle with the remaining dressing. Serve immediately.

Nutrition Tip

Jicama is a root vegetable that is over 80% water, so it doesn't have as much starch and carbohydrates as potatoes. It is also a good source of the prebiotic inulin, which helps support the balance of "good" and "bad" bacteria in our intestines — which, in turn, supports the immune system. Jicama is great sliced as a crudité for a delicious dip like Green Goddess Dressing (page 253) or Creamy Lemon Tahini Dressing (page 255).

Shredded Kale Salad with Pecan Parmesan

Raw kale can be tough and bitter, but not this time! The secret of this salad is the thinly sliced kale and massaging the dressing into the leaves. No more tough bitter greens for you.

Tip

If you don't have a mini food processor or spice grinder, you can finely chop the cooled toasted pecans, then mix them well in a bowl with the yeast, salt and oil.

- Preheat oven to 325°F (160°C)
- Mini food processor or spice grinder (see tip, at left)

Pecan Parmesan

¾ cup	pecan halves	175 mL
2 tbsp	nutritional yeast	30 mL
⅛ tsp	sea salt	0.5 mL
1 tbsp	extra virgin olive oil	15 mL

Salad

2	medium bunches Lacinato kale (about 10 to 12 leaves per bunch)	2
¼ cup	freshly squeezed lemon juice	60 mL
¼ cup	extra virgin olive oil	60 mL
¼ tsp	sea salt	1 mL
¼ tsp	freshly ground black pepper	1 mL

1. *Pecan Parmesan:* Spread pecans in a single layer on a baking sheet. Toast in preheated oven for 10 minutes or until fragrant and golden. Transfer to a plate to cool.

2. In mini food processor, combine cooled pecans, yeast, salt and oil; pulse to the consistency of rice. (Be careful not to overprocess; you want a nice crunchy texture, not a powder.)

3. *Salad:* Remove stems and thick ribs from kale leaves and cut leaves in half lengthwise. Stack 6 halved kale leaves and slice as thinly as you can (aim for about ⅛ inch/3 mm thick). Repeat with the remaining kale. Place shredded kale in a large bowl. You should end up with 8 to 9 cups (2 to 2.25 L) of chopped kale.

NUTRIENTS PER SERVING	
Calories	305
Fat	30 g
Carbohydrate	7 g
Fiber	3 g
Protein	4 g

Tips

There are two main types of kale sold in the stores or farmers' markets: curly kale and Lacinato kale, also called dinosaur kale, black kale, Tuscan kale or cavolo nero. Curly kale has bright green leaves that are sometimes curled so tightly it can be hard to chop them. It has a light peppery flavor that can become a bit bitter as it loses freshness. Lacinato kale has long, spear-shaped deep blue-green leaves with a pebbled texture just like you might imagine dinosaur skin to be! It has a deep, earthy flavor with what some describe as a nutty sweetness. You can chop Lacinato kale into thin ribbons much more easily than curly kale, but both types work well in this salad.

This salad is best eaten the day it is made; for the best flavor, don't let it sit in the fridge overnight.

4. In a small bowl, whisk together lemon juice, oil, salt and pepper. Pour over kale and toss with your hands, massaging the kale to help soften it, for 2 minutes. Let stand for 15 minutes.

5. Sprinkle three-quarters of the pecan parmesan over the salad and toss well. Top with the remaining pecan parmesan.

Nutrition Tip

Kale deserves all the hype it has generated as a superfood. Research and studies have identified almost four dozen different flavonoids in kale, making it an antioxidant superstar. As a member of the cruciferous vegetable family, it also contains isothiocyanates that play a key role in reducing the risk of cancer and supporting our detoxification systems.

Warm Spinach Salad with Eggs and Bacon

Tossing a warm lemony dressing with spinach softens the greens up, and the addition of a bit of bacon turns this salad into a comfort food dish.

Tip

To hard-cook eggs, place them in a single layer in a saucepan and cover with water. Bring to a boil over high heat. Turn off the heat, keep the pan on the hot burner, cover and let stand for 10 to 12 minutes. Drain the hot water and run cold water over the eggs to cool them. If the eggs are difficult to peel cleanly, crack them all over and place them in a pan of cold water for 5 minutes. The water will help to separate the membrane from the egg white.

2 tbsp	extra virgin olive oil	30 mL
2 tbsp	freshly squeezed lemon juice	30 mL
2 tsp	Dijon mustard	10 mL
¼ tsp	sea salt	1 mL
¼ tsp	freshly ground black pepper	1 mL
2	slices pasture-raised bacon (or turkey bacon), cut into 1-inch (2.5 cm) pieces	2
1	large shallot, minced (about ⅓ cup/75 mL)	1
6 cups	loosely packed baby spinach	1.5 L
3	large free-range eggs, hard-cooked, peeled and quartered (see tip, at left)	3

1. In a small bowl, whisk together oil, lemon juice, mustard, salt and pepper. Set aside.

2. In a small skillet, cook bacon over medium-high heat, stirring often, for 5 to 8 minutes or until golden brown and crisp. Using a slotted spoon, transfer bacon to a plate lined with paper towels.

3. Add shallot to the fat in the pan and cook, stirring, for about 1 minute or until softened. Remove from heat and let cool slightly, then add dressing, whisking well.

4. Place spinach in a large bowl. Add warm dressing and toss to coat. Divide spinach among serving plates and top with eggs and bacon. Serve immediately.

Nutrition Tip

Two of the antioxidant carotenoids in spinach are lutein and zeaxanthin, both of which are found in larger concentrations in the macula and retina of the eye than in any other tissue in the body. The role of lutein in diabetic retinopathy has not yet been well studied in human subjects, but one study did show that the serum concentrations of lutein and zeaxanthin were significantly lower in the subject with diabetic retinopathy than in subjects without diabetic retinopathy. When these subjects were given supplementation of lutein and zeaxanthin, they did experience improved visual acuity, suggesting a therapeutic benefit.

NUTRIENTS PER SERVING	
Calories	393
Fat	31 g
Carbohydrate	14 g
Fiber	4 g
Protein	16 g

Modern Cobb Salad

The Cobb salad was created in 1937 by Bob Cobb, the owner of the Brown Derby Restaurant in Hollywood. Legend has it that Bob was rummaging in the restaurant refrigerator, looking for a midnight snack. He grabbed what was there, threw it all together, and the Cobb salad was born.

Tip

Poaching a chicken breast is very quick. Place a boneless skinless chicken breast in a medium saucepan and add enough water to cover (or use stock for added flavor). Bring to a boil, then cover, reduce heat to low and simmer gently for 10 to 12 minutes or until chicken is no longer pink.

1 tbsp	finely minced shallot	15 mL
1/2 tsp	freshly ground black pepper	2 mL
1/4 tsp	sea salt	1 mL
3 tbsp	extra virgin olive oil	45 mL
2 tbsp	white wine vinegar	30 mL
2 tsp	Dijon mustard	10 mL
5 cups	coarsely chopped romaine lettuce	1.25 L
1 cup	chopped watercress	250 mL
1	avocado, sliced	1
2	large free-range eggs, hard-cooked, peeled and quartered (see tip, page 138)	2
2	small tomatoes, quartered	2
1 cup	sliced cucumber	250 mL
1 cup	cubed cooked chicken (see tip, at left)	250 mL
4	slices pasture-raised bacon (or turkey bacon), cooked crisp and crumbled	4

1. In a small bowl, whisk together shallot, pepper, salt, oil, vinegar and mustard.

2. In a large bowl, combine romaine and watercress. Add half the dressing and toss to coat.

3. Divide romaine mixture among four plates. Arrange equal portions of avocado, egg, tomato, cucumber and chicken on top. Drizzle with the remaining dressing and top with bacon.

Nutrition Tip

The peppery flavor of watercress comes from gluconasturtiin, one of its phytonutrients. As a close cousin to cabbage, watercress contains isothiocyanates, one of which, called phenylethyl isothiocyanate (PEITC), has been studied for its anticancer properties. Watercress is also rich in vitamins and minerals, with one of the standouts being vitamin K, which is important for proper blood clotting and the development and remodeling of our bones.

NUTRIENTS PER SERVING	
Calories	343
Fat	26 g
Carbohydrate	10 g
Fiber	6 g
Protein	20 g

Fennel, Grapefruit and Mint Salad

Makes 2 servings

This super-fresh salad will keep your digestive system happy! Fennel and mint are wonderful for calming and soothing the muscles in the intestine and promoting good digestion.

Tip

Chiffonade (which means "made of rags" in French) is a chopping technique useful for flat leafy herbs and vegetables that you are going to eat fresh. Stack about 10 leaves at a time on top of each other. Roll the stack lengthwise into a fairly tight cigar shape. Starting at one end, cut across the roll in thin strips. Gently fluff the strips with your fingers to separate them.

1	red grapefruit	1
2	stalks celery, cut into ½-inch (1 cm) pieces (about 1 cup/250 mL)	2
1	fennel bulb, trimmed and cut into ½-inch (1 cm) pieces (about 2 cups/500 mL)	1
¼ cup	finely chopped fresh flat-leaf (Italian) parsley	60 mL
¼ cup	fresh mint chiffonade (see tip, at left)	60 mL
1 tbsp	freshly squeezed lemon juice	15 mL
1 tbsp	extra virgin olive oil	15 mL
¼ tsp	sea salt	1 mL

1. Slice off enough of both ends of the grapefruit that you see the ends of the fruit segments. Set the grapefruit on a cut end and slice off the remaining peel and pith, one section at a time, following the curve of the fruit from top to bottom. Set a colander or strainer over a bowl. Carefully cut along both sides of each membrane, freeing the segments and letting them fall into the colander. Once all segments are done, squeeze as much juice as possible from the membranes. Measure out 1 tbsp (15 mL) juice and reserve any extra for another use. (If there isn't enough juice, squeeze 1 or 2 of the segments to get the required amount.) Cut the segments into 1-inch (2.5 cm) pieces.

2. In a medium bowl, combine grapefruit segments, celery, fennel, parsley and mint.

3. In a small bowl, whisk together grapefruit juice, lemon juice, oil and salt. Add dressing to salad and toss to coat.

Nutrition Tip

Lycopene is the phytonutrient that gives pink and red grapefruits their wonderful colors; as such, it is not present in white grapefruits. Lycopene has been studied for its effect on the development of prostate cancer in men. In one study, men who more frequently consumed lycopene-rich foods were 82% less likely to have prostate cancer than men who ate the least amount of lycopene-containing foods.

NUTRIENTS PER SERVING	
Calories	155
Fat	7 g
Carbohydrate	23 g
Fiber	6 g
Protein	3 g

Watermelon Salad

Makes 6 servings

Nothing says summer like slices of watermelon. Inspired by Jill's friend Marie-Pierre, who is an exceptional hostess, this salad takes watermelon to a new level.

Tip

For ¼ cup (60 mL) lime juice, you will need about 2 limes, but you'll likely only need to zest one of them to get the 2 tsp (10 mL) zest.

2 lbs	watermelon, cut into 1-inch (2.5 cm) cubes (about 6 cups/1.5 L)	1 kg
1 tbsp	mint chiffonade (see tip, page 140)	15 mL
2 tsp	grated lime zest	10 mL
¼ cup	freshly squeezed lime juice	60 mL
	Chili powder (optional)	

1. In a large bowl, using a wooden spoon, toss together watermelon, mint, lime zest and lime juice. (The salad can be covered and refrigerated at this point for up to 6 hours.) If desired, sprinkle with chili powder just before serving.

Nutrition Tip

Choosing a fully ripe watermelon really pays off in terms of antioxidant content. The biggest jump in the lycopene content of the watermelon flesh happens when it turns from pink to that really deep, delicious red. When you purchase a whole watermelon, look at the bottom (the spot where it was resting on the ground). A fully ripe watermelon will have a "ground spot" that is creamy yellow in color. If that spot is still green or white, the fruit is not yet ripe. For those of you who like to give the watermelon a knock to test its ripeness, apparently you are looking for a bass sound rather than a soprano sound.

NUTRIENTS PER SERVING	
Calories	49
Fat	0 g
Carbohydrate	12 g
Fiber	0 g
Protein	0 g

All Fruit Chop

We often forget that avocados and tomatoes are really fruits, not vegetables. This is a very casual yet refreshing salad — the only thing you need is a cutting board and a sharp knife. Serve it on mixed greens or as a salsa for chicken or fish.

Tips

If you are making this to use as a salsa, chop everything a little smaller than if serving it as a salad.

You can use 1 cup (250 mL) halved cherry tomatoes in place of the chopped tomato.

1	medium mango	1
1	medium avocado	1
1	medium tomato	1
1 tsp	balsamic vinegar	5 mL
6 to 10	fresh mint leaves, minced	6 to 10
$\frac{1}{8}$ tsp	sea salt	0.5 mL

1. Chop mango, avocado and tomato into pieces of about the same size.

2. In a large bowl, gently combine mango, avocado and tomato. Drizzle with vinegar and sprinkle with mint to taste and salt; stir gently to combine. Let stand for 15 minutes to blend the flavors.

Nutrition Tip

Besides containing almost two dozen different vitamins and minerals, mangos are also rich in antioxidant flavonoids that help protect our skin and vision. One cup (250 mL) of chopped mango provides 100% of the required daily intake of vitamin C, another antioxidant that is important for immune function and collagen formation for our joints and connective tissues.

NUTRIENTS PER SERVING	
Calories	137
Fat	8 g
Carbohydrate	18 g
Fiber	5 g
Protein	2 g

Vegetables

Green Beans with Shiitakes, Shallots and Toasted Almonds

Makes 4 servings

Although they are legumes and therefore not technically paleo, green beans are included in this book because we are actually eating the big green seed pod that contains the much smaller amount of legumes inside. We bet it's been a long time since you really looked inside a green bean!

• **Steamer basket**

1 lb	green beans, trimmed	500 g
2 tbsp	extra virgin olive oil	30 mL
2	large shallots, thinly sliced	2
2	cloves garlic, finely chopped	2
2 cups	thinly sliced shiitake mushroom caps	500 mL
½ tsp	sea salt	2 mL
¼ tsp	freshly ground black pepper	1 mL
½ cup	slivered almonds, toasted (see tip, page 127)	125 mL

1. Fill a saucepan with 2 inches (5 cm) of cold water and fit with a steamer basket. Bring to a boil over high heat. Add beans and steam for 2 minutes. Drain, rinse under cold water to stop the cooking and drain again. Set aside.

2. In a large skillet, heat oil over medium heat. Add shallots and cook, stirring occasionally, for 2 to 3 minutes or until starting to soften. Stir in garlic. Add shiitakes, salt and pepper; cook, stirring occasionally, for 5 to 6 minutes or until mushrooms are lightly browned. Add green beans and cook, stirring, for 1 to 2 minutes or until heated through.

3. Just before serving, stir in toasted almonds, or sprinkle them on top of each serving.

Nutrition Tip

Green beans have been studied mainly for their antioxidant content. They contain a wide variety of carotenoids, like lutein and beta-carotene, that we most often associate with the yellow/orange/red group of vegetables. They also provide good amounts of vitamin C and manganese to round out the antioxidant profile.

NUTRIENTS PER SERVING	
Calories	178
Fat	13 g
Carbohydrate	14 g
Fiber	6 g
Protein	6 g

Brown Butter Green Beans with Pine Nuts

Makes 4 servings

Browning butter is a great shortcut that really enhances the flavor of what might otherwise be an ordinary vegetable dish. When the butter foams, the water is boiling out and leaving the fat and milk proteins, which are what actually turn brown. The butter can go from golden to burnt quickly, so try not to be doing too many other things while you are making this recipe!

2 tbsp	grass-fed butter	30 mL
½ cup	raw pine nuts	125 mL
1 lb	green beans, trimmed	500 g
2 tsp	freshly squeezed lemon juice	10 mL
	Sea salt and freshly ground black pepper	

1. In a large saucepan, melt butter over medium heat. As it melts, keep a close eye on it and swirl it gently as it foams, watching the color. As it just starts to turn golden brown, stir in pine nuts and cook, stirring, for about 3 minutes or until pine nuts are golden brown.

2. Reduce heat to medium-low and add beans, stirring to coat with butter. Cover with a tight-fitting lid and steam for 3 to 5 minutes or until beans are tender-crisp. Remove from heat and stir well, then sprinkle with lemon juice and season to taste with salt and pepper.

Nutrition Tip

Pine nuts are a good source of magnesium, which is needed for hundreds of biochemical reactions in the body. People with diabetes are more likely to be low in magnesium than those without, likely because a higher level of magnesium is excreted in the urine when blood glucose levels are elevated.

NUTRIENTS PER SERVING	
Calories	201
Fat	18 g
Carbohydrate	11 g
Fiber	4 g
Protein	4 g

Beets in Mustard Sauce

Cold beets are a great accompaniment to sliced meat for a fresh summer meal, and are also wonderful as a side to the classic Flattened Roast Chicken (page 198). This recipe must be made 24 hours in advance to allow the flavors to marry, so plan ahead — you won't be sorry.

Tips

To cut an onion into crescents, first cut it in half lengthwise from bulb to root. Remove the outer skin. Place the onion, cut side down, on a chopping board. Cut off and discard bulb end. Cut the onion lengthwise at a slight angle into thin wedges.

Beets can stain your hands, so you may want to wear gloves or use a paper towel when slipping off the skins.

1 lb	red beets (about 5 medium)	500 g
	Cold water	
3 tbsp	Dijon or whole-grain mustard	45 mL
3 tbsp	red wine vinegar	45 mL
¼ cup	extra virgin olive oil	60 mL
1	medium onion, cut in half and then into thin crescents (see tip, at left)	1
	Sea salt and freshly ground black pepper	

1. If beets have their tops, cut them off, leaving about 1 inch (2.5 cm) of stem attached (reserve tops for another use, such as Easy Sautéed Greens, page 160). Place beets in a large saucepan, add enough cold water to cover and bring to a boil over high heat. Reduce heat to medium and boil for 45 to 60 minutes (depending on the size of the beets) or until the beets can easily be pierced with a sharp knife.

2. Meanwhile, in a large bowl, combine mustard and vinegar. Whisk in oil in a steady stream until sauce is smooth and creamy. Stir in onion.

3. Drain beets and submerge in several changes of cold water until they are cool enough to handle. Cut off the roots and tops and slip off the skins. Cut beets into slices that are just over ¼ inch (0.5 cm) and add to the onion mixture, stirring well. Cover and refrigerate for 24 hours. Stir well again and season to taste with salt and pepper before serving.

Nutrition Tip

When onions are cut or crushed, the phytochemical compounds allium and allyl disulfide are converted, by enzyme activity, to allicin. Allicin has been shown to help lower total and LDL cholesterol, decrease triglycerides and increase HDL cholesterol, all of which supports heart health and may reduce the risk of atherosclerosis and stroke.

NUTRIENTS PER SERVING	
Calories	188
Fat	14 g
Carbohydrate	12 g
Fiber	4 g
Protein	3 g

Roasted Beets and Pearl Onions

It's a good thing this recipe makes a lot — you'll find it delicious served cold with tomorrow's lunch.

Tip

To peel pearl onions, plunge them into a pot of boiling water and blanch for 30 seconds. Using a strainer or a slotted spoon, immediately transfer onions to a bowl of ice water. When cooled, cut off the root end of each onion and, holding the other end, squeeze it out of its skin.

Nutrition Tip

Although beets contain more sugar than other vegetables, they also have more fiber, which helps reduce the effects of carbohydrates on blood sugar. Beets are also a source of magnesium, which helps regulate blood sugar and insulin.

NUTRIENTS PER SERVING	
Calories	265
Fat	15 g
Carbohydrate	30 g
Fiber	8 g
Protein	6 g

- Preheat oven to 375°F (190°C), with rack in the bottom position
- 1 or 2 rimmed baking sheets, lined with parchment paper

4½ lbs	golden and/or red beets, peeled and cut into 1-inch (2.5 cm) thick wedges	2.25 kg
2 tbsp	extra virgin olive oil	30 mL
¼ tsp	sea salt	1 mL
⅛ tsp	freshly ground black pepper	0.5 mL
8 oz	pearl onions, peeled (see tip, at left)	250 g
¼ cup	shelled pistachios, chopped	60 mL

Lemon Parsley Dressing

1	shallot, minced	1
¼ tsp	sea salt	1 mL
¼ tsp	freshly ground black pepper	1 mL
¼ cup	freshly squeezed lemon juice	60 mL
2 tsp	Dijon mustard	10 mL
⅓ cup	extra virgin olive oil	75 mL
½ cup	loosely packed fresh flat-leaf (Italian) parsley leaves, chopped	125 mL

1. In a large bowl, toss together beets, oil, salt and pepper. Spread in a single layer on prepared baking sheet. (If using both golden and red beets, use two separate bowls and separate baking sheets so the red beets don't color the golden ones.)

2. Roast in preheated oven for 30 minutes, turning once halfway through. Add pearl onions and roast for 30 to 40 minutes, stirring once halfway through, until onions are golden and beets are tender.

3. *Dressing:* Meanwhile, in a bowl, whisk together shallot, salt, pepper, lemon juice and mustard. Whisk in oil in a steady stream until well combined. Whisk in parsley.

4. Transfer beets and onions to a large bowl, add dressing and toss to coat. Serve warm or at room temperature, topped with pistachios.

Garlicky Roasted Broccoli

Makes 4 servings

This is a fantastic, fast, nutritious and delicious vegetable recipe for those times when everyone in the house seems to be going in different directions. It is an ideal match for Flattened Roast Chicken (page 198).

Tips

Don't throw out the broccoli stems! Peel them and cut them lengthwise into ½-inch (1 cm) slices for a perfect dipper for Classic Guacamole (page 247). You can also julienne the stems and add them to any of the coleslaws (pages 128–130) or the Jicama, Avocado, Radish and Orange Salad with Cilantro (page 134).

You can substitute the oil of your choice for the avocado oil.

- **Preheat oven to 400°F (200°C)**
- **Rimmed baking sheet, lined with parchment paper or sprayed with olive oil cooking spray**

2	bunches broccoli, cut into florets (about 8 cups/2 L)	2
10	cloves garlic, finely chopped	10
2 tbsp	avocado oil	30 mL
½ tsp	sea salt	2 mL
½ tsp	freshly ground black pepper	2 mL
½ tsp	hot pepper flakes (optional)	2 mL
	Squeeze of fresh lemon juice	

1. In a large bowl, toss broccoli with garlic, oil, salt, black pepper and hot pepper flakes (if using). Spread in a single layer on prepared baking sheet.

2. Roast in preheated oven for 15 to 20 minutes, stirring once halfway through, until broccoli is tender and edges are brown. Squeeze lemon juice over broccoli before serving.

Nutrition Tip

Most broccoli studies have focused on its effects on cancer. Broccoli gives us a unique combination of antioxidant, anti-inflammatory and detoxification-supporting compounds that make it an important food for cancer prevention. Some studies have focused on just how much broccoli we might need to eat for certain preventive effects, and the answer seems to be: the more the better! On a daily basis, that means don't skimp on the broccoli. Make a lot, so you can load up your plate.

NUTRIENTS PER SERVING	
Calories	174
Fat	8 g
Carbohydrate	23 g
Fiber	8 g
Protein	9 g

Roasted Broccolini with Creamy Lemon Tahini Dressing

Broccolini might look like baby broccoli, but it's actually a hybrid of broccoli and Chinese broccoli (*kai-lan*), first bred in 1993. It is a bit milder than broccoli, but tastes best cooked.

- **Preheat oven to 425°F (220°C)**
- **Rimmed baking sheet, lined with parchment paper or sprayed with olive oil cooking spray**

1 lb	broccolini, trimmed	500 g
2 tbsp	extra virgin olive oil	30 mL
¼ tsp	sea salt	1 mL
¼ tsp	freshly ground black pepper	1 mL
	Creamy Lemon Tahini Dressing (page 255)	

1. Place broccolini on prepared baking sheet, toss with oil and season with salt and pepper. Spread broccolini out evenly so there is as little overlap as possible.

2. Roast in preheated oven for 10 to 15 minutes, turning and tossing halfway through, until broccolini is tender-crisp.

3. Arrange broccolini on a serving platter and drizzle with some of the Creamy Lemon Tahini Dressing. Serve immediately, with the rest of the dressing on the side for those who want more.

Nutrition Tip

Just like broccoli, broccolini is a member of the Brassica family of vegetables, and just like broccoli, the nutrients in broccolini support the detoxification systems of the body. Broccolini is a good source of the antioxidant vitamins A and C and is rich in folate, which supports heart health.

NUTRIENTS PER SERVING (WITHOUT DRESSING)	
Calories	107
Fat	7 g
Carbohydrate	8 g
Fiber	1 g
Protein	4 g

Cauliflower Steaks

The first time you prepare these for guests, they may think you are taking this whole nutrition thing too far. But once they see how fabulous these steaks look and how incredible they taste, they'll be asking for more.

Tip

Use a large spatula when you turn the cauliflower steaks over so that you can get under the whole piece. As cauliflower cooks, it becomes softer and can fall apart if you are not careful.

1	large head cauliflower (about 3 lbs/1.5 kg)	1
2 to 4 tbsp	extra virgin olive oil	30 to 60 mL
1 tsp	ground turmeric	5 mL
	Sea salt and freshly ground black pepper	

1. Clean cauliflower, discarding outside leaves. Cut cauliflower lengthwise through the core into 4 "steaks" about $1/2$ inch (1 cm) thick. Cut any large florets that may fall off the same way (reserve any smaller pieces for another use). Brush 1 to 2 tbsp (15 to 30 mL) oil over one side of the cauliflower steaks, sprinkle with $1/2$ tsp (2 mL) turmeric and season with salt and pepper.

2. In a large skillet, heat 1 tbsp (15 mL) oil over medium-high heat. Working with one or two steaks at a time (as room permits without overlapping), add cauliflower, oiled side down, and cook for 3 to 4 minutes or until browned on the bottom. Sprinkle the top with the remaining turmeric and season with salt and pepper. Using a large spatula, gently turn steak over and cook for 3 to 4 minutes or until cauliflower is tender and browned on both sides. Repeat with the remaining steaks, adding oil as needed between batches. Serve immediately.

Nutrition Tip

Turmeric, a powerful anti-inflammatory that has long been used to treat a wide variety of medical conditions, has achieved mainstream recognition in the past few years. The key to turmeric is its active ingredient, curcumin. Thousands of peer-reviewed scientific articles have been published about the activity and effectiveness of curcumin, including those demonstrating that curcumin can protect against oxidative stress, reduce blood cholesterol levels, protect against cognitive decline and induce cell death in various types of cancer cells.

NUTRIENTS PER SERVING	
Calories	114
Fat	7 g
Carbohydrate	11 g
Fiber	4 g
Protein	4 g

Roasted Cauliflower and Garlic

Makes 4 servings

Roasted cauliflower makes a delicious vegetable option to go with your protein. This super-easy dish will be a big hit with the whole family and may make you a new fan of cauliflower!

Tips

You can use the fat of your choice in place of the olive oil.

To turn this recipe into a mash, roast the cauliflower until very tender, then transfer to a food processor and process until smooth and creamy.

- Preheat oven to 400°F (200°C)
- Rimmed baking sheet, lined with parchment paper or sprayed with olive oil cooking spray

1	large head cauliflower (about 3 lbs/ 1.5 kg), cut into medium-size uniform pieces	1
5	cloves garlic, minced	5
2 tbsp	extra virgin olive oil	30 mL
½ tsp	sea salt	2 mL
¼ tsp	freshly ground black pepper	1 mL

1. In a large bowl, toss cauliflower with garlic, oil, salt and pepper. Spread in a single layer on prepared baking sheet.

2. Roast in preheated oven for 15 to 20 minutes, turning occasionally, until tender-crisp and starting to brown at the edges. Serve immediately.

Nutrition Tip

Along with other cruciferous vegetables (broccoli, cabbage, kale), cauliflower provides a number of anti-inflammatory nutrients, including indole-3-carbinol (I3C). This compound appears to act at the genetic level in the body by changing the expression of some of the genes involved in the formation and progression of certain cancers. Eaten regularly, cruciferous vegetables can be a good tool in the fight against cancer.

NUTRIENTS PER SERVING	
Calories	118
Fat	7 g
Carbohydrate	12 g
Fiber	4 g
Protein	4 g

Cauliflower Garlic Mash

Mashed potatoes used to be a staple with the Sunday night roast beef in many households across North America. But times have changed, and cauliflower mash is the new mashed potato! It is wonderful as a side dish or as the secret ingredient that keeps New Classic Meatballs (page 220) tender and juicy.

Tip

You can use the fat of your choice in place of the butter.

- Steamer basket
- Food processor

1	large head cauliflower (about 3 lbs/ 1.5 kg), cut into medium-size uniform pieces	1
5	cloves garlic (or to taste), peeled	5
½ tsp	sea salt	2 mL
¼ tsp	freshly ground black pepper	1 mL
2 tbsp	grass-fed butter	30 mL

1. In a covered steamer basket set over a large pot of boiling water, steam cauliflower and garlic for 8 to 10 minutes, checking the water level occasionally and replenishing as needed, until cauliflower is very tender. Drain cauliflower and garlic.

2. In food processor, combine cauliflower, garlic, salt, pepper and butter; process until smooth.

Nutrition Tip

Potatoes have plenty of vitamins and minerals, but they also have a lot of carbohydrates that can have a negative effect on blood sugar and insulin levels. According to the USDA National Nutrient Database (from which come the numbers for the nutritional analyses in this book), 1 cup (250 mL) of commercial ready-to-eat mashed potatoes has about 30 grams of carbs, while homemade mashed potatoes have about 35 grams in the same size serving. This cauliflower mash has about 12 grams. The difference in the total carbohydrates can have a dramatic effect on your blood sugar. Plus, this mash is delicious!

NUTRIENTS PER SERVING	
Calories	109
Fat	6 g
Carbohydrate	12 g
Fiber	4 g
Protein	4 g

Fried Cauliflower Rice

Fried rice has always been a great way to use up the ends of the vegetables that are in the fridge. This fried cauliflower rice is no exception, plus you'll use up the cauliflower, too.

Tips

You can use an equal amount of the fat of your choice in place of the olive oil.

The eggs add some protein to this dish, but to make it a complete meal, you will need 2 eggs per person. For a large number of eggs, cook them in another pan as you would scrambled eggs. Then stir the cooked eggs into the fried cauliflower rice at the end.

- Food processor

1	medium head cauliflower (about 2 lbs/ 1 kg), cut into 2-inch (5 cm) pieces	1
3 tbsp	extra virgin olive oil	45 mL
1/2 cup	chopped onion	125 mL
1/2 cup	chopped carrot	125 mL
2	cloves garlic, minced	2
1 cup	chopped cremini or button mushrooms	250 mL
1/2 cup	chopped red bell pepper	125 mL
1/2 cup	chopped yellow bell pepper	125 mL
1/2 cup	chopped green onions	125 mL
2	large free-range eggs, beaten	2
2 tbsp	organic gluten-free tamari or coconut amino acids	30 mL

1. In food processor, pulse half the cauliflower to the consistency of rice. Pour into a large bowl and repeat with the remaining cauliflower (see tip, page 154).

2. In a large skillet, heat oil over medium heat. Add onion and carrot; cook, stirring, for 3 minutes. Add garlic and mushrooms; cook, stirring, for 2 minutes. Add red pepper, yellow pepper and green onions; cook, stirring, for 1 minute. Stir in cauliflower rice until well combined. Cover and cook for 3 minutes.

3. Stir rice well and push it to one side of the skillet. Pour eggs onto the empty side and cook, stirring and scraping from the bottom of the pan, until well scrambled. Mix the entire mixture together until well combined. Sprinkle with tamari and mix well. Serve immediately.

NUTRIENTS PER SERVING	
Calories	134
Fat	9 g
Carbohydrate	10 g
Fiber	3 g
Protein	5 g

Nutrition Tip

Cauliflower is part of the cruciferous family of vegetables, which have been well studied for their role in detoxification and cancer prevention. Consumption of cauliflower has been linked to prevention of bladder, ovarian, colon, prostate and breast cancers. By including other nutritious vegetables, this recipe builds on the antioxidant power of the cauliflower, making it the healthiest "fried rice" you've ever had.

Cilantro Cauliflower Rice

Makes 8 servings

Cauliflower is a wonderful low-carbohydrate alternative to rice. When you serve it with saucy dishes, such as Butter Chicken (page 204), the only difference you will notice is in your blood sugar numbers.

Tips

Not everyone likes cilantro; if you are among the cilantro-averse, substitute an equal amount of chopped fresh parsley.

Do not overfill the food processor or some of the cauliflower rice will be too small and will become mushy. You can also grate the cauliflower with the medium side of a box grater, or you can chop it by hand.

• **Food processor**

1	large head cauliflower (about 3 lbs/ 1.5 kg), cut into 2-inch (5 cm) pieces	1
2 tbsp	coconut oil	30 mL
½ cup	minced fresh cilantro	125 mL

1. In food processor, pulse half the cauliflower to the consistency of rice. Pour into a large bowl and repeat with the remaining cauliflower (see tip, at left).

2. In a large skillet, heat coconut oil over medium heat. Add cauliflower rice, stirring to coat. Cook, stirring, for 4 to 6 minutes or until tender. Remove from heat and stir in cilantro.

Nutrition Tip

Researchers from the United States and Mexico have isolated an antibacterial compound called dodecanal from both the seeds (coriander seeds) and fresh leaves (cilantro) of the coriander plant. Most herbs do have some antimicrobial activity, due to their volatile oils, but the researchers were surprised by the potency of dodecanal.

NUTRIENTS PER SERVING	
Calories	57
Fat	4 g
Carbohydrate	5 g
Fiber	2 g
Protein	2 g

Cauliflower Couscous with Lemon and Pine Nuts

Makes 4 servings

The flavors of olives, pine nuts and lemon zest lend a Mediterranean feel to this low-carbohydrate take on couscous, featuring cauliflower in place of wheat couscous.

Tips

Make sure to purchase organic lemons when you're planning to grate the zest.

Do not overfill the food processor or some of the cauliflower couscous will be too small and will become mushy. You can also grate the cauliflower with the medium side of a box grater, or you can chop it by hand.

• Food processor

1	medium head cauliflower (about 2 lbs/1 kg), cut into florets	1
2 tbsp	extra virgin olive oil	30 mL
1/2 cup	finely chopped onion	125 mL
1	clove garlic, minced	1
1/2 cup	toasted pine nuts (see tip, page 127)	125 mL
1/4 cup	pitted drained black olives, roughly chopped	60 mL
1 tbsp	chopped fresh cilantro	15 mL
1 tbsp	grated lemon zest	15 mL
1/2 tsp	sea salt	2 mL
Pinch	cayenne pepper (optional)	Pinch

1. In food processor, pulse half the cauliflower to the consistency of couscous. Pour into a large bowl and repeat with the remaining cauliflower (see tip, at left).

2. In a large skillet, heat oil over medium heat. Add onion and cook, stirring, for 2 minutes. Add garlic and cook, stirring, for 2 minutes. Add cauliflower couscous and cook, stirring, for about 3 minutes or until tender. Remove from heat and stir in pine nuts, olives, cilantro, lemon zest, salt and cayenne (if using).

Nutrition Tip

Although technically classified as fruits, we tend to use olives more as a zesty vegetable or pickle. Olives are unique in their fat content in that almost three-quarters of their fat is from oleic acid, a monounsaturated fat that is associated with a reduced risk of cardiovascular disease. Olives also contain a diverse range of antioxidant and anti-inflammatory phytonutrients, which adds to their value for heart health.

NUTRIENTS PER SERVING	
Calories	246
Fat	15 g
Carbohydrate	14 g
Fiber	5 g
Protein	6 g

Cauliflower Tortillas

These tortillas are a great option when you want a wrap or a taco (such as Fish Tacos, page 180). Change the spices in any way you like, depending on what you are putting inside.

Tip

If you don't have a blender or food processor, you can use the side of your box grater with the smallest holes to grate the cauliflower in step 1.

- Preheat oven to 375°F (190°C), with racks placed in the upper and lower thirds of the oven
- Blender or food processor (see tip, at left)
- Steamer basket, lined with cheesecloth
- 2 baking sheets, lined with parchment paper

1	large head cauliflower (about 3 lbs/ 1.5 kg), stems removed, cut into chunks	1
2	large free-range eggs, beaten	2
1/2 tsp	dried oregano	2 mL
1/2 tsp	paprika	2 mL
1/2 tsp	sea salt	2 mL
1/4 tsp	freshly ground black pepper	1 mL

1. In blender, pulse half the cauliflower to a texture finer than rice. Pour into a large bowl and repeat with the remaining cauliflower.

2. Place cauliflower in prepared steamer basket and set over a large pot of boiling water. Cover and steam for 5 minutes. Remove from heat and let stand until cool enough to handle.

3. Drain cauliflower, place on a clean dish towel and squeeze out as much liquid as you can. (Squeeze hard so you don't end up with soggy tortillas later on!)

4. Transfer cauliflower to a large bowl and add eggs, oregano, paprika, salt and pepper, mixing well. Divide mixture into 6 balls of equal size.

NUTRIENTS PER TORTILLA	
Calories	60
Fat	2 g
Carbohydrate	7 g
Fiber	3 g
Protein	5 g

Tip

Store the tortillas in an airtight container in the refrigerator for up to 3 days. To reheat, place in a dry skillet over low heat for a few minutes, flipping once to make sure they are heated through.

5. Place 3 balls on each prepared baking sheet and flatten into circles about $\frac{1}{4}$ inch (0.5 cm) thick.

6. Place one baking sheet on each oven rack and bake in preheated oven for 10 minutes. Carefully flip tortillas over and switch the positions of the baking sheets on the racks. Bake for 5 to 6 minutes or until cooked through.

Nutrition Tip

Commercial taco shells and tortillas have very little to offer in terms of nutritious ingredients and, in fact, contain things that are harmful to our health, including hydrogenated vegetable oils and high-fructose corn syrup. These cauliflower tortillas, on the other hand, provide vitamins, minerals and phytonutrients to support your detoxification system and the health of your entire body.

Cauliflower Zucchini Hash Browns

Think you can't enjoy a crispy hash brown with your eggs anymore? Think again! These low-carb hash browns taste like the real thing and don't wreak havoc with your blood sugar. But they aren't just for breakfast — enjoy them as you would a potato side with the Classic Rack of Lamb (page 235) or the Baked Haddock with Peppers and Tomatoes (page 184).

Tips

Grate the cauliflower and zucchini on the side of your box grater with the largest holes. Cut the cauliflower in half or into quarters first, so it doesn't slip against the grater.

You can use the fat of your choice in place of the olive oil; this recipe is great with grass-fed bacon fat.

1 cup	grated cauliflower (see tip, at left)	250 mL
1 cup	grated zucchini	250 mL
1/4 cup	minced onion	60 mL
1/2 tsp	sea salt	2 mL
1/4 tsp	freshly ground black pepper	1 mL
1/8 tsp	garlic powder or minced garlic (optional)	0.5 mL
1	large free-range egg, beaten	1
1 tbsp	extra virgin olive oil	15 mL

1. In a large bowl, combine cauliflower and zucchini. Add onion, salt, pepper, garlic (if using) and egg, mixing well.

2. In a large skillet, heat oil over medium heat. Drop hash brown mixture into the skillet in 4 portions and press down with the back of a spatula. Cook for 3 to 5 minutes or until bottoms are nicely browned. Gently flip hash browns over and cook for 2 to 3 minutes or until browned and hot in the center.

Nutrition Tip

It goes without saying that these hash browns are more nutritious than those of a major fast-food chain, but we're going to say it anyway. There are twice as many fat grams in the big-chain hash browns, and the fats they use are industrial seed oils. There are also four times as many carbohydrates as in ours, and only one-third the amount of protein. Bottom line? You will have better blood sugar results and less inflammation when you make ours — not to mention all the additional vitamins, minerals and phytonutrients.

NUTRIENTS PER HASH BROWN	
Calories	64
Fat	5 g
Carbohydrate	3 g
Fiber	1 g
Protein	3 g

Roasted Fennel and Onions

Makes 4 servings

Roasting fennel and onions mellows them and brings out their natural sweetness. This vegetable dish is a perfect accompaniment to Skillet-Grilled Flank Steak (page 222), Flattened Roast Chicken (page 198) or Pumpkin Seed–Crusted Rainbow Trout (page 190).

Tips

Cut off the fennel stems just at the top of the bulb. Cut ¼ inch (0.5 cm) off the root end. If there are black markings on the outer layer of the bulb, you can remove the entire layer or use a vegetable peeler to remove just the discolored areas. Cut the bulb in half through the root. Cut the halves into ½-inch (1 cm) thick wedges.

Leave the root end intact when you peel the onion. Cut the onion in half through the root. Cut each half into wedges, with a piece of the root end on each wedge to hold it together.

NUTRIENTS PER SERVING	
Calories	98
Fat	5 g
Carbohydrate	14 g
Fiber	5 g
Protein	2 g

- **Preheat oven to 450°F (230°C)**
- **Rimmed baking sheet, lined with parchment paper**

2	medium fennel bulbs, trimmed and cut into ½-inch (1 cm) thick wedges (see tip, at left)	2
2	medium onions, halved lengthwise and cut into ½-inch (1 cm) thick wedges (see tip, at left)	2
4 tsp	extra virgin olive oil	20 mL
½ tsp	sea salt	2 mL
¼ tsp	freshly ground black pepper	1 mL

1. Keeping them separate, brush fennel and onions with oil and season with salt and pepper. Arrange fennel in a single layer on prepared baking sheet. Spread onions in a single layer over fennel.

2. Roast in preheated oven, turning every 10 minutes, for 30 to 40 minutes or until vegetables are very tender and fennel is lightly browned. Serve warm or at room temperature.

Nutrition Tip

Onions are a rich source of flavonoids, and these phytonutrients tend to be concentrated in the outer layers of the skin. To maximize onions' health benefits, try to remove as little as possible when peeling the skin.

Easy Sautéed Greens

This recipe works well with any type of leafy green. Use your favorite or branch out and try what is in season. Spinach requires the least amount of cooking; kale, Swiss chard, beet greens and dandelion greens take a minute or two longer.

Tip

You can use the fat of your choice in place of the olive oil.

2 tbsp	extra virgin olive oil	30 mL
1	medium onion, thinly sliced	1
1/4 tsp	hot pepper flakes (optional)	1 mL
6	cloves garlic, thinly sliced	6
8 cups	dark leafy greens (tough stems and ribs removed as needed)	2 L
1 to 2 tsp	balsamic vinegar	5 to 10 mL
1/4 tsp	sea salt	1 mL
1/4 tsp	freshly ground pepper	1 mL

1. In a large skillet, heat oil over medium heat. Add onions and cook, stirring occasionally, for 2 to 3 minutes or until translucent. Stir in hot pepper flakes (if using). Add garlic and cook, stirring, for 1 to 2 minutes or until softened. Add greens and cook, tossing with kitchen tongs, until wilted, about 2 to 5 minutes depending on the type of green. Sprinkle with vinegar to taste and toss well. Remove from heat and season with salt and pepper. Serve immediately.

Nutrition Tip

All types of dark leafy greens are incredibly rich in phytonutrients, so you can't go wrong with any of them. However, each has its own unique profile. Swiss chard, for example, contains over a dozen different antioxidant polyphenols, including syringic acid, which is concentrated in the leaves. Syringic acid inhibits an enzyme called alpha-glucosidase, which means that fewer carbohydrates are broken down into simple sugar molecules, making Swiss chard a valuable tool in blood sugar management.

NUTRIENTS PER SERVING	
Calories	91
Fat	7 g
Carbohydrate	7 g
Fiber	2 g
Protein	2 g

Kale and Sweet Potato Sauté

The sweet taste of sweet potatoes, the heartiness of kale, and the spice of chili and cumin combine for a delicious side dish that is perfect with grilled chicken, lamb or beef, or with Almond-Crusted Salmon (page 185). If there is any left over, top it with some fried or scrambled eggs for a breakfast hash that will keep you going all morning.

Tip

If the sweet potato cubes are larger than $1/2$ inch (1 cm), they may take longer to cook.

2 tbsp	extra virgin olive oil (approx.), divided	30 mL
$1^1/_2$ lbs	sweet potatoes (2 medium), peeled and cut into $1/_2$-inch (1 cm) cubes	750 g
$4^1/_2$ tsp	ground cumin, divided	22 mL
3 tsp	chili powder, divided	15 mL
$3/_4$ tsp	sea salt (approx.), divided	3 mL
2	cloves garlic, minced	2
1	bunch curly or Lacinato kale (about 10 oz/300 g), center ribs and tough stems removed, leaves shredded	1
1 tbsp	filtered water	15 mL
	Freshly ground black pepper (optional)	

1. In a large skillet, heat 1 tbsp (15 mL) oil over medium heat. Add sweet potatoes and cook, stirring occasionally, for about 5 minutes or until starting to soften. Stir in 1 tsp (5 mL) cumin, 2 tsp (10 mL) chili powder and $1/_2$ tsp (2 mL) salt. Add more oil if the pan seems dry. Cook, stirring occasionally, for 8 to 10 minutes or until sweet potatoes are golden brown and tender. Transfer sweet potatoes to a bowl.

2. In the same skillet, heat the remaining 1 tbsp (15 mL) oil and garlic over medium heat. When the garlic starts to sizzle (do not let it brown), add kale, a little at a time, until it all fits in the pan. Turn kale with tongs to coat with oil. Add the remaining cumin, chili powder and salt. Stir in water and cook for about 5 minutes or until kale is wilted and tender.

3. Return sweet potatoes to the pan and toss together. Cook for about 2 minutes or until heated through. Taste and adjust seasoning with salt and pepper as desired. Serve hot.

Nutrition Tip

This dish hits it out of the park with its many nutrients, especially beta-carotene. We know that yellow/orange-pigmented vegetables have beta-carotene, but so does kale — the pigments are just hidden by the dark green color. Beta-carotene is an important carotenoid that the body can convert to vitamin A (retinol). Vitamin A helps maintain healthy skin and plays a vital role in our eye health.

NUTRIENTS PER SERVING	
Calories	165
Fat	8 g
Carbohydrate	21 g
Fiber	6 g
Protein	5 g

Nut-Crusted Portobello Slices

Makes 4 servings

These wonderfully meaty slices are incredibly flavorful and satisfying. They make a great side dish but can also be enjoyed as a hearty snack, served with The Best Paleo Mayo (page 249), sprinkled with capers, or with Classic Guacamole (page 247).

Tips

Portobellos are cremini mushrooms that have been allowed to grow to full maturity.

Mushrooms of all types will get soggy if you use water to clean them. Use a pastry brush or a damp paper towel to wipe away any dirt.

You can use 1 tsp (5 mL) garlic powder in place of the fresh garlic. Add it in step 3, with the salt and pepper.

Feel free to add any other ground spices or dried herbs you enjoy to the almond meal in step 3.

- Blender or food processor (optional)

4	portobello mushrooms	4
1 cup	raw almonds	250 mL
1	clove garlic	1
$\frac{1}{2}$ tsp	sea salt	2 mL
$\frac{1}{4}$ tsp	freshly ground black pepper	1 mL
3	large free-range eggs, beaten	3
4 tbsp	extra virgin olive oil (approx.)	60 mL

1. Remove mushroom stems and cut caps into long thin slices, about $\frac{3}{4}$ inch (2 cm) thick.

2. In blender, pulse almonds and garlic to the consistency of cornmeal. (Or chop them by hand using a large knife and a large cutting board.)

3. Transfer almond meal to a plate and stir in salt and pepper.

4. Place eggs in a wide, shallow container (such as a pie plate).

5. In a large skillet, heat half the oil over medium heat. Working with one mushroom slice at a time, dip both sides in egg, shaking off excess, then press firmly into almond meal, coating well. As they are coated, immediately add slices to the skillet, arranging as many in the skillet as will fit in a single layer. Cook for 3 to 4 minutes per side, turning once, or until golden brown on both sides. Transfer mushroom slices to a wire rack. Repeat with the remaining mushroom slices, egg and almond meal, adding oil and adjusting the heat as needed between batches. Discard any excess egg and almond meal. Serve hot, warm or at room temperature.

Nutrition Tip

It is the alpha- and beta-glucan molecules that are responsible for the beneficial effects of mushrooms, including positive immune and cardiovascular effects.

NUTRIENTS PER SERVING	
Calories	399
Fat	35 g
Carbohydrate	12 g
Fiber	6 g
Protein	14 g

Portobello Mushroom Cap Buns

Makes 4 "buns"

These buns are a wonderfully rich and meaty substitution for wheat flour buns. They are terrific with the Classic Turkey Burgers (page 215) and as a base for Roasted Ratatouille (page 170).

Tips

Never run mushrooms under water; they absorb water like a sponge. Instead, wipe them with a damp paper towel or use a pastry brush to remove any dirt.

Be careful not to use too much oil, as the mushroom caps can get soggy.

- Preheat oven to 400°F (200°C)
- Rimmed baking sheet, lined with foil, with a wire rack set on top

8	portobello mushroom caps	8
1 tbsp	extra virgin olive oil	15 mL
	Sea salt and freshly ground black pepper	

1. Brush both sides of each mushroom cap lightly with oil and season with salt and pepper. Place caps, gill side up, on rack over prepared baking sheet. Bake in preheated oven for 10 minutes. Flip mushrooms over and bake for 8 to 10 minutes or until browned.

Nutrition Tip

An average wheat flour hamburger bun has about 34 grams of carbohydrates, while a portobello bun has just 7 grams. There is a tremendous difference in the effect these two buns will have on blood sugar. In addition, with portobello buns you are also getting immune-supporting phyto-nutrients as opposed to enriched wheat flour and glucose-fructose.

NUTRIENTS PER BUN (2 MUSHROOM CAPS)	
Calories	67
Fat	4 g
Carbohydrate	7 g
Fiber	2 g
Protein	2 g

Rustic Sautéed Onions and Mushrooms

This recipe goes with any protein you are preparing and takes the Skillet-Grilled Flank Steak (page 222) into gourmet territory. You can change up the flavor using different types of mushrooms and herbs until you find your favorite combination.

Tips

You can use bacon fat or any fat of your choice in place of the butter.

Never run mushrooms under water; they absorb water like a sponge. Instead, wipe them with a damp paper towel or use a pastry brush to remove any dirt.

2 tbsp	grass-fed butter	30 mL
1	large onion, cut in half and then into thin crescents (see tip, page 146)	1
1	small clove garlic, minced (optional)	1
3 cups	sliced mixed mushrooms (button, cremini, oyster, shiitake caps)	750 mL
½ tsp	chopped fresh thyme, rosemary and/or parsley (optional)	2 mL
¼ tsp	sea salt	1 mL
¼ tsp	freshly ground black pepper	1 mL

1. In a large skillet, melt butter over medium heat. Add onion and cook, stirring occasionally, for 3 minutes. Add garlic (if using) and mushrooms; cook, stirring occasionally, for 8 to 10 minutes or until onion is tender and mushrooms have started to brown. Stir in herbs (if using), salt and pepper. Serve warm.

Nutrition Tip

There is evidence to support the health benefits of including onions and garlic in your diet on a regular basis, daily if possible. The combination of sulfur-containing compounds and flavonoids in all of the members of the onion and garlic family support the detoxification system, which operates 24 hours a day, 7 days a week. Mushrooms provide support for the immune system, so we should also be eating them more often.

NUTRIENTS PER SERVING	
Calories	79
Fat	6 g
Carbohydrate	5 g
Fiber	1 g
Protein	2 g

Caramelized Onions

Caramelized onions bring a sweet-and-savory taste to almost anything. Once you start keeping them on hand, you'll wonder how you ever made out without them. You can store them in the fridge for about 3 days, but we're guessing they'll be gone before that.

Tips

The onions shrink down a lot during this process, so you may need more to start with than you think. But be careful about overcrowding the pan. You want the onions to sauté, not steam. A 12-inch (30 cm) skillet can handle 2 large sweet onions.

Be patient; don't be tempted to turn the heat up above medium-low, or the onions will burn.

2 tbsp	grass-fed butter	30 mL
2	large Vidalia or sweet Spanish onions, cut into ⅛-inch (3 mm) thick slices	2
	Water, Warming Chicken Stock (page 116) or Beef Bone Broth (page 114)	
	Sea salt and freshly ground black pepper	
½ tsp	balsamic vinegar (optional)	2 mL

1. In a large skillet, melt butter over medium heat. Add onions, stirring well. Reduce heat to medium-low and cook, stirring occasionally, for 30 to 45 minutes (depending on the water content of the onions) or until onions are deep golden brown. If onions start to stick, add 2 to 3 tbsp (30 to 45 mL) water or stock and scrape up the browned bits from the bottom of the pan (you may need to do this more than once). In the last few minutes, season to taste with salt and pepper and stir in vinegar (if using).

Nutrition Tip

Onions are a valuable source of the prebiotic inulin, a water-soluble fiber that helps feed the beneficial bacteria in our gut. In turn, these good bacteria assist with the digestion and absorption of nutrients and play a significant role in healthy immune function. A 2013 study published in the journal *Diabetes & Metabolism* demonstrated improved glycemic control and increased antioxidant activity among women with type 2 diabetes who consumed inulin.

NUTRIENTS PER ½ CUP (125 ML)	
Calories	140
Fat	8 g
Carbohydrate	17 g
Fiber	2 g
Protein	2 g

Slow-Roasted Tomatoes

Slow-roasting
caramelizes and
intensifies the flavor of
the tomatoes and gives
them a meatier and
more robust texture.
These are great as a
stand-alone side, in the
Roasted Salsa (page 241)
or in a tossed green
salad. If there are any
left over, cover them
completely with olive
oil and store them in
the fridge for up to
2 weeks.

Tip

This recipe can be made
with any type of ripe
tomato, from beefsteak to
grape. The larger or more
moist ones may need
longer; the smaller ones
won't need as long.

- **Preheat oven to 225°F (110°C)**
- **Rimmed baking sheet, lined with parchment paper**

6	plum (Roma) tomatoes, cut in half lengthwise	6
2 tbsp	extra virgin olive oil	30 mL
	Sea salt and freshly ground black pepper	
	Dried oregano or basil (optional)	

1. Place tomatoes, cut side up, on prepared baking sheet. Drizzle with oil and sprinkle lightly with salt, pepper and oregano (if using).

2. Roast in preheated oven for about 3 hours or until tomatoes are shriveled and browned around the edges but still have a little juice in the middle.

Nutrition Tip

Tomatoes are a great source of lycopene, an antioxidant carotenoid that has been associated with reduced risk of prostate cancer. Lycopene is fat-soluble, so unless fat is eaten at the same time, the lycopene is not efficiently absorbed and can pass right through the intestine. The low, slow cooking of these tomatoes with olive oil makes for well-absorbed and therefore effective lycopene.

NUTRIENTS PER TOMATO HALF	
Calories	25
Fat	2 g
Carbohydrate	1 g
Fiber	0 g
Protein	0 g

Zucchini Noodles

Makes 4 servings

These noodles are great raw (as in the Thai Zucchini Noodle Salad, page 133) or quickly sautéed (as in the Sautéed Shrimp with Zucchini Noodles and Creamy Avocado Pesto, page 194). You can even blanch them in a pot of boiling water for 1 minute, drain well and use them with Basic Marinara Sauce (page 239) or in place of the spaghetti squash in Spaghetti Squash Bolognese (page 232).

Tips

If you have a vegetable spiralizer, you can use it instead of the julienne peeler to create zucchini noodles. You can also make zucchini noodles with a mandolin or by hand.

We prefer not to use the seedy core, as it gets a bit mushy if you heat the zucchini.

Whichever way you decide to use the zucchini noodles, you will need at least 1 zucchini per person.

NUTRIENTS PER SERVING	
Calories	33
Fat	1 g
Carbohydrate	6 g
Fiber	2 g
Protein	2 g

- **Julienne peeler**

4	medium zucchini (each about 7 oz/200 g)	4

1. Using the julienne peeler, make long slices along one side of a zucchini until you get to the seeded core. Rotate the zucchini and peel another side in the same way. Continue until you have done all four sides. Discard the seeded core. Repeat with the remaining zucchini.

2. Place zucchini noodles in a colander and let drain for a few minutes. If desired (especially if you plan to cook the noodles), use paper towels to squeeze the moisture out of the zucchini.

Nutrition Tip

Zucchini provides good levels of many of the nutrients needed for healthy blood sugar regulation, including vitamins B_1, B_2, B_3 and B_6, as well as the minerals zinc and magnesium. It also contains a type of fiber called pectin that has been shown to be helpful for insulin metabolism and keeping blood sugar levels in balance.

Roasted Spaghetti Squash Noodles

Serve as is with a dollop of grass-fed butter and some salt and pepper, or use as noodles for Basic Marinara Sauce (page 239) or Spinach Hemp Pesto (page 244).

Tip

Instead of discarding the seeds, try roasting them with a bit of olive oil and salt.

- Preheat oven to 400°F (200°C)
- Rimmed baking sheet

| 1 | large spaghetti squash (about 4 lbs/2 kg) | 1 |
| 1 tbsp | coconut oil (optional) | 15 mL |

1. Cut spaghetti squash in half lengthwise. Scrape out and discard seeds and pulp (see tip, at left). Place squash, cut side up, on baking sheet. If desired, brush cut sides of squash with oil.

2. Roast in preheated oven for 45 to 55 minutes or until squash can be easily pierced with a fork. Let stand until cool enough to handle (or hold the squash with an oven mitt). Using a fork, scrape out the squash flesh into spaghetti-like strands.

Nutrition Tip

Substituting spaghetti squash noodles or zucchini noodles (page 167) for wheat flour noodles makes a big difference in the body. Cup for cup, there are a lot less carbohydrates in the vegetable noodles than there are in wheat pasta. One cup (250 mL) of cooked wheat spaghetti has 38 grams of carbohydrates, while 1 cup of spaghetti squash has 23 grams and 1 cup of zucchini noodles has about 6 grams. (And who eats just 1 cup of cooked spaghetti?) Try the spaghetti squash and zucchini noodles — your blood sugar will thank you.

NUTRIENTS PER 1 CUP (250 ML)	
Calories	123
Fat	4 g
Carbohydrate	23 g
Fiber	5 g
Protein	2 g

Balsamic Roasted Vegetables

Roasting vegetables is the best way to bring out their sweetness, and the balsamic vinegar gives them an extra burst of flavor. You don't need to be limited by the veggies we've called for; use what is in season, what you like or what you have on hand. This is a tasty way to use up the ends of all your vegetables.

Tips

Yellow summer squash (also known as yellow zucchini) and Japanese eggplant can be hard to find, so just substitute more zucchini and Italian eggplants, or other vegetables of your choice.

To make nice wedges of onions that hold together, leave the root end intact when you peel the onion. Cut the onion in half through the root. Cut each half into wedges, with a piece of the root end on each wedge to hold it together.

NUTRIENTS PER SERVING	
Calories	187
Fat	8 g
Carbohydrate	29 g
Fiber	12 g
Protein	6 g

- Preheat oven to 450°F (230°C)
- Large rimmed baking sheet, lined with parchment paper

1 tsp	dried basil	5 mL
½ tsp	sea salt	2 mL
½ tsp	freshly ground black pepper	2 mL
2 tbsp	extra virgin olive oil	30 mL
2 tbsp	balsamic vinegar	30 mL
2	medium zucchini, halved lengthwise and cut into 2-inch (5 cm) pieces	2
2	medium yellow summer squash, halved lengthwise and cut into 2-inch (5 cm) pieces	2
2	Japanese eggplants, halved lengthwise and cut into 2-inch (5 cm) pieces	2
1	medium red onion, cut through the root into 8 wedges (see tip, at left)	1
1	large red bell pepper, cut into 2-inch (5 cm) pieces	1

1. In a small bowl, combine basil, salt, pepper, oil and vinegar.

2. In a large bowl, combine zucchini, summer squash, eggplants, onion and red pepper. Add dressing and toss to coat. Spread vegetable mixture in a single layer on prepared baking sheet, making sure not to crowd them.

3. Roast in preheated oven for 30 to 40 minutes, stirring occasionally, until vegetables are tender and lightly browned. Serve warm or at room temperature.

Nutrition Tip

Eggplants are a good source of many different nutrients, including vitamins K, C, B_6 and folate, and the minerals potassium, manganese and phosphorus. Research shows that nasunin, an anthocyanin found in the skin of the eggplant, is a strong antioxidant that, in animal studies, protects the fats in the brain cell membranes from free radical damage.

Roasted Ratatouille

When you can't decide what vegetable to make, this is the solution. Although we've called for specific vegetables, you can use whatever you have in the fridge. This dish becomes a delicious complete meal when topped with a protein such as the New Classic Meatballs (page 220).

Tip

If you don't have fresh basil on hand, you can use 1 tbsp (15 mL) dried basil in its place. Add the dried basil to the fire-roasted tomatoes before you bring them to a boil.

- **Preheat oven to 450°F (230°C)**
- **Rimmed baking sheet, lined with parchment paper**

2	large cloves garlic, peeled	2
2	medium zucchini, sliced or chopped into 1-inch (2.5 cm) pieces	2
1	medium eggplant (unpeeled), sliced or chopped into 2-inch (5 cm) pieces	1
1	medium onion, coarsely chopped	1
1	red bell pepper, sliced	1
1	yellow bell pepper, sliced	1
1 cup	cherry tomatoes	250 mL
1/4 cup	extra virgin olive oil	60 mL
1 tsp	hot pepper flakes (optional)	5 mL
1/4 tsp	sea salt	1 mL
1/4 tsp	freshly ground black pepper	1 mL
1	can (14 oz/398 mL) diced fire-roasted tomatoes, with juice	1
2 tbsp	minced fresh basil	30 mL

1. In a large bowl, combine garlic, zucchini, eggplant, onion, red pepper, yellow pepper and cherry tomatoes. Add oil, hot pepper flakes (if using), salt and black pepper, tossing to coat evenly. Spread in a single layer on prepared baking sheet. Roast in preheated oven for 20 minutes, stirring occasionally, until tender.

2. In a large saucepan, bring fire-roasted tomatoes to a boil over medium-high heat. Boil for 5 minutes to reduce the amount of liquid. Stir in roasted vegetables and basil; reduce heat to medium and cook, stirring occasionally, for 5 minutes. Serve hot, or let cool, cover and refrigerate for up to 3 days and serve cold.

Nutrition Tip

This ratatouille is a wonderful combination of antioxidants and phytonutrients. The peppers are excellent sources of vitamin C, the onions and garlic provide sulfur compounds, and the canned tomatoes are rich in lycopene. Once it's all combined, this dish supports immunity, cardiovascular and overall health.

NUTRIENTS PER SERVING	
Calories	223
Fat	15 g
Carbohydrate	23 g
Fiber	8 g
Protein	5 g

Eggs

Eggs in a Hole

This is my take on shakshuka, a traditional baked egg dish with origins in North Africa and the Middle East. Because eggs are featured, it is often thought of as a breakfast recipe, but you won't want to limit it to just the morning. Additions such as artichoke hearts, spicy sausage and even fish pieces can easily be incorporated.

- **Preheat oven to 400°F (200°C)**
- **Ovenproof skillet**

¼ cup	extra virgin olive oil	60 mL
1	large onion, halved and thinly sliced	1
1	large red bell pepper, thinly sliced	1
1	large yellow or orange bell pepper, thinly sliced	1
3	cloves garlic, minced	3
1 tsp	ground cumin	5 mL
½ tsp	smoked paprika	2 mL
½ tsp	hot pepper flakes (optional)	2 mL
2	cans (each 14 oz/398 mL) diced fire-roasted tomatoes, with juice	2
6	large free-range eggs	6
¼ cup	chopped fresh flat-leaf (Italian) parsley	60 mL
¼ cup	chopped fresh basil	60 mL
¼ tsp	sea salt	1 mL
¼ tsp	freshly ground black pepper	1 mL

1. In ovenproof skillet, heat oil over medium heat. Add onion, red pepper and yellow pepper; cook, stirring, for 4 minutes. Add garlic, cumin, paprika and hot pepper flakes (if using); cook, stirring, for 2 minutes.

2. Stir in tomatoes and bring to a boil. Reduce heat and simmer for 10 minutes or until thickened. Make 6 evenly spaced holes in the tomato mixture. Crack 1 egg into each hole.

3. Transfer skillet to preheated oven and bake for 7 to 10 minutes or until egg whites are set but yolk is still runny. (If you like your eggs more firm, cook to desired consistency.) Remove skillet from oven and sprinkle with parsley, basil, salt and black pepper. Serve immediately.

Nutrition Tip
Egg yolks are one of the best sources of choline, an essential micronutrient especially needed in the body for healthy brain function and the formation of neurotransmitters. It is also important for nerve signaling and detoxification.

NUTRIENTS PER SERVING	
Calories	403
Fat	28 g
Carbohydrate	23 g
Fiber	5 g
Protein	17 g

Basic Scrambled Eggs with Roasted Salsa

The Cauliflower Zucchini Hash Browns (page 158) are a wonderful accompaniment to these tasty eggs.

1	avocado, cut in half lengthwise, pitted and peeled	1
6	large free-range eggs	6
¼ tsp	sea salt	1 mL
¼ tsp	freshly ground black pepper	1 mL
1 tbsp	grass-fed butter	15 mL
1½ cups	Roasted Salsa (page 241)	375 mL

1. Cut avocado into long slices and divide evenly among serving plates.

2. In a medium bowl, whisk together eggs, salt and pepper.

3. In a large skillet, heat butter over medium heat. Add eggs and cook, stirring and scraping from the bottom of the pan, until eggs are fluffy and still look a little wet but are not runny.

4. Serve eggs beside avocado slices, topped with Roasted Salsa.

Nutrition Tip

Many people are aware that the yolk contains the majority (90%) of the fat content in an egg, but they may not realize that the yolk also contains 40% of the protein. As for vitamins and minerals, certain ones — like the fat-soluble vitamins A, D, E and K — are found exclusively in the yolk; others, such as vitamins B_2 and B_3, are mostly found in the white.

NUTRIENTS PER SERVING	
Calories	400
Fat	30 g
Carbohydrate	19 g
Fiber	8 g
Protein	16 g

Scrambled Eggs Florentine

Eggs Florentine isn't just for weekends, especially when you scramble the eggs and make the ultra-quick Easy Hollandaise. Bump up the protein a bit with some bacon or a slice of smoked salmon. Remember, eggs aren't only for breakfast — enjoy this at lunch or dinner, too.

1 tbsp	extra virgin olive oil	15 mL
4 cups	packed baby spinach	1 L
1 tsp	grass-fed butter	5 mL
4	large free-range eggs, beaten	4
1	tomato, sliced	1
	Easy Hollandaise (page 251), kept warm	
	Freshly ground black pepper	

1. In a large skillet, heat oil over medium heat. Add spinach and cook, turning spinach with tongs, for about 2 minutes or until dark green and wilted. Remove from heat and cover to keep warm.

2. In another skillet, melt butter over medium heat. Add eggs and cook, stirring and scraping from the bottom of the pan, until eggs are fluffy and still look a little wet but are not runny.

3. Place half the tomato slices on each plate. Pour off any liquid from the spinach, give the spinach a little squeeze and place on top of the tomatoes. Place scrambled eggs on top, dividing evenly. Top each plate with 4 tbsp (60 mL) Easy Hollandaise and season with pepper.

Nutrition Tip

When we use eggs from free-range, pasture-raised hens that have scavenged for bugs and shoots in the outdoors, we are getting a healthier ratio of omega-3 to omega-6 fats, which is important to help reduce inflammation in the body. Free-range eggs have also been shown to be higher in the antioxidant vitamin E and up to two times higher in immune-friendly vitamin D.

NUTRIENTS PER SERVING (WITHOUT HOLLANDAISE)	
Calories	114
Fat	7 g
Carbohydrate	5 g
Fiber	2 g
Protein	9 g

Basic Vegetable Frittata

Frittatas are so easy and fast, and you can customize them any way you want. Eat this one for breakfast, lunch or dinner; it tastes good hot, at room temperature and even cold. Just as with the Egg and Pancetta Muffins (page 178), you can add any vegetables you like, including leftovers, to this frittata.

Tips

You can substitute the fat of your choice for the butter.

A classic frittata is baked in a cast-iron skillet, but it comes out a bit cleaner when you use a baking dish.

A larger baking dish will make a shallower frittata and would require a shorter cooking time.

- **Preheat oven to 350°F (180°C)**
- **8-inch (20 cm) square glass baking dish, greased**

1 tbsp	grass-fed butter	15 mL
½ cup	chopped onion	125 mL
½ cup	chopped asparagus	125 mL
½ cup	chopped red bell pepper	125 mL
¼ tsp	sea salt	1 mL
¼ tsp	freshly ground black pepper	1 mL
8	large free-range eggs, beaten	8
¼ cup	finely chopped fresh parsley	60 mL
¼ cup	chopped pitted drained kalamata olives	60 mL

1. In a medium skillet, heat butter over medium heat. Add onion and cook, stirring, for 2 minutes. Add asparagus and cook, stirring, for 2 minutes. Add red pepper and cook, stirring, for 2 minutes. Stir in salt and pepper.

2. Pour eggs into prepared baking dish. Spoon in onion mixture, distributing evenly. Sprinkle with parsley and olives.

3. Bake in preheated oven for 20 to 30 minutes or until eggs are set and a knife inserted in the center comes out clean. Serve immediately or let cool slightly and serve warm.

Nutrition Tip

Eggs are a source of all of the B vitamins, including B_1 (thiamine), B_2 (riboflavin), B_3 (niacin), B_5 (pantothenic acid), B_6 (pyridoxine), B_{12} (cobalamin), choline, biotin and folate. B vitamins often work together to perform their various jobs in the body, such as supporting metabolism and immune function, converting food into fuel, repairing DNA and making red blood cells. Because they are all so interdependent, having all the B vitamins in one source is a bonus.

NUTRIENTS PER SERVING	
Calories	199
Fat	14 g
Carbohydrate	5 g
Fiber	2 g
Protein	14 g

Peppers Stuffed with Eggs, Mushrooms and Broccoli

Baking bell peppers makes them sweet and tender, especially red bell peppers. Don't save this dish for breakfast. It makes a quick and easy lunch or dinner served with a mound of crisp green lettuce and our Classic Vinaigrette (page 258).

Tip

You can substitute the fat of your choice for the butter.

- Preheat oven to 375°F (190°C)
- Rimmed baking sheet, lined with parchment paper

2 tbsp	grass-fed butter	30 mL
1 cup	chopped onion	250 mL
1 cup	chopped broccoli	250 mL
1	clove garlic, minced	1
1 cup	chopped mushrooms	250 mL
¼ tsp	sea salt	1 mL
¼ tsp	freshly ground black pepper	1 mL
1 cup	hot cooked ground meat of choice (optional)	250 mL
2	red bell peppers, stemmed, cut in half lengthwise and seeded	2
4	large free-range eggs, beaten	4

1. In a large skillet, heat butter over medium heat. Add onion and cook, stirring, for 4 minutes. Add broccoli and cook, stirring, for 2 minutes. Add garlic, mushrooms, salt and pepper; cook, stirring occasionally, for 3 minutes. Stir in meat (if using).

2. Place red peppers, cut side up, on prepared baking sheet. Pack filling into peppers, dividing evenly. Pour eggs into peppers over filling, dividing evenly.

3. Bake in preheated oven for about 40 minutes or until peppers are tender, eggs are set and a knife inserted in the middle of the filling comes out clean.

Nutrition Tip

Lutein and zeaxanthin are carotenoids found in the macula of the eye that help filter out the harmful blue light that can damage this area over time. Eggs and broccoli contain both of these antioxidants, helping to protect against cataracts and macular degeneration.

NUTRIENTS PER SERVING

Calories	282
Fat	22 g
Carbohydrate	23 g
Fiber	4 g
Protein	23 g

Nori Egg Rolls

Makes 1 serving

"Nori" is the Japanese name for dried edible seaweed sheets used in most kinds of sushi. It is made by shredding the edible seaweed porphyra, then pressing it into thin sheets — just like making paper. You can find it in any Asian grocery store, and most large grocery stores now stock it too.

Tips

In place of the arugula, you can use any leafy green you have on hand in the fridge.

Those of you who don't like nori can still enjoy this dish by arranging the avocado and arugula across the egg, drizzling with dressing and rolling the egg up.

NUTRIENTS PER SERVING	
Calories	391
Fat	33 g
Carbohydrate	11 g
Fiber	6 g
Protein	17 g

1 tsp	grass-fed butter	5 mL
2	large free-range eggs, beaten	2
1	sheet nori seaweed	1
1/4	avocado, sliced	1/4
1 cup	arugula	250 mL
1 tbsp	Creamy Lemon Tahini Dressing (page 255)	15 mL

1. In a medium skillet, melt butter over medium heat. Add eggs, swirling to form an even layer on the bottom of the skillet. Cover and cook for 1 minute, then turn off heat and leave the skillet on the burner until the egg is cooked through and no liquid remains on top, about 3 minutes.

2. Place nori on a work surface with one corner closest to you. Slide egg out of the skillet into the middle of the nori. Arrange avocado in a straight line across the egg, starting 1 inch (2.5 cm) from the corner closest to you. Arrange arugula on top and drizzle with dressing. Fold up the corner of the nori closest to you, then fold in the left corner over the fillings and roll to the right side so everything is tucked in.

Nutrition Tip

Sea vegetables contain a broad range of minerals, including the ultra-trace mineral vanadium. As sodium vanadate, vanadium was used to treat people with diabetes before the discovery of insulin in 1921. In a few studies, vanadium has been shown to increase the cells' sensitivity to insulin, but there are no official guidelines and research is ongoing.

Egg and Pancetta Muffins

Egg muffins are a fun way to eat eggs and a great option for a nutritious grab-and-go breakfast. Make a double batch and freeze them so you never have to be without a good protein for breakfast again.

Tips

For the mushrooms, either creminis or button mushrooms will be delicious.

This recipe is very adaptable. Use whatever vegetables you have on hand, even leftovers from last night's dinner.

To freeze these muffins, place them on a baking sheet lined with waxed paper and freeze until firm. Once frozen, transfer to a sealable freezer bag or airtight container and store in the freezer for up to 1 month.

- Preheat oven to 350°F (180°C)
- 12-cup muffin pan, greased or lined with paper liners

8 oz	pancetta, chopped	250 g
½ cup	finely chopped onion	125 mL
1 cup	chopped mushrooms	250 mL
1 cup	chopped baby spinach	250 mL
¼ tsp	freshly ground black pepper	1 mL
12	large free-range eggs	12

1. In a large skillet over medium-high heat, cook pancetta, stirring occasionally, for 8 to 10 minutes or until starting to crisp. Using a slotted spoon, transfer pancetta to a bowl. Drain most of the fat from the skillet, leaving just enough to cook the onion.

2. Add onion to the fat remaining in the skillet and cook, stirring, for 2 minutes. Add mushrooms and cook, stirring, for 2 minutes. Stir in spinach and pepper; remove from heat.

3. In a large bowl, beat eggs. Stir in onion mixture and pancetta. Spoon or pour into prepared muffin cups, dividing evenly.

4. Bake in preheated oven for 20 to 25 minutes or until eggs are set and a knife inserted in the center of a muffin comes out clean. Serve immediately or let cool and store in an airtight container in the refrigerator for up to 4 days.

Variation

Substitute 8 oz (250 g) ground pork mixed with 2 tsp (10 mL) Italian Spice Blend (page 261) for the pancetta; in step 1, cook the pork, breaking it up with a spoon, until no longer pink.

Nutrition Tip

Eggs are recognized by the World Health Organization as the standard against which all other proteins are evaluated. The protein in eggs is known as HBV protein: protein with high biological value. On a scale of 0 to 100, eggs come in with a score of 94, meaning that all essential amino acids are present in the egg in a proportion similar to that required by the body for growth and repair.

NUTRIENTS PER MUFFIN	
Calories	131
Fat	9 g
Carbohydrate	2 g
Fiber	3 g
Protein	9 g

Fish and Seafood

Fish Tacos

Who doesn't love fish tacos? This delicious grain-free take is sure to please the whole family.

Tip

The Cauliflower Tortillas are a great way to serve these tacos, but if you are in a hurry, simply use Boston lettuce leaves that have been washed and dried well. Other lettuces, such as romaine or iceberg, work too, but are less pliable and may crack. You can use two layers of leaves to help with any cracks in the lettuce.

White Sauce

½ cup	The Best Paleo Mayo (page 249)	125 mL
1 tbsp	freshly squeezed lime juice	15 mL
½ tsp	ground cumin	2 mL
¼ tsp	cayenne pepper (optional)	1 mL
	Filtered water	

Fish

1 lb	skinless white fish fillets (such as cod, haddock or halibut)	500 g
½ cup	coconut flour	125 mL
2 tsp	ground cumin	10 mL
1 tsp	sea salt	5 mL
1 tsp	garlic powder	5 mL
1 tsp	paprika	5 mL
½ tsp	chili powder	2 mL
1	large free-range egg	1
4 tbsp	coconut oil	60 mL

Taco Fixings

8	Cauliflower Tortillas (page 156) or lettuce leaves (see tip, at left)	8
1	medium avocado, sliced	1
1 cup	Fresh Tomato Salsa (page 240)	250 mL
8	lime wedges	8
¼ cup	chopped fresh cilantro	60 mL

1. *Sauce:* In a small bowl, combine mayo, lime juice, cumin and cayenne (if using). Thin with water to desired consistency. Set aside.

2. *Fish:* Pat fish dry and cut into 3- by 1-inch (7.5- by 2.5 cm) strips, removing any bones.

3. In a medium bowl, combine coconut flour, cumin, salt, garlic powder, paprika and chili powder. In a shallow dish, beat egg.

NUTRIENTS PER SERVING	
Calories	450
Fat	25 g
Carbohydrate	26 g
Fiber	12 g
Protein	35 g

Tips

For those of you who are still developing a taste for fish, you can substitute boneless skinless chicken breasts in this recipe. In step 2, cut the chicken as described for the fish. Continue with the remaining steps, ensuring that the chicken is no longer pink inside in step 5.

Feel free to improvise with additional taco fillings, including sliced bell peppers, thinly sliced sweet or red onion, or our Classic Guacamole (page 247).

4. Dip fish strips in egg, shaking off excess, then dredge in flour mixture, pressing to coat evenly. Place coated fish sticks on a separate plate. Discard any excess egg and flour mixture.

5. In a large skillet, heat 2 tbsp (30 mL) coconut oil over medium heat. Add half the fish strips, leaving space in between, and cook for 4 to 5 minutes or until golden on the bottom. Using a spatula, carefully turn fish over and cook for 2 to 3 minutes or until coating is golden brown and fish flakes easily when tested with a fork. Transfer fish to a wire rack. Repeat with the remaining coconut oil and fish strips, adjusting heat as necessary to prevent burning.

6. *Tacos:* Divide fish strips, avocado and salsa evenly among tortillas. Top with white sauce, a squeeze of lime juice and cilantro.

Nutrition Tip

Many commercial brands of tortilla shells contain trans fats to keep them flexible. You need to look beyond the nutritional panel and read the ingredients list to really know whether a food contains trans fats, as certain labeling laws allow a product to say it has zero trans fats per serving if the level of trans fats is below a certain amount. If you see hydrogenated vegetable oil, partially hydrogenated vegetable oil or shortening listed in the ingredients, the item has trans fats; put it back on the shelf.

Roasted Black Cod with Warm Tomato Vinaigrette on Seared Rapini

Black cod, also known as sablefish, is a mild-tasting white fish that adapts well to many flavors. Sustainable black cod is caught in the ocean off Alaska and British Columbia.

Tip

If you don't have fresh thyme leaves on hand, you can use 1/2 tsp (2 mL) dried thyme in their place.

- **Preheat oven to 400°F (200°C)**
- **Rimmed baking sheet, lined with parchment paper**

4	pieces skinless black cod (each about 4 oz/125 g)	4
	Sea salt and freshly ground black pepper	
	Sweet paprika	
1 tsp	fresh thyme leaves	5 mL
4 tbsp	extra virgin olive oil, divided	60 mL
1 cup	cherry tomatoes	250 mL
1/4 tsp	hot pepper flakes	1 mL
2 tbsp	slivered pitted drained kalamata olives	30 mL
2 tsp	balsamic vinegar	10 mL
2 tbsp	minced fresh basil	30 mL
1	large clove garlic, thinly sliced	1
1	large bunch rapini, rough ends trimmed and larger stalks peeled (about 6 cups/1.5 L)	1
1/3 cup	filtered water	75 mL

1. Place fish on prepared baking sheet and season with salt, pepper and paprika. Sprinkle with thyme and drizzle with 1 tbsp (15 mL) oil. Roast in preheated oven for 8 to 10 minutes or until fish is opaque and flakes easily when tested with a fork.

2. Meanwhile, in a medium skillet, heat 2 tbsp (30 mL) oil over medium-high heat. Add tomatoes and hot pepper flakes; cook, stirring, for 3 to 4 minutes or until tomatoes are just starting to shrivel. Add olives and vinegar; cook, stirring, for 1 to 2 minutes or until olives are heated through. (At this point, if the fish is not finished cooking, turn off the heat.) Just before serving, reheat tomato mixture and stir in basil.

NUTRIENTS PER SERVING	
Calories	244
Fat	15 g
Carbohydrate	6 g
Fiber	4 g
Protein	24 g

A general rule of thumb for fish is to cook it for 10 minutes per inch (2.5 cm) of thickness. A thinner tail piece will take less time, and a full fillet a little longer. Look for cracks starting to form on the surface of the fish, then cook a minute or two longer. The fish flakes should separate cleanly from one another when the fish is done.

3. Meanwhile, in a large skillet, heat the remaining oil over medium heat. Add garlic and cook, stirring, until golden, about 1 minute. Add rapini and water; bring to a simmer. Reduce heat to low, cover and simmer, stirring occasionally, for about 5 minutes or until rapini is tender. Increase heat to medium and sauté, uncovered, until any remaining water evaporates. Season with salt and pepper.

4. Divide rapini among serving plates. Place fish on rapini and spoon tomato mixture over fish.

Nutrition Tip

Rapini, an Italian staple also known as broccoli rabe or raab, looks like thin broccoli with clusters of buds. It is a powerhouse of nutrition, with extraordinary levels of potassium, vitamin C and vitamin K (phylloquinone), which is an important vitamin for protecting against osteoporosis. The amount of protein and carbohydrates in rapini is about the same, and rapini is chock-full of fiber, all of which make it a top choice for balanced blood sugar.

Baked Haddock
with Peppers and Tomatoes

Haddock's flavor is mild
and its texture flaky —
a perfect fit for those
developing a new taste
for fish.

Tip

A general rule of thumb
for fish is to cook it for
10 minutes per inch (2.5 cm)
of thickness. A thinner tail
piece will take less time, and
a full fillet a little longer.
Look for cracks starting to
form on the surface of the
fish, then cook a minute or
two longer. The fish flakes
should separate cleanly
from one another when
the fish is done.

- Preheat oven to 375°F (190°C)
- 13- by 9-inch (33 by 23 cm) baking dish

3 tbsp	extra virgin olive oil	45 mL
3	cloves garlic, minced	3
1	red onion, minced	1
4	tomatoes, chopped	4
1	green bell pepper, cut lengthwise into $\frac{1}{2}$-inch (1 cm) slices	1
1	yellow bell pepper, cut lengthwise into $\frac{1}{2}$-inch (1 cm) slices	1
1 tsp	dried basil	5 mL
$\frac{1}{2}$ tsp	sea salt	2 mL
$\frac{1}{4}$ tsp	freshly ground black pepper	1 mL
2 lbs	skinless haddock fillets	1 kg
2 tbsp	freshly squeezed lemon juice	30 mL
1 tsp	chopped fresh dill	5 mL
6 tbsp	chopped fresh parsley	90 mL

1. In a heavy skillet, heat oil over medium heat. Add garlic and onion; cook, stirring, for about 4 minutes or until onion is tender. Add tomatoes, green pepper, yellow pepper, basil, salt and pepper; cook, stirring, for 3 to 4 minutes or until softened. Remove from heat.

2. Spread half the tomato mixture over the bottom of the baking dish. Place fish on top. Spoon remaining tomato mixture over fish. Sprinkle with lemon juice, then with dill. Cover dish with foil.

3. Bake in preheated oven for 10 to 15 minutes or until fish is opaque and flakes easily when tested with a fork. Serve sprinkled with parsley.

NUTRIENTS PER SERVING	
Calories	302
Fat	10 g
Carbohydrate	11 g
Fiber	3 g
Protein	42 g

Nutrition Tip

Haddock is an excellent source of phosphorus and selenium and a good source of magnesium and potassium, all of which contribute to overall health and aid in blood sugar management. It is also an excellent source of vitamins B_6 and B_{12}, which are important for heart health.

Almond-Crusted Salmon

This simple and delicious way to prepare salmon is one of our favorites. It's easy enough for a family meal and will bring rave reviews at your next dinner party when served alongside the Kale and Sweet Potato Sauté (page 161).

Tips

Grainy mustard is another good option in place of the Dijon. Some grainy mustards are drier than others, and the nuts won't stick to the drier ones very well. Mix a little Dijon in with the grainy mustard to make a better consistency for the nuts to stick to. Either way, the mustard adds a wonderful taste with the almonds.

Always purchase organic lemons when you plan to grate the zest. Most of the pesticides will be concentrated in the skin, and it is best to minimize your exposure.

- **Preheat oven to 400°F (200°C)**
- **Food processor (optional)**
- **Rimmed baking sheet, lined with parchment paper**

⅓ cup	raw almonds	75 mL
4	skin-on wild salmon fillets (each about 4 oz/125 g)	4
½ tsp	sea salt	2 mL
¼ tsp	freshly ground black pepper	1 mL
4 tsp	Dijon mustard (see tip, at left)	20 mL
¼ cup	chopped fresh flat-leaf (Italian) parsley	60 mL
1 tsp	grated lemon zest	5 mL
2 tbsp	freshly squeezed lemon juice	30 mL
2 tbsp	extra virgin olive oil	30 mL

1. In food processor, pulse almonds until the pieces are the size of rice (or chop them by hand with a large knife). Transfer to a plate.

2. Season salmon with salt and pepper. Brush the flesh side of each fillet with 1 tsp (5 mL) mustard. Dip the mustard side in almonds, pressing firmly to help the nuts adhere. Place fish, nut side up, on prepared baking sheet.

3. Bake in preheated oven for 10 to 15 minutes or until nuts are browned and fish flakes easily when tested with a fork.

4. In a small bowl, combine parsley, lemon zest, lemon juice and oil. Spoon over fish and serve immediately.

Variation

Substitute other nuts or seeds, such as pistachios, pecans or sesame seeds, for a different flavor.

Nutrition Tip

Salmon is well known for its omega-3 fatty acid content. At the same time, it has a relatively small amount of omega-6s. The standard North American diet is skewed too heavily in the direction of omega-6 fatty acids, which can promote inflammation in the body. Eating wild salmon on a regular basis can help us achieve a better balance between these two essential fatty acids.

NUTRIENTS PER SERVING	
Calories	357
Fat	25 g
Carbohydrate	6 g
Fiber	3 g
Protein	28 g

Classic Fish Sticks

Makes 4 servings

Nothing from the freezer aisle tastes as good as these fish sticks. Serve with The Best Tartar Sauce (page 250) and you have an instant classic.

Tips

You can substitute the fat of your choice for the butter.

In step 4, resist the temptation to flip the fish sticks too early — you may lose the breading if you do.

1½ lbs	skinless white fish fillets (such as cod, haddock, halibut or snapper)	750 g
1 cup	almond flour	250 mL
1 tsp	sea salt	5 mL
2	large free-range eggs	2
4 tbsp	grass-fed butter	60 mL

1. Pat fish dry and cut into 4- by 1-inch (10 by 2.5 cm) pieces, removing any bones.

2. In a shallow dish, combine almond flour and salt. In another shallow dish, beat eggs.

3. Dip fish pieces in egg, shaking off excess, then dredge in flour mixture, pressing to coat evenly. Place coated fish sticks on a separate plate. Discard any excess egg and flour mixture.

4. In a large skillet, melt 2 tbsp (30 mL) butter over medium heat. Add half the fish sticks, leaving space in between, and cook for 4 to 5 minutes or until golden on the bottom. Using a spatula, carefully turn fish over and cook for 2 to 3 minutes or until coating is golden brown and fish flakes easily when tested with a fork. Transfer fish to a wire rack. Repeat with the remaining butter and fish, adjusting heat as necessary to prevent burning.

Nutrition Tip

When you make your own food, you know exactly what's in it. What may be surprising is what *isn't* in it. Here are just some of the possible ingredients in brand-name frozen fish sticks: modified starch, sugar, maltodextrin (sugar), wheat flour, corn flour, canola oil and cottonseed oil. What are you putting in your fish sticks? Fish, almond flour, salt, eggs and butter. Enough said.

NUTRIENTS PER SERVING	
Calories	287
Fat	16 g
Carbohydrate	7 g
Fiber	0 g
Protein	7 g

Salmon Cakes

**Makes about
12 small patties**

You'll want to make a double batch of these yummy cakes — they reheat well and can be used for a quick protein-packed breakfast.
They pair well with the Roasted Asparagus Salad with Arugula and Hazelnuts (page 126) and a dollop of The Best Tartar Sauce (page 250).

Tips

If you don't have fresh dill and parsley on hand, you can substitute 1 tsp (5 mL) dried dillweed and ½ tsp (2 mL) dried parsley.

You can substitute the fat of your choice for the avocado oil.

Cooked salmon cakes can be stored in an airtight container in the refrigerator for up to 3 days. To reheat, place them on a wire rack over a baking sheet and bake in a 325°F (160°C) oven for 10 to 15 minutes. You can also reheat them in a skillet over medium heat, flipping once or twice, for 4 to 5 minutes.

NUTRIENTS PER PATTY	
Calories	80
Fat	5 g
Carbohydrate	1 g
Fiber	0 g
Protein	8 g

- **Preheat oven to 250°F (120°C)**
- **Rimmed baking sheet, with a wire rack set on top**

2	cans (each 7.5 oz/231 g) wild salmon, drained	2
1	large free-range egg, beaten	1
1	clove garlic, minced	1
½	large sweet onion, finely chopped (about ½ cup/125 mL)	½
1 tbsp	chopped fresh dill	15 mL
1 tsp	finely chopped fresh parsley	5 mL
½ tsp	sea salt	2 mL
¼ tsp	freshly ground black pepper	1 mL
1 tbsp	The Best Paleo Mayo (page 249)	15 mL
2 tbsp	avocado oil (approx.)	30 mL
1 tbsp	chopped green onion	15 mL

1. In a large bowl, combine salmon, egg, garlic, onion, dill, parsley, salt, pepper and mayo, mixing well. Form into 2-inch (5 cm) diameter patties.

2. In a large skillet, heat 1 tbsp (15 mL) oil over medium heat. Working in batches, add salmon cakes, without crowding them, and cook, turning once, for 6 to 7 minutes per side or until browned and crispy on both sides, adding more oil as needed between batches. As they are cooked, transfer the cakes to the wire rack on the baking sheet and keep warm in preheated oven. When all of the cakes are cooked, serve immediately, topped with green onion.

Nutrition Tip

Drain the liquid from canned salmon, but hang on to the skin and those bones! A half-can serving of salmon with the bones has about 250 mg of calcium. The canning process softens the bones, so they break apart easily and can be mashed up with the skin so no one will notice. Calcium and vitamin D may have direct effects on pancreatic beta cells to enhance insulin secretion. The skin contains a lot of the beneficial anti-inflammatory omega-3 oils that are so important in the diet.

Smoked Salmon Nori Rolls

This is a great take on a hand roll, without the sweetened sticky rice. With the smoked salmon, these rolls are a great meal, but they can also be made with vegetables alone and used as a side for another protein, even chicken wings!

Tip

Use a very sharp knife when cutting your roll, as a dull one will crush it. Keeping the blade slightly wet will also help. A good way to do this it to dip the knife tip into a bowl of water, then turn it so that the tip points straight up. Tap the handle of the knife on the table and gravity will send the water down the cutting edge.

8	sheets toasted nori	8
$\frac{1}{2}$ cup	Zucchini Wasabi Spread (page 248)	125 mL
8	pieces smoked wild salmon (each about 1 oz/30 g)	8
2	avocados, each thinly sliced lengthwise into 8 pieces	2
1	English cucumber, thinly sliced lengthwise into 16 pieces and trimmed to fit the nori sheets	1
1	large red bell pepper, thinly sliced lengthwise into 16 pieces	1
24	fresh mint leaves, chopped	24
24	fresh cilantro leaves, chopped	24
	Warm water	

1. Place 1 sheet of nori on a work surface, with the rough side facing up. Carefully spread 2 tbsp (30 mL) Zucchini Wasabi Spread over nori, leaving $1\frac{1}{2}$ inches (4 cm) bare along the bottom edge (the edge closest to you).

2. Place 1 piece of salmon, 2 slices of avocado, 2 slices of cucumber and 2 slices of red pepper about $1\frac{1}{2}$ inches (4 cm) from the bottom edge. Top with some of the mint and cilantro.

3. Starting with the bare edge, roll nori around the fillings, pressing gently to make a compact roll. Moisten a finger with warm water and run it along the inside edge of the flap that remains at the top of the roll, then press the moistened edge against the roll to seal.

4. Repeat steps 1 to 3 with the remaining ingredients.

5. Using a very sharp serrated knife, cut each roll into 6 pieces (see tip, at left).

Nutrition Tip

Nori is about one-third fiber, making it a good addition to a meal to help regulate blood sugar. Including more fiber in our meals helps us feel full longer, and the nori and avocado in this recipe are a great fiber combination.

NUTRIENTS PER ROLL	
Calories	261
Fat	18 g
Carbohydrate	13 g
Fiber	16 g
Protein	13 g

Lemon and Herb Sardines

Makes 2 servings

This is an adaptation of a recipe Jill made at a Center for Mind-Body Medicine conference. After tasting this recipe, sardine skeptics will become converts. This is a fast, nutritious meal for any time of day. Serve with Seed Crackers (page 269) and Belgian endive spears or cucumber rounds.

1 tbsp	minced red onion	15 mL
1 tbsp	finely chopped fresh parsley	15 mL
1 tbsp	finely chopped fresh basil	15 mL
2 tsp	finely chopped fresh mint	10 mL
1 tbsp	grated lemon zest	15 mL
4 tsp	freshly squeezed lemon juice	20 mL
1 tsp	extra virgin olive oil	5 mL
1 tsp	Dijon mustard	5 mL
	Sea salt	
1	can (4.35 oz/120 g) sardines packed in water or olive oil, drained	1

1. In a medium bowl, combine onion, parsley, basil, mint, lemon zest, lemon juice, oil and mustard. Season to taste with salt. Add sardines, flaking them with a fork and stirring to combine.

Nutrition Tip

Sardines are powerful little packages containing many nutrients that support overall health. One serving contains almost 50% of the daily value of the anti-inflammatory omega-3 fatty acids EPA and DHA, and over 300% of the daily value for vitamin B_{12}, which is important for the formation of red blood cells and the myelin sheaths around our nerves that allow nerve impulses to travel smoothly. Sardines are near the bottom of the marine food chain, so they don't contain as much mercury as large predatory fish do.

NUTRIENTS PER SERVING	
Calories	156
Fat	9 g
Carbohydrate	1 g
Fiber	1 g
Protein	15 g

Pumpkin Seed–Crusted Rainbow Trout

This is an adaptation of a recipe from Jill's friend Angela, who eats paleo and loves to try new dishes. Think of it as a foundational recipe for baked fish. Serve it with Kale and Sweet Potato Sauté (page 161) for a complete meal.

Tips

If you don't have a food processor or blender, you can grind the seeds in small batches in a clean coffee or spice grinder, or finely chop them by hand with a sharp knife and a large cutting board.

Try nuts or other types of seeds, such as pecan halves or sesame seeds, in place of the pumpkin seeds. You can even throw in some of your favorite fresh or dried herbs with the seeds.

You can replace the trout with any white fish, such as haddock, halibut or cod.

NUTRIENTS PER SERVING	
Calories	321
Fat	20 g
Carbohydrate	4 g
Fiber	2 g
Protein	34 g

- Preheat oven to 350°F (180°C)
- Food processor or blender (see tip, at left)
- Rimmed baking sheet, lined with parchment paper

1 cup	raw green pumpkin seeds (pepitas)	250 mL
4	pieces skin-on rainbow trout fillet (each about 4 oz/125 g)	4
2 tbsp	organic gluten-free tamari or coconut amino acids	30 mL

1. Place pumpkin seeds in a dry skillet over medium heat and stir occasionally as the pan heats up. When seeds are aromatic and starting to brown, reduce heat to medium-low and cook, stirring constantly, until seeds are golden brown. Transfer seeds to a plate and let cool completely.

2. Transfer seeds to a food processor or blender and process until finely ground (but stop before seeds start to turn into seed butter).

3. Place fish, skin side down, on prepared baking sheet and brush the top and sides with tamari. Coat the top and sides well with ground seeds, pressing them into the fish to help them stick.

4. Bake in preheated oven for 15 to 20 minutes, depending on thickness, until fish flakes easily when tested with a fork.

Nutrition Tip

Pumpkin seeds are good way to add zinc to your diet. You may be aware of zinc's importance in supporting the immune system — many of us take zinc lozenges for a cold, for example. In addition, zinc is concentrated in the islet cells of the pancreas, where insulin is produced, so adequate zinc intake helps promote healthy insulin production and secretion, for the balanced management of blood sugar.

Modern Tuna Salad with Avocado and Ginger

Makes 2 servings

Tuna sandwiches are a lunchtime staple for most kids. With the delicious additions of spicy ginger and cooling avocado, this version is all grown up. We bet this tuna salad will quickly become a new comfort food in your household.

Tip

Chunk light tuna is predominantly skipjack tuna, but it could also contain yellowfin, tongol or bigeye. It has lower mercury levels than white (albacore) tuna, and is generally cheaper. Be sure to buy tuna packed in water to avoid industrial seed oils.

1	stalk celery, finely chopped	1
1	green onion, thinly sliced on the diagonal	1
¼ cup	finely minced sweet onion	60 mL
1 tsp	grated gingerroot	5 mL
¼ cup	The Best Paleo Mayo (page 249)	60 mL
1 tbsp	freshly squeezed lime juice	15 mL
1	can (6 oz/170 g) water-packed chunk light tuna, drained	1
1	avocado, roughly chopped	1
	Sea salt and freshly ground black pepper	
4 cups	mixed salad greens	1 L
2 tsp	chopped fresh cilantro (optional)	10 mL

1. In a medium bowl, combine celery, green onion, sweet onion, ginger, mayo and lime juice, mixing well. Gently mix in tuna and avocado. Season to taste with salt and pepper.

2. Divide salad greens between two plates and top with tuna mixture. If desired, garnish with cilantro.

Nutrition Tip

Researchers have recently discovered that tuna contains the mineral selenium in a novel form called selenoniene. This compound has a strong antioxidant capacity that protects the fish's red blood cells from damage from free radicals. In vitro (test tube) studies are ongoing to determine how much of this antioxidant protection we might get from eating tuna.

NUTRIENTS PER SERVING	
Calories	413
Fat	17 g
Carbohydrate	11 g
Fiber	7 g
Protein	20 g

Pan-Seared Sea Scallops

Tender, mild and buttery, pan-seared scallops are a delight. Irresistible for a romantic dinner for two, they are also surprisingly quick for a beautifully balanced meal.

Tips

Be sure to purchase dry or dry-packed scallops. Avoid those that don't specify "dry," as they have likely been preserved with sodium tripolyphosphate, which results in bloated scallops that are full of water and won't sear to a golden brown.

Scallops sometimes have a small white muscle attached to their sides, which you can just pull off and discard.

3 cups	packed arugula or frisée	750 mL
2 tbsp	extra virgin olive oil, divided	30 mL
	Sea salt and freshly ground black pepper	
8	dry-packed sea scallops (see tips, at left)	8
2 tbsp	grass-fed butter, divided	30 mL
1	small clove garlic, minced	1
1	shallot, minced	1
2 tbsp	freshly squeezed lemon juice	30 mL
2 tbsp	minced fresh flat-leaf (Italian) parsley	30 mL

1. In a large bowl, toss arugula with 1 tbsp (15 mL) oil and season to taste with salt and pepper. Divide greens between two plates.

2. Pat scallops with a paper towel until they are very dry. (This is important so the scallops sear nicely instead of boiling in their own water.)

3. In a large skillet, heat 1 tbsp (15 mL) butter and the remaining oil over medium-high heat. Working in batches if necessary, add scallops, leaving space in between. Sear scallops, undisturbed, for about 3 minutes or until deep golden brown on the bottom. Turn scallops over and sear for 2 to 3 minutes or until scallops are firm and golden brown. Place 4 scallops on top of the greens on each plate.

4. Let the skillet cool slightly, then melt the remaining butter over medium-low heat. Add garlic, shallot and lemon juice; cook, scraping the pan and stirring, for 1 to 2 minutes or until shallot is tender. Spoon shallot mixture over scallops and sprinkle with parsley.

Nutrition Tip

Scallops are an excellent source of iodine, and 1 serving of this recipe provides almost 90% of the daily value for this important mineral. Iodine is the key component of thyroid hormones — which control the body's metabolism, energy production and energy use — so it's essential that we get enough.

NUTRIENTS PER SERVING	
Calories	298
Fat	25 g
Carbohydrate	7 g
Fiber	1 g
Protein	11 g

Roasted Black Cod with Warm Tomato
Vinaigrette on Seared Rapini (page 182)

Smoked Salmon Nori Rolls (page 188)

Butter Chicken with
Cilantro Cauliflower Rice (page 204)

Lemon Pepper Chicken Wings (page 212) and
Rainbow Roots Slaw with Tahini Parsley Dressing (page 130)

Thai Basil Beef (page 226) and
Fried Cauliflower Rice (page 153)

Spaghetti Squash Bolognese (page 232)

Skillet-Grilled Lamb with
Avocado Mint Sauce (page 236)

Coconut Banana Soft-Serve
(raspberry variation, page 276)

Mediterranean Shrimp with Wilted Spinach

This classic dish is the perfect way to use frozen shrimp. Most shrimp is frozen soon after being caught, so it is likely fresher than the unfrozen shrimp at the fish counter. For quick thawing, remove the frozen shrimp from the bag and place it in a bowl of cold water under a slowly running tap. The shrimp should be ready to cook in about 15 to 20 minutes.

24	large wild shrimp, peeled and deveined	24
	Sea salt and freshly ground black pepper	
2 tbsp	extra virgin olive oil	30 mL
2 tbsp	minced garlic	30 mL
1	large red onion, sliced	1
2 cups	grape or cherry tomatoes, halved	500 mL
½ cup	drained kalamata olives, pitted and sliced	125 mL
2 tbsp	thinly sliced fresh basil	30 mL
8 cups	baby spinach	2 L

1. Rinse shrimp and pat dry with paper towels. Season with salt and pepper; set aside.

2. In a large skillet, heat oil over medium heat. Add garlic and onion; cook, stirring, for 5 minutes or until onion is tender. Add tomatoes and cook, stirring, for 1 to 2 minutes or until softened.

3. Add shrimp and cook, turning once, for 1 to 2 minutes per side or until pink, firm and opaque. Stir in olives and basil. Remove from heat and gently toss in spinach until wilted. Serve immediately.

Nutrition Tip

All vegetables contain a wide variety of phytonutrients, but spinach is a special case. Over a dozen different flavonoid compounds that function as anti-inflammatory agents have been identified in spinach. Studies show that spinach promotes heart health by boosting the functions of nitric oxide, which improves circulation, blood pressure and blood vessel health.

NUTRIENTS PER SERVING	
Calories	375
Fat	19 g
Carbohydrate	31 g
Fiber	9 g
Protein	26 g

Sautéed Shrimp with Zucchini Noodles and Creamy Avocado Pesto

Makes 4 servings

Who says you can't have noodles? These delicious zucchini noodles are a terrific low-carb way to keep your blood sugar balanced while enjoying creamy pesto and (zucchini) pasta.

Tip

If you have a vegetable spiralizer, you can use it instead of the julienne peeler to create zucchini noodles. You can also make zucchini noodles with a mandolin or by hand.

- **Julienne peeler**

5	medium zucchini (each about 7 oz/200 g)	5
2 tbsp	grass-fed butter (approx.)	30 mL
32	large wild shrimp, peeled and deveined	32
1 tbsp	extra virgin olive oil	15 mL
¾ cup	Creamy Avocado Pesto (page 245)	175 mL

1. Using the julienne peeler, make long slices along one side of a zucchini until you get to the seeded core. Rotate the zucchini and peel another side in the same way. Continue until you have done all four sides. Discard the seeded core. Repeat with the remaining zucchini.

2. Place zucchini noodles in a colander and let drain for 20 to 30 minutes, using paper towels to squeeze the moisture out of the zucchini a couple of times.

3. In a large skillet, melt 1 tbsp (15 mL) butter over medium heat. Working in batches, add shrimp and cook, turning once, for 1 to 2 minutes per side or until pink, firm and opaque, adding more butter as needed between batches. Transfer shrimp to a large bowl and cover to keep warm. Drain off any liquid remaining in skillet.

NUTRIENTS PER SERVING	
Calories	282
Fat	22 g
Carbohydrate	14 g
Fiber	5 g
Protein	14 g

Tips

We prefer not to use the seedy core, as it gets a bit mushy when you heat the zucchini.

You can prepare the Creamy Avocado Pesto while the zucchini noodles are draining.

4. In the same skillet, heat oil over medium heat. Add zucchini noodles, stirring to coat with oil. Cook, stirring, for 1 to 3 minutes, depending on how crunchy you like your noodles (the longer you cook them, the softer they will get). Turn off heat and add pesto, tossing until noodles are evenly coated.

5. Divide noodles among serving plates and top with shrimp. Serve immediately.

Nutrition Tip

Astaxanthin is the pigment that gives shrimp, krill and lobster their pink, red and orange shades. Studies show that astaxanthin has general antioxidant properties in eye tissue and, along with lutein and zeaxanthin, may play a protective role against age-related macular degeneration. Like all carotenoids, astaxanthin is best absorbed alongside dietary fat, so the Creamy Avocado Pesto is a perfect accompaniment to the shrimp in this recipe.

Cooked Shrimp Ceviche

This cooked ceviche is a great option for anyone who won't eat raw seafood. For those that need to avoid shellfish altogether, you can also prepare this recipe with cooked white fish, such as sole or snapper. Serve with small spoons or Belgian endive spears as scoops.

Tip

English cucumbers, with their small seeds and thin skin, are perfect for this ceviche, but you can use field cucumbers instead. The skin is a lot thicker on field cucumbers, so peel most of it off, but leave a little because you want some green in the ceviche. Cut the cucumber in half lengthwise and scoop out the seeds, as they can make the ceviche too liquidy, then dice the remaining flesh.

Variation

Substitute 1 lb (500 g) sole or snapper, cooked and cooled, for the shrimp.

NUTRIENTS PER SERVING	
Calories	209
Fat	12 g
Carbohydrate	8 g
Fiber	4 g
Protein	19 g

1 lb	large wild shrimp, peeled, deveined, cooked and cooled	500 g
½	red bell pepper, finely chopped	½
½	jalapeño pepper, seeded and minced	½
½ cup	diced jicama	125 mL
½ cup	diced English cucumber (see tip, at left)	125 mL
½ cup	diced celery	125 mL
2 tbsp	finely minced red onion	30 mL
	Juice of 1 lemon	
	Juice of 1 lime	
¼ cup	minced fresh cilantro	60 mL
3 tbsp	extra virgin olive oil	45 mL
1	avocado, diced	1

1. In a large non-reactive (non-metal) bowl, combine shrimp, red pepper, jalapeño, jicama, cucumber, celery, onion, lemon juice and lime juice. Cover and refrigerate for 30 to 60 minutes to blend the flavors.

2. Add cilantro and oil to shrimp mixture, mixing well. Gently stir in avocado just before serving.

Nutrition Tip

Wild shrimp are less likely to harbor bacteria or contain the chemicals and antibiotics that are often found in farmed shrimp. But the environmental implications of buying wild are a problem because of the damage to the sea bottom and anything that lives there. According to a 2015 Consumer Report, when it comes to safety and sustainability, responsibly caught U.S. wild shrimp are the best bet. Check out the "Best Choices" or "Good Alternatives" on the Monterey Bay Aquarium's Seafood Watch Guide, at www.seafoodwatch.org.

Chicken and Turkey

Flattened Roast Chicken

Makes 6 servings

Flattening the chicken reduces the cooking time and helps ensure more even cooking so that every piece of chicken is moist and tender. Roasting vegetables with the chicken makes an easy all-in-one meal. You'll love how tender and mild the roasted garlic cloves are!

Tips

You can substitute the fat of your choice for the olive oil.

Save the backbone to make Warming Chicken Stock (page 116).

Nutrition Tip

Chicken is an excellent source of vitamin B_3 (niacin), which is important for energy production and the conversion of dietary proteins, carbohydrates and fats into usable energy.

NUTRIENTS PER SERVING	
Calories	277
Fat	14 g
Carbohydrate	13 g
Fiber	3 g
Protein	27 g

- **Preheat oven to 375°F (190°C)**
- **Shallow roasting pan or large rimmed baking sheet, lined with parchment paper**

1	whole free-range chicken (3 to 4 lbs/1.5 to 2 kg), patted dry	1
3 tbsp	extra virgin olive oil	45 mL
1 tsp	sea salt	5 mL
1 tsp	dried oregano	5 mL
½ tsp	freshly ground black pepper	2 mL
½ tsp	paprika	2 mL
8	cloves garlic, peeled	8
6	medium carrots, quartered	6
2	medium onions, quartered	2
2	red bell peppers, quartered	2

1. Place chicken, breast side down, on a cutting board. Using kitchen shears, cut along both sides of the backbone, from end to end; reserve backbone for another use. (You will be cutting through ribs, so use a firm grip and be careful of the cut ends of the ribs, which can be very sharp.) Turn the chicken breast side up and press down hard on the breasts to flatten and open the chicken completely. Place chicken, breast side up, in prepared pan.

2. In a small bowl, combine oil, salt, oregano, pepper and paprika. Use half of this mixture to rub the chicken all over.

3. In a large bowl, combine garlic, carrots, onions, red peppers and the remaining oil mixture, tossing well to coat. Scatter the vegetables around the chicken.

4. Roast in preheated oven for 50 to 60 minutes or until an instant-read thermometer inserted in the thickest part of the thigh registers 165°F (74°C) and vegetables are tender. Transfer chicken to a cutting board, cover with a sheet of parchment paper and then a sheet of foil, so only the parchment paper is touching the chicken (see page 62), and let rest for 10 minutes before carving. Serve chicken with vegetables on the side.

Chicken Thighs with Artichokes and Capers

Makes 6 servings

Even though the recipe title calls for chicken thighs, you can make this recipe with chicken breasts, whole chicken legs or a combination, to suit everyone's taste. Bone-in skin-on chicken gives extra flavor to the finished dish, plus it's cheaper! You can remove the skin after serving.

Tips

If you don't have an ovenproof skillet, use a casserole dish or a shallow roasting pan for the chicken. Prepare the shallots, artichokes, capers and lemon juice in a skillet, then transfer them to the casserole with the chicken before baking.

You can substitute the fat of your choice for the olive oil.

- Preheat oven to 375°F (190°C)
- Large ovenproof skillet (see tip, at left)

1 tbsp	extra virgin olive oil	15 mL
3	large shallots, sliced (about 1 cup/250 mL)	3
2 cups	drained canned or thawed frozen artichoke hearts	500 mL
1/4 cup	drained capers	60 mL
1/2 cup	freshly squeezed lemon juice	125 mL
12	bone-in skin-on free-range chicken thighs (about 4 1/2 lbs/2.25 kg)	12
1 tsp	freshly ground black pepper	5 mL
1/4 tsp	sea salt	1 mL

1. In ovenproof skillet, heat oil over medium heat. Add shallots and cook, stirring, for 3 to 4 minutes or until tender. Stir in artichoke hearts, capers and lemon juice. Add chicken, skin side up, making sure the pieces don't overlap. Season with pepper and salt.

2. Transfer skillet to preheated oven and bake for 45 minutes or until an instant-read thermometer inserted in the thickest part of a thigh registers 165°F (74°C). Serve chicken with the artichoke mixture on the side.

Nutrition Tip

Fiber-rich artichokes are a great addition to your diet to help manage your blood sugar. Not only does fiber slow the absorption of glucose into the bloodstream, it also binds with cholesterol in the intestine and escorts it out of the body before it can be reabsorbed. A compound called cynarin in artichokes increases bile production in the liver, which also helps remove cholesterol from the body.

NUTRIENTS PER SERVING	
Calories	334
Fat	13 g
Carbohydrate	13 g
Fiber	4 g
Protein	41 g

Chicken with Almond Satay Sauce

Makes 4 servings

This simple marinated chicken is an easy alternative to grilling. The delicious satay sauce uses almonds instead of peanuts. Serve the chicken on a platter lined with lettuce leaves, with a bowl of the satay sauce on the side.

Tip

Slicing chicken is easier if you place it in the freezer for 5 to 10 minutes first.

NUTRIENTS PER SERVING OF CHICKEN	
Calories	139
Fat	4 g
Carbohydrate	1 g
Fiber	0 g
Protein	24 g

NUTRIENTS PER 1 TBSP (15 ML) SATAY SAUCE	
Calories	51
Fat	5 g
Carbohydrate	1 g
Fiber	1 g
Protein	1 g

- **Rimmed baking sheet, lined with parchment paper**

1	small onion, minced	1
1	clove garlic, minced	1
1 tbsp	minced or grated gingerroot	15 mL
2 tsp	chili powder	10 mL
¼ tsp	sea salt	1 mL
2 tbsp	organic gluten-free tamari or coconut amino acids	30 mL
1 tbsp	freshly squeezed lemon juice	15 mL
1 tbsp	extra virgin olive oil	15 mL
1 lb	boneless skinless free-range chicken breasts, cut into 1-inch (2.5 cm) thick strips	500 mL

Almond Satay Sauce

1	can (14 oz/400 mL) full-fat coconut milk	1
⅓ cup	almond butter (smooth or crunchy)	75 mL
1 tbsp	fish sauce (see tip, opposite)	15 mL
2 tsp	freshly squeezed lime juice (or to taste)	10 mL
¼ tsp	hot pepper flakes (or to taste)	1 mL
	Sea salt and freshly ground black pepper	

1. In a large glass bowl, combine onion, garlic, ginger, chili powder, salt, tamari, lemon juice and oil. Add chicken, mixing well. Cover and refrigerate for 1 to 2 hours, until chilled, stirring occasionally.

2. Preheat broiler.

3. *Satay Sauce:* In a medium saucepan, combine coconut milk, almond butter, fish sauce, lime juice and hot pepper flakes. Season to taste with salt and pepper. Bring to a boil over medium-high heat. Reduce heat and simmer for 5 minutes. Remove from heat and let cool or keep warm, as desired.

Tips

Make sure the fish sauce has only three ingredients: fish, salt and water. Steer clear of non-paleo ingredients such as sugar and hydrolyzed wheat protein.

Leftover almond satay sauce will keep well in an airtight container in the refrigerator for up to 1 week. It is terrific warm or cold with pork, chicken and shrimp. For a quick lunch, drizzle it over one of these proteins rolled up in a couple of lettuce leaves.

4. Using tongs, transfer chicken to prepared baking sheet, spreading it out so it overlaps as little as possible. Discard marinade. Broil for 4 minutes. Turn chicken over and broil for 3 to 5 minutes or until no longer pink inside. Serve chicken drizzled with cool or warm satay sauce.

Nutrition Tip

There's a lot of evidence to support the idea that eating nuts on a regular basis reduces the risk of heart disease. A review published in the *British Journal of Nutrition* looked at four large epidemiological studies and determined that the risk of coronary heart disease was 37% lower for people who consumed nuts more than four times per week than for those who never or seldom consumed nuts. Almonds are also a good source of magnesium, which helps reduce resistance in the blood vessels — which, in turn, improves the flow of blood, nutrients and oxygen throughout the body.

Jerk Chicken Kebabs

These kebabs are great done on the grill for a nice al fresco dinner when it's warm out, but the oven-baked method is just as delicious and doesn't require a parka!

Tip

If you don't have fresh thyme on hand, you can use 1 tsp (5 mL) dried thyme instead.

- Preheat barbecue grill to high or preheat oven to 400°F (200°C)
- Blender or food processor
- Four 8- to 10-inch (20 to 25 cm) bamboo skewers, soaked in water for about 1 hour
- Baking sheet, lined with parchment paper (optional)

4	green onions, sliced	4
3	cloves garlic, sliced	3
1	jalapeño pepper, seeded and roughly chopped (optional)	1
1 tbsp	chopped fresh thyme	15 mL
1½ tsp	sea salt	7 mL
1½ tsp	freshly ground black pepper	7 mL
¾ tsp	ground cinnamon	3 mL
½ tsp	ground cloves	2 mL
¼ tsp	ground nutmeg	1 mL
3 tbsp	freshly squeezed lime juice	45 mL
3 tbsp	extra virgin olive oil	45 mL
2 tbsp	organic gluten-free tamari or coconut amino acids	30 mL
1½ lbs	boneless skinless free-range chicken breasts or thighs, cut into 1-inch (2.5 cm) pieces	750 g

1. In blender, combine green onions, garlic, jalapeño (if using), thyme, salt, pepper, cinnamon, cloves, nutmeg, lime juice, oil and tamari; blend until smooth.

2. Place chicken in a large bowl and pour sauce over top, tossing well to coat. Cover and refrigerate for at least 2 hours, until chilled, or for up to 6 hours.

3. Remove chicken from marinade, discarding marinade, and thread 5 or 6 pieces of chicken onto each skewer. (If baking, place skewers on prepared baking sheet.)

NUTRIENTS PER SERVING	
Calories	213
Fat	6 g
Carbohydrate	1 g
Fiber	0 g
Protein	36 g

Tip

To increase your vegetable intake, add bell pepper and onion pieces to the skewers with the chicken. Cut the pepper and onion into pieces about 1½ inches (4 cm) square and thread one piece of each onto the skewers in between each piece of chicken in step 3.

4. Place skewers on preheated grill, reduce heat to medium and grill, turning occasionally, for about 10 minutes (or bake in preheated oven, turning occasionally, for about 15 minutes), until juices run clear when chicken is pierced (for thighs) or chicken is no longer pink inside (for breasts).

Nutrition Tip

Garlic is a member of the Allium family, which also includes onions and leeks. It has a variety of sulfur-containing compounds that are responsible for its characteristic smell, and for many of its health benefits. Sulfur is the third most abundant mineral in the body, lending flexibility and elasticity to connective tissue, cartilage and joints.

Butter Chicken with Cilantro Cauliflower Rice

Makes 6 to 8 servings

Butter chicken is without a doubt one of the best-known Indian dishes. Instead of high-carbohydrate rice, this version is served with cauliflower rice. We challenge you to tell the difference!

Nutrition Tip

Turmeric is used as a powerful anti-inflammatory in both Chinese and Indian traditional medicine. Curcumin, the active ingredient in turmeric, has been shown to inhibit the COX-2 enzymes that promote inflammation and pain. These are the same enzymes inhibited by non-steroidal anti-inflammatory drugs (NSAIDs).

NUTRIENTS PER SERVING	
Calories	427
Fat	32 g
Carbohydrate	8 g
Fiber	2 g
Protein	31 g

2 tbsp	coconut oil	30 mL
1	large onion, chopped	1
5	cloves garlic, minced	5
2 tbsp	grated gingerroot	30 mL
2 tsp	garam masala (store-bought or see recipe, page 262)	10 mL
1 tsp	sea salt	5 mL
1 tsp	ground coriander	5 mL
1 tsp	ground cumin	5 mL
1 tsp	ground turmeric	5 mL
½ tsp	paprika	2 mL
½ tsp	cayenne pepper	2 mL
¼ tsp	chili powder	1 mL
2 lbs	boneless skinless free-range chicken thighs, cut into 1-inch (2.5 cm) chunks	1 kg
1	large green bell pepper, chopped	1
1	can (14 oz/398 mL) tomato purée	1
1	can (14 oz/400 mL) full-fat coconut milk	1
2 tbsp	freshly squeezed lemon juice	30 mL
	Cilantro Cauliflower Rice (page 154)	

1. In a large skillet, heat coconut oil over medium heat. Add onion and cook, stirring, for 5 to 10 minutes or until golden brown. Add garlic and ginger; cook, stirring, for 1 to 2 minutes. Add garam masala, salt, coriander, cumin, turmeric, paprika, cayenne and chili powder; cook, stirring, for 1 minute.

2. Add chicken and cook, stirring occasionally, for 3 minutes. Add green pepper and tomato purée, stirring well. Cover and cook, stirring occasionally, for 15 minutes or until juices run clear when chicken is pierced.

3. Add coconut milk and lemon juice; simmer, uncovered, for 5 minutes. Serve with Cilantro Cauliflower Rice.

Chicken Chili

Sometimes called white chili, this chicken and peppers concoction is a nice change from the usual beans and beef — even for chili aficionados.

Tip

If you are rushed for time, use a fully cooked barbecue chicken from the grocery store. These are generally about 2 to 3 lbs (1 to 1.5 kg) and will provide 3 to 5 cups (750 mL to 1.25 L) of meat when you use both the light and dark meat. Remove all the skin and bones, cut the meat into $3/4$-inch (2 cm) chunks and add as instructed in step 4.

Nutrition Tip

Tomatoes are packed full of antioxidants, which are very important for our overall heart health.

NUTRIENTS PER SERVING (1 OF 8)	
Calories	279
Fat	8 g
Carbohydrate	18 g
Fiber	4 g
Protein	35 g

- Preheat oven to 350°F (180°C)
- 13- by 9-inch (33 by 23 cm) glass casserole or baking dish, lightly sprayed with olive oil cooking spray

4	bone-in skin-on free-range chicken breasts	4
	Sea salt and freshly ground black pepper	
2 tbsp	extra virgin olive oil	30 mL
4 cups	chopped onions (about 3 large)	1 L
2	cloves garlic, minced	2
2	red bell peppers, chopped	2
1	yellow bell pepper, chopped	1
1	orange bell pepper, chopped	1
1 tsp	chili powder	5 mL
1 tsp	ground cumin	5 mL
$1/4$ tsp	hot pepper flakes (or to taste)	1 mL
$1/4$ tsp	cayenne pepper (optional)	1 mL
2	cans (each 28 oz/796 mL) diced tomatoes, with juice	2
$1/4$ cup	minced fresh basil	60 mL
4	green onions, finely chopped	4

1. Place chicken in casserole dish and season with salt and pepper. Roast in preheated oven for 35 to 40 minutes or until chicken is no longer pink inside. Remove skin and bones, and cut meat into $3/4$-inch (2 cm) chunks.

2. Meanwhile, in a large pot or Dutch oven, heat oil over medium-low heat. Add onions and cook, stirring, for 10 to 15 minutes or until tender. Add garlic and cook, stirring, for 2 minutes. Add red peppers, yellow pepper, orange pepper, $1^1/2$ tsp (7 mL) salt, chili powder, cumin, hot pepper flakes and cayenne (if using); cook, stirring, for 2 minutes.

3. Stir in tomatoes and basil; bring to a boil over high heat. Reduce heat and simmer, stirring occasionally, for 30 minutes.

4. Stir in chicken and any accumulated juices and simmer, stirring occasionally, for 15 minutes. Serve topped with green onions.

Chicken Fajita Wraps

Everyone loves fajitas, so gather family and friends around the table for some very social eating. These get a light touch with crisp lettuce leaves for wrapping.

Tips

Slicing chicken is easier if you place it in the freezer for 5 to 10 minutes first.

If you don't have homemade stock on hand, you can use ready-to-use organic chicken broth.

Nutrition Tip

The peppers, salsa and lime juice in this recipe all combine to give you a good dose of vitamin C. Vitamin C transforms both animal and plant dietary iron into a form that is more easily absorbed in the intestine. To increase your iron levels, try eating vitamin C–rich foods along with iron-containing foods.

NUTRIENTS PER SERVING	
Calories	276
Fat	11 g
Carbohydrate	11 g
Fiber	2 g
Protein	33 g

2 tbsp	extra virgin olive oil, divided	30 mL
1 cup	thinly sliced onion, divided	250 mL
1 tsp	ground cumin	5 mL
1 tsp	chili powder	5 mL
2	boneless skinless free-range chicken breasts (each about 5 oz/150 g), cut into thin strips	2
½ tsp	sea salt	2 mL
¼ tsp	freshly ground black pepper	1 mL
¾ cup	Fresh Tomato Salsa (page 240)	175 mL
½ cup	Warming Chicken Stock (page 116)	125 mL
1	large green bell pepper, thinly sliced	1
	Juice of 1 lime	
	Leafy lettuce	

1. In a medium saucepan, heat 1 tbsp (15 mL) oil over medium heat. Add half the onion and cook, stirring, for 4 to 5 minutes or until translucent. Stir in cumin and chili powder. Stir in chicken, salt, pepper, salsa and stock; bring to a boil. Reduce heat and simmer, stirring occasionally, for 15 to 20 minutes or until chicken is no longer pink inside.

2. Meanwhile, in a skillet, heat the remaining oil over medium heat. Add green pepper and the remaining onion; cook, stirring, for 5 to 6 minutes or until slightly softened. Set aside.

3. Using a slotted spoon, transfer chicken to a bowl and let cool slightly, then shred it with two forks.

4. Bring the liquid in the saucepan to a boil over medium-high heat and boil, stirring occasionally, for about 5 minutes or until thickened. Reduce heat to low and return chicken to the pot, along with any accumulated juices, stirring well. Stir in lime juice.

5. Serve chicken mixture on lettuce leaves, topped with sautéed pepper and onion.

Buffalo-Inspired Chicken Lettuce Wraps

Makes 4 servings

Dinner doesn't get much faster than these quick, finger-licking-good bundles. Boston (butter) lettuce is great for wraps, but really you can use any kind of lettuce. Be sure to double up on the leaves if they are small or have any holes.

Tip

You can substitute the oil of your choice for the avocado oil.

2 tbsp	avocado oil	30 mL
1 lb	boneless skinless free-range chicken breasts or thighs, cut into 1-inch (2.5 cm) cubes	500 g
2 tsp	chili powder (or to taste)	10 mL
1/2 tsp	onion powder	2 mL
1/4 tsp	sea salt	1 mL
1/4 tsp	freshly ground black pepper	1 mL
1	head Boston (butter) lettuce, separated into leaves	1
1	avocado, chopped	1
1/2 cup	cherry tomatoes, halved	125 mL
2	green onions, chopped	2
	Ranch Dressing (page 252) (optional)	

1. In a medium skillet, heat oil over medium-high heat. Add chicken, stirring to coat with oil. Stir in chili powder, onion powder, salt and pepper; cook, stirring, for 8 to 10 minutes or until chicken is no longer pink inside (for breasts) or juices run clear when chicken is pierced (for thighs).

2. Fill lettuce leaves with chicken, avocado, tomatoes and green onions, dividing evenly. Drizzle with Ranch Dressing (if using).

Nutrition Tip

A meal that results in good blood sugar numbers without a large post-meal spike is one that combines adequate protein, nutritious fat, slow carbohydrates and a good amount of fiber. Look no further than these chicken wraps. The chicken contributes good protein, the tomatoes and lettuce provide slow carbohydrates, and the avocado seals the deal with monounsaturated fat, high fiber and slow carbs.

NUTRIENTS PER SERVING	
Calories	270
Fat	13 g
Carbohydrate	7 g
Fiber	5 g
Protein	31 g

Asian Chicken Lettuce Cups

These wraps are terrific
for entertaining or a
family meal. Just be
sure to have plates or
napkins available to
catch any drips.

Tip

Make sure the fish sauce has
only three ingredients: fish,
salt and water. Steer clear of
non-paleo ingredients such
as sugar and hydrolyzed
wheat protein.

Sauce

2	cloves garlic, minced	2
1 tbsp	minced gingerroot	15 mL
1 tbsp	minced fresh cilantro (optional)	15 mL
1 tbsp	sesame seeds, toasted (see tip, opposite)	15 mL
¼ cup	organic gluten-free tamari or coconut amino acids	60 mL
1 tbsp	freshly squeezed lime juice	15 mL
1 tbsp	unseasoned rice vinegar	15 mL
1 tsp	fish sauce (see tip, at left)	5 mL
1 tsp	toasted (dark) sesame oil	5 mL

Stir-Fry

1 tbsp	olive oil or avocado oil	15 mL
1 lb	ground free-range chicken	500 g
2	stalks celery, finely chopped	2
1	carrot, finely chopped	1
½	red bell pepper, finely chopped	½
1 cup	sugar snap peas or snow peas, finely chopped	250 mL
½ cup	finely chopped onion	125 mL
1	clove garlic, minced	1
½ cup	finely chopped shiitake mushroom caps	125 mL
1 tsp	minced gingerroot	5 mL
2	green onions, finely chopped	2

Lettuce Cups

12	Boston (butter) lettuce leaves (see tip, opposite)	12
1 cup	bean sprouts	250 mL
¼ cup	chopped fresh cilantro (optional)	60 mL
¼ cup	cashews, toasted and chopped (see tip, opposite)	60 mL

1. *Sauce:* In a small bowl, combine garlic, ginger, cilantro (if using), sesame seeds, tamari, lime juice, vinegar, fish sauce and sesame oil.

NUTRIENTS PER SERVING (1 OF 6)	
Calories	226
Fat	13 g
Carbohydrate	11 g
Fiber	2 g
Protein	17 g

Tips

Lettuce leaves often have little holes or rips, so you may want to double up on the lettuce for the lettuce cups so that nothing leaks out.

To toast nuts or seeds, place them in a dry skillet over medium heat and stir occasionally until aromatic (about 2 to 4 minutes, depending on the nut or seed). At this point, reduce the heat to medium-low and cook, stirring constantly to ensure even browning, until nuts or seeds are evenly golden brown (about 2 to 5 minutes, depending on the nut or seed). Transfer to a plate or cutting board to cool. (If you leave them in the pan, they will continue to cook and may burn.)

2. *Stir-Fry:* In a large skillet, heat olive oil over medium-high heat. Add chicken and cook, breaking it up with a spoon, for 6 to 8 minutes or until no longer pink. Add celery, carrot, red pepper, peas and onion; stir-fry for 3 minutes. Stir in garlic, mushrooms and ginger. Stir sauce and add half the sauce to the pan; cook, stirring, for 1 to 2 minutes or until thickened. Transfer stir-fry to a large bowl and top with green onions.

3. *Lettuce Cups:* Fill lettuce leaves with stir-fry, dividing evenly, and top with bean sprouts, cilantro (if using) and cashews. Stir the remaining sauce and drizzle over top, as desired.

Nutrition Tip

A recipe doesn't often have more ingredients than this one, but it sure is worth it. With all these vegetables, herbs, nuts, seeds and poultry, you are getting a diverse range of vitamins, minerals and especially phytonutrients. Each nutrient is valuable in and of itself, but the real nutritional power of whole foods comes from the synergy of how what we eat works together in the body. There's a lot to work with here!

Greek Chicken Salad

This is a perfect way to use leftover Flattened Roast Chicken (page 198). To make it even easier, you can use whatever leafy greens you have on hand. It is good with a gentle spring mix or some zesty bitter greens (like arugula, baby kale and baby chard), but it is also delightfully refreshing with simple romaine lettuce. It's almost like a new salad every time you make it!

10	cherry tomatoes, halved	10
8	kalamata olives	8
1	small cucumber, chopped (about 1 cup/250 mL)	1
1 cup	diced cooked free-range chicken	250 mL
2 tsp	drained capers	10 mL
	Sea salt and freshly ground black pepper	
2 tbsp	extra virgin olive oil	30 mL
2 tbsp	freshly squeezed lemon juice	30 mL
5 cups	loosely packed leafy greens	1.25 L
2 tbsp	chopped fresh flat-leaf (Italian) parsley	30 mL

1. In a medium bowl, combine tomatoes, olives, cucumber, chicken and capers, mixing well. Season to taste with salt and pepper.

2. In another medium bowl, combine oil and lemon juice. Add leafy greens and toss to coat.

3. Divide leafy greens between two plates and top with chicken mixture, dividing evenly. Sprinkle with parsley.

Nutrition Tip

Any leftover cooked protein (meat, poultry, fish or seafood) can be made into a salad like this one. Plan for leftovers when you are planning meals so you don't have to prepare three meals from scratch every day. That way, you are not stuck wondering what to eat, which can lead to consumption of foods high in carbohydrates and low in nutrient density.

NUTRIENTS PER SERVING	
Calories	297
Fat	18 g
Carbohydrate	10 g
Fiber	3 g
Protein	24 g

Curried Chicken Salad

This salad is delicious just served on a plate with a fork, but it is also a great filling for a collard or lettuce wrap. To use collard leaves, select the smaller, younger leaves. Wash the leaves, pat them dry, cut out the thick stems at the bottom, add a dollop of chicken salad and roll away. Be sure to tuck the bottom of the leaf in first and then roll from one side so everything is contained.

Tip

To toast nuts or seeds, place them in a dry skillet over medium heat and stir occasionally until aromatic (about 2 to 4 minutes, depending on the nut or seed). At this point, reduce the heat to medium-low and cook, stirring constantly to ensure even browning, until nuts or seeds are evenly golden brown (about 2 to 5 minutes, depending on the nut or seed). Transfer to a plate or cutting board to cool.

NUTRIENTS PER SERVING	
Calories	301
Fat	19 g
Carbohydrate	7 g
Fiber	3 g
Protein	23 g

3 tbsp	The Best Paleo Mayo (page 249) (approx.)	45 mL
1 tsp	curry powder	5 mL
1/4 tsp	paprika	1 mL
2	green onions, chopped (about 1/4 cup/60 mL)	2
1	red bell pepper, finely chopped	1
1	apple, diced (optional)	1
1 cup	diced celery	250 mL
1 cup	diced cooked free-range chicken	250 mL
	Sea salt and freshly ground black pepper	
1/4 cup	toasted cashews or almonds, coarsely chopped (optional)	60 mL

1. In a medium bowl, combine mayo, curry powder and paprika, mixing well. Add green onions, red pepper, apple (if using), celery and chicken, mixing well. Add more mayo if needed. Season to taste with salt and pepper. If desired, stir in cashews just before serving.

Nutrition Tip

It's time to stop thinking of celery as just a low-carb food without much in it except water. Research has identified apiuman, a non-starchy polysaccharide that appears to have anti-inflammatory benefits, especially for the digestive tract. Use celery within 5 days of purchase to benefit from its maximum nutrient potential.

Lemon Pepper Chicken Wings

For many of us, chicken wings are about the sauce — and lots of it. But we're confident you'll become a convert to this simple, fresh, delicious version.

Tip

For 2 tbsp (30 mL) lemon zest, you'll need to grate the zest from 2 to 3 lemons.

- **Preheat oven to 375°F (190°C)**
- **Large baking sheet, lined with foil, with a wire rack set on top**

2 lbs	free-range chicken wings (see tip, page 213)	1 kg
2 tbsp	grated lemon zest	30 mL
2 tbsp	freshly squeezed lemon juice	30 mL
1 tbsp	freshly ground black pepper	15 mL
1 tsp	sea salt	5 mL

1. Pat chicken dry with paper towels, removing as much moisture as you can. Arrange on the wire rack over the prepared baking sheet, leaving space in between, if possible.

2. Roast in preheated oven for 30 to 35 minutes, flipping them over halfway through, until juices run clear when chicken is pierced.

3. Meanwhile, in a large bowl, combine lemon zest, lemon juice, pepper and salt.

4. Add wings to the lemon sauce and toss until evenly coated. Serve hot.

Nutrition Tip

Black pepper is such a commonly used spice, we don't give a second thought to its nutritional value, but we should. Known as a carminative, black pepper triggers our taste buds to send a message to our stomach to increase the production of hydrochloric acid, which helps us digest protein. As a bonus, black pepper also reduces the formation of intestinal gas.

NUTRIENTS PER SERVING	
Calories	291
Fat	20 g
Carbohydrate	2 g
Fiber	1 g
Protein	27 g

Barbecue-Rubbed Chicken Wings

Makes 4 servings

Make these tasty barbecue wings into a complete meal with our Classic Coleslaw (page 128).

Tip

Chicken wings come in three parts: the drumette, the wing flat or wingette, and the tip. If you are buying your chicken wings already cut up, there may not be any tips included, but if you are cutting them yourself, you can choose to use the tip or not. Many people recommend freezing the tips to use for making stock, but I think they are a crunchy and chewy delight! They cook faster than the other two parts, so watch that they don't burn.

- Preheat oven to 375°F (190°C)
- Large rimmed baking sheet, lined with foil, with a wire rack set on top

2 lbs	free-range chicken wings (see tip, at left)	1 kg
3 tbsp	Barbecue Spice Blend (page 260)	45 mL

1. Pat chicken dry with paper towels, removing as much moisture as you can. Place wings in a large bowl, add spice blend and toss well to coat.

2. Arrange wings on the wire rack over the prepared baking sheet, leaving space in between, if possible.

3. Roast in preheated oven for 30 to 35 minutes, flipping them over halfway through, until juices run clear when chicken is pierced. Serve hot.

Nutrition Tip

Most brand-name barbecue sauces contain a lot of sugar — about 16 g per 2 tbsp (30 mL), the equivalent of sprinkling three spoonfuls of granulated sugar on your wings. Not great for your blood sugar! Our chicken wing recipes are full of taste, without any sugar. Give them a try; you'll be happy with your postprandial numbers!

NUTRIENTS PER SERVING	
Calories	341
Fat	23 g
Carbohydrate	9 g
Fiber	6 g
Protein	30 g

Turkey-Stuffed Peppers

Makes 4 servings

This dish is very adaptable and is a great way to use up bits of vegetables in the fridge. Other ground meats, such as beef, work well too. The Italian Spice Blend is the key, so be sure you always have some on hand.

Nutrition Tip

Turkey provides the full spectrum of B vitamins, which all have a synergistic relationship with each other. Niacin is especially well represented, with 4 oz (125 g) of meat providing about 80% of the daily value or dietary reference intake. It is also an excellent source of B_6, at over 50% in the same amount of meat. B vitamins help convert our food into fuel and support carbohydrate metabolism.

NUTRIENTS PER SERVING	
Calories	294
Fat	16 g
Carbohydrate	14 g
Fiber	4 g
Protein	26 g

- Preheat oven to 350°F (180°C)
- 8-inch (20 cm) square casserole dish

4	green bell peppers	4
1 lb	ground free-range turkey	500 g
2 tbsp	extra virgin olive oil	30 mL
1 cup	sliced button or cremini mushrooms	250 mL
1 cup	chopped zucchini	250 mL
1/2 cup	chopped red bell pepper	125 mL
1/2 cup	chopped yellow bell pepper	125 mL
1/2 cup	chopped onion	125 mL
1 tsp	minced garlic	5 mL
1 cup	packed spinach leaves, trimmed and coarsely chopped	250 mL
1	can (14 oz/398 mL) diced tomatoes, drained	1
5 tsp	Italian Spice Blend (page 261)	25 mL
	Sea salt and freshly ground black pepper	

1. Cut tops off green peppers, discard the stems and chop the tops. Pull out and discard seeds and membranes from the pepper bottoms.

2. In a large skillet over medium heat, cook turkey, breaking it up with a spoon, for about 10 minutes or until no longer pink. Using a slotted spoon, transfer turkey to a bowl and set aside. Discard any fat remaining in the pan.

3. In the same skillet, heat oil over medium-high heat. Add mushrooms, zucchini, chopped green pepper, red pepper, yellow pepper, onion and garlic; cook, stirring, for about 5 minutes or until tender.

4. Return turkey to the pan, along with any accumulated juices, and stir in spinach and tomatoes. Season with Italian Spice Blend, stirring well.

5. Stuff green pepper shells with turkey mixture, dividing evenly. Place stuffed peppers upright in casserole dish.

6. Bake in preheated oven for 30 minutes or until peppers are soft enough to be pierced with a fork.

Classic Turkey Burgers

Burgers aren't just for summer or for the grill. Enjoy these quick and easy skillet burger patties for a change of pace. Serve them with Portobello Mushroom Cap Buns (page 163) and The Best Paleo Mayo (page 249).

Tips

You can substitute the fat of your choice for the butter.

Use a light touch when mixing ground meat. You want all of the ingredients to be evenly incorporated, but overhandling can make the patties dense and tough.

Pressing a dimple into the middle of each patty helps prevent the meat from shrinking too much and forming a dense ball of cooked meat.

1 lb	ground free-range turkey	500 g
1	clove garlic, minced	1
1/2 cup	chopped fresh Italian parsley	125 mL
1/4 cup	minced green onions	60 mL
1 tsp	dried oregano	5 mL
1/2 tsp	sea salt	2 mL
1/2 tsp	freshly ground black pepper	2 mL
2 tbsp	grass-fed butter	30 mL

1. In a large bowl, using your hands, combine turkey, garlic, parsley, green onions, oregano, salt and pepper just until all ingredients are evenly incorporated. Shape into 4 patties about 1/2 inch (1 cm) thick. Using two fingers, press a shallow dimple into the middle of each patty.

2. In a large skillet, heat butter over medium heat. Add patties, in batches if necessary, and cook, turning once, for about 6 minutes per side or until patties are no longer pink inside and an instant-read thermometer inserted horizontally in the center of a patty registers 165°F (74°C).

Nutrition Tip

Four ounces (125 g) of turkey provides over 60% of the dietary reference intake of selenium. This essential trace mineral is important for the proper functioning of our thyroid gland because it is required for the production of active thyroid hormones. When we consider that the thyroid is in charge of our whole operating system, including appetite, temperature, metabolism, sleep and energy, we can see how important selenium is.

NUTRIENTS PER PATTY	
Calories	226
Fat	15 g
Carbohydrate	1 g
Fiber	1 g
Protein	23 g

Greek-Style Turkey Burgers

Makes 4 patties

Here's a nice Mediterranean twist on the Classic Turkey Burgers (page 215). Serve them with Portobello Mushroom Cap Buns (page 163) and The Best Paleo Mayo (page 249).

Tips

Use a light touch when mixing ground meat. You want all of the ingredients to be evenly incorporated, but overhandling can make the patties dense and tough.

Pressing a dimple into the middle of each patty helps prevent the meat from shrinking too much and forming a dense ball of cooked meat.

1 lb	ground free-range turkey	500 g
1	clove garlic, minced (about 1 tsp/5 mL)	1
¼ cup	minced red onion	60 mL
¼ cup	chopped drained kalamata olives	60 mL
2 tbsp	finely chopped fresh parsley	30 mL
2 tbsp	finely chopped drained oil-packed sun-dried tomatoes	30 mL
1	large free-range egg, beaten	1
2 tbsp	extra virgin olive oil	30 mL

1. In a large bowl, using your hands, combine turkey, garlic, onion, olives, parsley, sun-dried tomatoes and egg just until all ingredients are evenly incorporated. Shape into 4 patties about $^1/_2$ inch (1 cm) thick. Using two fingers, press a shallow dimple into the middle of each patty.

2. In a large skillet, heat oil over medium heat. Add patties, in batches if necessary, and cook, turning once, for about 6 minutes per side or until patties are no longer pink inside and an instant-read thermometer inserted horizontally in the center of a patty registers 165°F (74°C).

Nutrition Tip

For turkey, as with all animal proteins, the amount of omega-3 fats is determined by the animal's diet. When turkeys spend their time foraging for different sprouts and bugs, they eat more omega-3-containing plants, which translates into more of that beneficial fat in the meat. Increasing our intake of omega-3 fats is important to reduce inflammation in the body and to support healthy nerve function.

NUTRIENTS PER PATTY	
Calories	267
Fat	18 g
Carbohydrate	2 g
Fiber	1 g
Protein	24 g

Pork, Beef and Lamb

Dry-Rubbed Baby Back Ribs

Makes 2 to 3 servings

Slow and low is the way to go for fall-off-the-bone ribs. Make extra so you have some for leftovers. You'll be glad you did.

- **Preheat oven to 250°F (120°C)**
- **Shallow roasting pan or rimmed baking sheet**

1	rack baby back pork ribs	1
2 tbsp	Barbecue Spice Blend (page 260)	30 mL

1. Remove the membrane, sometimes called the silverskin, from the bone side of the ribs. Rub the meat and bone side with the spice blend. Wrap the rib rack first in a layer of parchment paper, then in foil, folding the foil to create a sealed package (see page 62). Place package, meat side down, in roasting pan.

2. Bake in preheated oven for about 3 hours or until pork is fall-off-the-bone tender. (As long as the foil is sealed, you can leave the ribs in for up to 5 hours; it just means they'll fall off of the bone more easily!) Open package carefully and drain and discard any accumulated juices and fat. Cut rack into individual ribs and serve immediately.

Nutrition Tip

Know what the first ingredient is for one of the best-ranked commercial barbecue sauces out there? You guessed it: high-fructose corn syrup. But that's not all. The ingredients go on to list pineapple juice concentrate (sugar), molasses (sugar) and corn syrup (sugar). I think you get the message. Try our Barbecue Spice Blend instead.

NUTRIENTS PER SERVING	
Calories	292
Fat	19 g
Carbohydrate	6 g
Fiber	4 g
Protein	26 g

Stuffed Mushrooms

Stuffed mushrooms are often served as an appetizer, but in this case we bumped up the size of the mushroom caps for a satisfying entrée. To prepare these as an appetizer, just use 16 to 20 cremini (baby portobello) mushroom caps instead.

Tip

You can substitute the fat of your choice for the bacon fat.

Nutrition Tip

Mushrooms are the highest non-animal source of vitamin D — which is not really a vitamin at all, but a pro-hormone. The body is capable of producing its own vitamin D through the action of sunlight on the skin, whereas vitamins are nutrients that our bodies can't make and must acquire through diet or supplements.

NUTRIENTS PER SERVING	
Calories	334
Fat	24 g
Carbohydrate	7 g
Fiber	2 g
Protein	25 g

- Preheat oven to 450°F (230°C)
- Rimmed baking sheet, lined with foil, with a wire rack set on top

¾ tsp	sea salt	3 mL
¾ tsp	fennel seeds, coarsely ground	3 mL
¾ tsp	garlic powder	3 mL
¾ tsp	onion powder	3 mL
¾ tsp	paprika	3 mL
½ tsp	dried oregano	2 mL
1 lb	ground pasture-raised pork	500 g
4	large portobello mushroom caps (about 4 inches/10 cm in diameter)	4
1 tbsp	bacon fat	15 mL
1	clove garlic, minced	1
½ cup	minced onion	125 mL
¼ cup	minced red bell pepper	60 mL
2 cups	loosely packed baby spinach, finely chopped	500 mL

1. In a medium bowl, combine salt, fennel seeds, garlic powder, onion powder, paprika and oregano. Add pork and mix well to combine. Set aside.

2. Place mushrooms, cup side down, on the wire rack over the prepared baking sheet. Bake in preheated oven for 10 to 12 minutes or until some of the moisture has released from the mushrooms. Remove from oven, leaving oven on, and turn mushrooms cup side up on the rack.

3. Meanwhile, in a large skillet, melt bacon fat over medium heat. Add minced garlic, onion and red pepper; cook, stirring, for 2 minutes. Add pork mixture and cook, breaking it up with a spoon, for about 5 minutes or until no longer pink. Stir in spinach.

4. Spoon pork mixture into mushroom caps. Bake for 20 minutes or until the tops start to brown.

Variation

Substitute ground free-range turkey for the pork.

New Classic Meatballs

The secret for keeping meatballs juicy without using milk-soaked bread — a cauliflower garlic purée — comes from Michelle Tam's book *Nom Nom Paleo.* Thank you, Michelle, for sharing this brilliant tip. Serve these as is or as spaghetti and meatballs with Basic Marinara Sauce (page 239) and Roasted Spaghetti Squash Noodles (page 168).

Tips

Use a light touch when mixing ground meat. You want all of the ingredients to be evenly incorporated, but overhandling can make the meatballs dense and tough.

Store any leftover meatballs in an airtight container in the refrigerator for up to 5 days or in the freezer for up to 1 month. Reheating them with a bit of water will help keep them moist.

2 lbs	ground pasture-raised pork	1 kg
2	cloves garlic, minced	2
1 cup	Cauliflower Garlic Mash (page 152)	250 mL
1/2 cup	minced onion	125 mL
1/2 cup	minced fresh flat-leaf (Italian) parsley	125 mL
1/4 cup	minced fresh basil	60 mL
2 tsp	sea salt	10 mL
2 tbsp	olive oil (approx.)	30 mL

1. In a large bowl, using your hands, combine pork, garlic, Cauliflower Garlic Mash, onion, parsley, basil and salt. Roll into 1-inch (2.5 cm) balls.

2. In a large skillet, heat 1 tbsp (15 mL) oil over medium-high heat. Working in batches, add meatballs and cook, turning occasionally, for 5 to 8 minutes or until browned on all sides and no longer pink inside, adding more oil as needed and adjusting heat between batches to prevent burning.

Variation

Substitute ground free-range turkey or ground grass-fed beef for the pork.

Nutrition Tip

The term "pasture-raised" is more appropriate than "grass-fed" when it comes to pork, because pigs are natural omnivores who eat a little bit of everything, not just grass. Wild pigs eat pretty much anything they can get their snouts into: grubs, roots, grass, nuts, berries, fruit and insects. On a farm where the animals are pastured, vegetables are added to the mix. The meat from pastured pigs has a higher omega-3 and vitamin E content, making it a better choice than grain-fed pork for reducing inflammation in the human body.

NUTRIENTS PER 4 MEATBALLS	
Calories	350
Fat	28 g
Carbohydrate	3 g
Fiber	1 g
Protein	20 g

Baked Bacon

This classic accompaniment to eggs is a snap when baked in the oven. It's delicious with our Basic Scrambled Eggs with Roasted Salsa (page 173) or the Scrambled Eggs Florentine (page 174).

Tip

The baking time depends on the thickness of the bacon and how crispy you like it.

- Preheat oven to 350°F (180°C)
- Rimmed baking sheet, lined with foil, with a wire rack set on top

1 lb	pasture-raised bacon strips (or turkey bacon strips)	500 g

1. Arrange bacon on the wire rack over the prepared baking sheet, spacing the strips evenly.

2. Bake in preheated oven for 20 to 30 minutes or until bacon is cooked to your liking.

Nutrition Tip

Unless you have a good source of pasture-raised pork, it is very hard to find bacon without any added sugar of some sort. Just as with beef and lamb, the healthiest bacon comes from pigs that spend the majority of their time outside. Pigs are omnivores, so they like to root around for whatever they can find, including old acorns, insects and clover. If they are raised on a small farm, they may even be lucky enough to get kitchen scraps!

NUTRIENTS PER 2 STRIPS	
Calories	89
Fat	7 g
Carbohydrate	0 g
Fiber	0 g
Protein	6 g

Skillet-Grilled Flank Steak

This steak is delicious with Rustic Sautéed Onions and Mushrooms (page 164). Serve leftovers cold with Shredded Kale Salad with Pecan Parmesan (page 136) or a green salad with Ranch Dressing (page 252). Thinly sliced, it is also a great protein substitute for the Chicken Fajita Wraps (page 206).

Tips

Cooking steak or burgers in a cast-iron skillet allows you to cook over higher direct heat so the meat quickly develops a delicious brown crust before overcooking. You can also grill them on the barbecue over medium-high heat, with the lid open, or under a preheated broiler with the rack 2 inches (5 cm) from the heat.

You can substitute the fat of your choice for the butter.

Resist the urge to move the meat or press it while it is cooking. Leaving it in one place allows the surface to form a delicious sear.

NUTRIENTS PER SERVING	
Calories	229
Fat	14 g
Carbohydrate	0 g
Fiber	0 g
Protein	26 g

- **Cast-iron skillet (see tip, at left)**

1 lb	grass-fed beef flank steak	500 g
	Sea salt and freshly ground black pepper	
2 tbsp	grass-fed butter	30 mL

1. Score steak in a crisscross pattern on both sides. (This prevents it from curling at the edges and cooking unevenly.) Season both sides with salt and pepper.

2. Heat the cast-iron skillet over medium-high heat. Add butter and swirl until melted. Add steak and cook, turning once, for 3 to 4 minutes per side for medium-rare (depending on the thickness of the meat) or until cooked to desired doneness.

3. Transfer steak to a cutting board, tent it loosely with foil (see tip, opposite) and let rest for 5 minutes so the juices are reincorporated. Slice diagonally against the grain and serve immediately.

> ## Nutrition Tip
>
> For people who don't get a lot of direct sunlight (without sunscreen) and don't regularly eat oily fish, red meat can contribute to overall vitamin D intake. Red meat contains a type of vitamin D called 25-hydroxycholecalciferol, which is assimilated into the body more easily than other dietary forms, such as vitamin D_2.

Marinated Flank Steak

The delicious marinade in this recipe is the perfect accent for the wonderfully rustic flavor of flank steak, complementing it without overpowering it.

Tips

Resist the urge to move the meat around or press on it while it is cooking. Leaving it in one place allows the skillet surface to form a delicious sear. The cooking time depends on the thickness of the steak.

When tenting meat with foil, you are simply trying to keep some of the heat around the meat while it reincorporates the juices. Ideally, you don't want the foil to touch the meat (see page 62), so just fold the foil in the middle to make a tent and place it over the meat. The sides don't need to be sealed shut. You can also place a piece of parchment paper between the meat and the foil, then wrap the meat more tightly to keep in more heat.

- Glass dish large enough for the steak to lie flat
- Cast-iron skillet (see tip, opposite)

2	large cloves garlic, minced	2
1/2 cup	finely chopped red onion	125 mL
1/4 cup	extra virgin olive oil	60 mL
1/4 cup	organic gluten-free tamari or coconut amino acids	60 mL
2 tbsp	red wine vinegar	30 mL
1 lb	grass-fed beef flank steak	500 g

1. In glass dish, combine garlic, onion, oil, tamari and vinegar.

2. Score steak in a crisscross pattern on both sides. (This prevents it from curling at the edges and cooking unevenly.) Place steak in glass dish, turning to coat. Cover and refrigerate for at least 1 hour or up to 4 hours, turning the steak occasionally.

3. Heat the cast-iron skillet over medium-high heat. Remove steak from marinade, discarding marinade, and cook steak, turning once, for 3 to 4 minutes per side for medium-rare (depending on the thickness of the meat) or until cooked to desired doneness.

4. Transfer steak to a cutting board, tent it loosely with foil (see tip, at left) and let rest for 5 minutes so the juices are reincorporated. Slice diagonally against the grain and serve immediately.

Nutrition Tip

Red meat is an important source of zinc in the diet, because other rich sources, such as shellfish and organ meats, are not eaten nearly as often. The form of zinc found in red meat is very bioavailable and is easily used by the body. Zinc is important for our sense of taste and smell, for optimal immune function and for prostate health.

NUTRIENTS PER SERVING	
Calories	169
Fat	7 g
Carbohydrate	0 g
Fiber	0 g
Protein	25 g

Ginger Beef with Broccoli and Shiitakes

Makes 4 servings

The combination of beef and broccoli is a perennial favorite. This version omits the sweeteners but delivers on the delicious classic Asian flavor.

Tip

Slicing raw meat is easier if you place it in the freezer for 5 to 10 minutes first.

- Steamer basket
- Large bowl of ice water

	Juice of 1 orange	
	Juice of 1 lime	
1 tsp	organic gluten-free tamari or coconut amino acids	5 mL
1 tsp	toasted (dark) sesame oil	5 mL
1 lb	broccoli florets	500 g
1 tbsp	coconut oil	15 mL
1/2 cup	thinly sliced green onions (both green and white parts)	125 mL
1 tbsp	minced garlic	15 mL
1 tbsp	minced gingerroot	15 mL
1/4 tsp	hot pepper flakes (optional)	1 mL
1 lb	grass-fed beef flank steak or boneless sirloin steak, cut into thin strips about 3 inches (7.5 cm) long	500 g
4 oz	shiitake mushroom caps (or portobello caps), thinly sliced (about 1 1/2 cups/375 mL)	125 g
1/4 cup	chopped toasted cashews or almonds (see tip, opposite)	60 mL

1. In a small bowl, combine orange juice, lime juice, tamari and sesame oil. Set aside.

2. In a steamer basket set over a pot of boiling water, steam broccoli for about 2 minutes or until slightly softened but still crunchy. Using a slotted spoon, transfer broccoli to the bowl of ice water to stop the cooking. Drain well and set aside.

NUTRIENTS PER SERVING	
Calories	436
Fat	21 g
Carbohydrate	22 g
Fiber	6 g
Protein	44 g

Tip

To toast nuts or seeds, place them in a dry skillet over medium heat and stir occasionally until aromatic (about 2 to 4 minutes, depending on the nut or seed). At this point, reduce the heat to medium-low and cook, stirring constantly to ensure even browning, until nuts or seeds are evenly golden brown (about 2 to 5 minutes, depending on the nut or seed). Transfer to a plate or cutting board to cool. (If you leave them in the pan, they will continue to cook and may burn.)

3. In a large skillet, heat coconut oil over medium-high heat. Add green onions and cook, stirring, for 30 seconds. Add garlic, ginger and hot pepper flakes (if using); cook, stirring, for 30 seconds. Add beef and cook, stirring, for about 2 minutes or until browned on all sides. Add the reserved broccoli and cook, stirring, for 1 minute. Add mushrooms and cook, stirring, for 1 to 2 minutes or until softened. Add orange juice mixture, stirring well. Serve immediately, topped with cashews.

Nutrition Tip

An unusual compound in shiitake mushrooms, called d-Eritadenine (also known as lentinacin or lentsine), has been shown to help lower total blood cholesterol. This cardiovascular benefit is likely augmented by the mushrooms' beta-glucans, which are also known to promote heart health.

Thai Basil Beef

This better-than-takeout dish is also quick and easy — perfect for a weeknight meal. Serve with Fried Cauliflower Rice (page 153).

Tips

Make sure the fish sauce has only three ingredients: fish, salt and water. Steer clear of non-paleo ingredients such as sugar and hydrolyzed wheat protein.

To make slicing raw meat easier, place it in the freezer for about 10 minutes first.

You can use an equal amount of the fat of your choice in place of the coconut oil.

3 tbsp	organic gluten-free tamari or coconut amino acids	45 mL
1 tbsp	fish sauce (see tip, at left)	15 mL
1 tbsp	filtered water	15 mL
1/2 tsp	freshly ground white pepper	2 mL
3 tbsp	coconut oil (approx.), divided	45 mL
1 lb	grass-fed beef flank steak, cut into thin strips	500 g
4	baby bok choy, leaves pulled apart and hearts halved	4
3	cloves garlic, minced	3
1	red bell pepper, cut into thin strips	1
1	yellow bell pepper, cut into thin strips	1
1	large onion, halved and sliced	1
1 1/2 cups	fresh Thai basil leaves	375 mL

1. In a medium bowl, combine tamari, fish sauce, water and pepper. Set aside.

2. In a large skillet, heat 2 tbsp (30 mL) coconut oil over medium heat. Add beef and cook, stirring, for about 5 minutes or until cooked to desired doneness. Transfer beef and any drippings to the bowl with the tamari mixture and stir to combine.

3. Return the skillet to medium heat and melt the remaining coconut oil. Add baby bok choy, garlic, red pepper, yellow pepper and onion; cook, stirring often and adding more coconut oil if needed, for about 8 minutes or until vegetables are softened.

4. Add beef mixture and cook, stirring, for 3 to 4 minutes or until beef is heated through. Turn off heat, add basil and cook, stirring, until basil is wilted.

Nutrition Tip

Eugenol is a compound found in the volatile oils of basil and other herbs. It has been well studied because it can block the activity of the cyclooxygenase (COX) enzyme, which is what many over-the-counter non-steroidal anti-inflammatory drugs (NSAIDs) do. Basil is therefore classified as an anti-inflammatory food that may help with conditions like arthritis.

NUTRIENTS PER SERVING	
Calories	352
Fat	21 g
Carbohydrate	11 g
Fiber	3 g
Protein	29 g

Sweet Potato Shepherd's Pie

Here, a traditional dish gets a modern upgrade with whipped sweet potatoes as the topping. You'll love it.

Tip

Grass-fed beef tends to be a bit leaner than conventionally raised beef, and most grass-fed meat is labelled as lean.

Nutrition Tip

Sweet potatoes are one of the best sources of the antioxidant beta-carotene, which is helpful for fighting free radical damage in the body. Research has shown that eating about 5 g of fat at the same meal will significantly increase your body's uptake of beta-carotene, maximizing its benefits. You'll enjoy maximum absorption with this meal.

NUTRIENTS PER SERVING	
Calories	414
Fat	25 g
Carbohydrate	23 g
Fiber	4 g
Protein	24 g

- **Potato masher or immersion blender**
- **8-inch (20 cm) square glass baking dish**

10 cups	cold filtered water	2.5 L
4	medium sweet potatoes, peeled and roughly chopped	4
2 tbsp	grass-fed butter	30 mL
1½ lbs	ground grass-fed beef	750 g
3	cloves garlic, minced	3
2	stalks celery, finely chopped	2
2	carrots, finely chopped	2
1 cup	finely chopped onion	250 mL
1 tsp	sea salt	5 mL
½ tsp	freshly ground black pepper	2 mL
½ tsp	dried thyme	2 mL
½ tsp	dried oregano	2 mL
1 tbsp	tomato paste	15 mL

1. Pour cold water into a large pot and add sweet potatoes. Bring to a boil over high heat. Reduce heat to medium-high and boil for 10 to 12 minutes or until sweet potatoes are fork-tender. Drain the water from the pot. Add butter and mash potatoes with the potato masher until creamy. Transfer to a large bowl and set aside.

2. Preheat oven to 375°F (190°C).

3. In the same pot, cook beef over medium heat, breaking it up with a spoon, for 7 to 10 minutes or until no longer pink. Using a slotted spoon, transfer beef to another large bowl and set aside. Discard all but 2 tbsp (30 mL) fat from the pot.

4. In the fat remaining in the pot, cook garlic, celery, carrots, onion, salt, pepper, thyme and oregano, stirring occasionally, for 5 minutes. Return beef to the pot, along with any accumulated juices, and add tomato paste, stirring well.

5. Spoon beef mixture into baking dish and spread sweet potato mash evenly on top. Bake for 30 minutes.

Paleo Cabbage Rolls

Nothing says comfort food like cabbage rolls. These make a great family dinner on a chilly or wintery night.

Tips

You can use an equal amount of the fat of your choice in place of the coconut oil.

Grate the cauliflower on the side of your box grater with the largest holes. Cut the cauliflower in half or into quarters first, so it doesn't slip against the grater.

- 13- by 9-inch (33 by 23 cm) casserole or baking dish

Cabbage Rolls

1	large head green or savoy cabbage	1
2 tbsp	coconut oil	30 mL
1	onion, finely chopped	1
2	cloves garlic, minced	2
1½ cups	grated cauliflower (see tip, at left)	375 mL
1 tsp	sea salt	5 mL
½ tsp	freshly ground black pepper	2 mL
1 tbsp	Dijon mustard	15 mL
1½ lbs	ground grass-fed beef	750 g

Sauce

1 tbsp	coconut oil	15 mL
1	small onion, minced	1
1	clove garlic, minced	1
1	can (28 oz/796 mL) crushed tomatoes	1
¼ cup	tomato paste	60 mL
½ tsp	sea salt	2 mL
½ tsp	freshly ground black pepper	2 mL

1. *Cabbage Rolls:* Bring a large pot of water to a boil over high heat. Meanwhile, cut the core out of the cabbage. When the water is boiling, add cabbage and reduce heat to a simmer. As the cabbage leaves soften, peel them off with a spoon and use tongs to remove them from the water, being careful not to rip them in half. Set the leaves on paper towels to dry. The whole process usually takes about 15 minutes. (Alternatively, you can let the whole cabbage simmer for 15 minutes, drain it in a colander, then remove the leaves.)

2. Meanwhile, in a large skillet, heat coconut oil over medium heat. Add onion and cook, stirring, for 3 minutes. Add garlic and cook, stirring, for 1 minute. Add cauliflower and cook, stirring, for 3 minutes or until slightly softened. Transfer cauliflower mixture to a large bowl and let cool slightly. Stir in salt, pepper and mustard.

NUTRIENTS PER SERVING	
Calories	242
Fat	14 g
Carbohydrate	10 g
Fiber	4 g
Protein	19 g

Tip

If there are unused cabbage leaves, slice them thinly and sauté them with a bit of butter or olive oil just before the cabbage rolls are done. You will only need to sauté them for about 5 minutes, as they are already partially cooked. Spread the cooked chopped cabbage on the plates and place the cabbage rolls on top.

Variation

Substitute ground free-range turkey or ground pasture-raised pork for the beef.

3. Preheat oven to 350°F (180°C).

4. *Sauce:* In the same skillet, heat coconut oil over medium heat. Add onion and cook, stirring, for 3 to 4 minutes or until softened. Add garlic and cook, stirring, for 1 minute. Stir in tomatoes, tomato paste, salt and pepper. Reduce heat to low and let simmer while you assemble the cabbage rolls.

5. Add beef to the cauliflower mixture and, using your hands, mix well to incorporate all ingredients.

6. Spoon a thin layer of the sauce into casserole dish.

7. Pat dry any remaining moisture on the cabbage leaves. Lay each leaf rib side down and spoon about $1/3$ cup (75 mL) of the meat mixture onto the base of each leaf. Firmly (but not too tightly) roll the leaf forward, folding in the sides as you go and ending with the seam down. As each roll is finished, place it seam side down in the casserole dish. Once all the rolls are in the dish, pour the remaining sauce over top. Cover the dish loosely with foil.

8. Bake for about 90 minutes or until very tender.

Nutrition Tip

Cabbage is a valuable ally in cardiovascular health. When we eat it, fiber-related nutrients bind with some of the bile acids in our intestines and are escorted out of the body instead of getting reabsorbed. The liver must replace the lost bile by using some of the existing cholesterol, and voila: our cholesterol levels fall. This cholesterol-lowering benefit occurs whether the cabbage is raw or cooked, but may be at its peak when cabbage is steamed.

Sloppy Joes

Makes 4 servings

You'll want to double this comfort food recipe and freeze some for when you are short on time but want something good and hearty. Serve as is or with Portobello Mushroom Cap Buns (page 163) or Roasted Spaghetti Squash Noodles (page 168).

2 tbsp	extra virgin olive oil	30 mL
1	large onion, chopped	1
3	stalks celery, chopped	3
2	bell peppers (any color), chopped	2
1 lb	ground grass-fed beef	500 g
3	cloves garlic, minced	3
1 tsp	chili powder	5 mL
1 tsp	ground cumin	5 mL
½ tsp	sea salt	2 mL
½ tsp	freshly ground black pepper	2 mL
1	can (14 oz/398 mL) diced tomatoes, with juice	1
¼ cup	tomato paste	60 mL
2 tsp	organic gluten-free tamari or coconut amino acids	10 mL

1. In a large skillet, heat oil over medium heat. Add onion and cook, stirring, for 4 minutes. Add celery and bell peppers; cook, stirring, for 4 minutes. Add beef, garlic, chili powder, cumin, salt and pepper; cook, breaking beef up with a spoon, for 8 to 10 minutes or until beef is no longer pink.

2. Stir in tomatoes, tomato paste and tamari; bring to a simmer. Reduce heat to medium-low and simmer, stirring occasionally, for 10 to 15 minutes or until thickened. (Add a splash of water to the pan if it gets too dry.)

Nutrition Tip

A 2006 study published in *The American Journal of Clinical Nutrition* showed that the amount of insulin required to lower blood sugar after a meal is reduced when the meal contains chili powder. You may want to add chili powder to your food more often, because the study also determined that when chili-containing meals are a regular occurrence, insulin drops even lower.

NUTRIENTS PER SERVING	
Calories	391
Fat	23 g
Carbohydrate	18 g
Fiber	4 g
Protein	28 g

Taco Salad

Makes 4 servings

Who doesn't love a good taco salad? This version gives you a tasty protein and a whole bunch of vegetables without the trans fats and additives in the commercial shells. For an even faster meal, chop up leftover Flattened Roast Chicken (page 198) or Skillet-Grilled Flank Steak (page 222) to use in place of the ground beef.

Variations

Substitute ground free-range turkey for the beef.

Try using ½ cup (125 mL) Classic Guacamole (page 247) in place of the avocados.

If you have cooked chicken or steak on hand, cut it into ¼-inch (0.5 cm) thick slices or chop it into bite-size pieces. Add to the skillet at the end of step 1 and cook, stirring, for 3 to 5 minutes or until heated through.

NUTRIENTS PER SERVING	
Calories	460
Fat	31 g
Carbohydrate	26 g
Fiber	16 g
Protein	33 g

1 lb	ground grass-fed beef	500 g
2	cloves garlic, minced	2
1	onion, finely chopped	1
	Sea salt and freshly ground black pepper	
2 tbsp	chili powder	30 mL
2 tsp	ground cumin	10 mL
1 tsp	dried oregano	5 mL
¼ tsp	cayenne pepper (optional)	1 mL
1 tbsp	tomato paste (optional)	15 mL
2	romaine hearts, chopped	2
2	avocados, sliced or chopped	2
3 cups	cherry or grape tomatoes, halved	750 mL
½ cup	Fresh Tomato Salsa (page 240)	125 mL
⅓ cup	chopped fresh cilantro	75 mL
	Lime wedges (optional)	

1. In a large skillet over medium heat, cook beef, breaking it up with a spoon, until starting to brown. Add garlic and onion; cook, stirring, for 5 minutes or until onion is translucent. Season with salt and black pepper. Stir in chili powder, cumin, oregano, cayenne (if using) and tomato paste (if using); cook, stirring, for 2 to 3 minutes or until beef is no longer pink.

2. Divide romaine hearts among serving plates and top with beef mixture, avocados, tomatoes and salsa. Sprinkle with cilantro and, if desired, squeeze lime juice over top.

Nutrition Tip

Taco shells are just one of many places where man-made trans fats hide. These fats are known to raise LDL cholesterol and lower HDL cholesterol, increase triglycerides and promote systemic inflammation. Even if the nutrition panel indicates zero trans fats, be sure to check the ingredient list. If hydrogenated or partially hydrogenated vegetable oils or shortenings are listed, the product contains commercial trans fats and should not be consumed.

Spaghetti Squash Bolognese

When you really feel like spaghetti, dive into this low-carb version. You will be hard-pressed to tell the difference from wheat pasta, and your blood sugar will be happy.

Tip

If you don't have fresh parsley and basil on hand, you can use 2 tbsp (30 mL) dried parsley and 1 tbsp (15 mL) dried basil in their place. Omit the parsley garnish.

• **Preheat oven to 400°F (200°C)**

1	large spaghetti squash (about 6 lbs/3 kg), halved lengthwise and seeded	1
1 tbsp	extra virgin olive oil or avocado oil	15 mL
	Sea salt and freshly ground black pepper	
1 lb	ground grass-fed beef	500 g
4	slices pasture-raised bacon or turkey bacon, chopped (optional)	4
1	large onion, finely chopped (about 1½ cups/375 mL)	1
3	cloves garlic, minced	3
3	medium carrots, diced (about 1½ cups/375 mL)	3
2	stalks celery, diced (about 1 cup/250 mL)	2
1 cup	sliced mushrooms	250 mL
1 tbsp	dried oregano	15 mL
¼ tsp	ground cinnamon	1 mL
¼ cup	chopped fresh parsley	60 mL
2 tbsp	chopped fresh basil	30 mL
1	can (28 oz/796 mL) crushed tomatoes	1
1	can (14 oz/398 mL) diced tomatoes, drained and juice reserved	1
	Additional chopped fresh parsley	

1. Place squash, cut side up, on a baking sheet. Brush cut sides of squash with oil and season with salt and pepper. Roast in preheated oven for 45 to 55 minutes or until squash can be easily pierced with a fork.

2. Meanwhile, in a large Dutch oven over medium heat, cook beef and bacon (if using), breaking beef up with a spoon, for 5 to 7 minutes or until beef is no longer pink and bacon is crisp. Using a slotted spoon, transfer meat to a bowl and set aside. Pour off all but 2 tbsp (30 mL) fat from the pot.

NUTRIENTS PER SERVING	
Calories	403
Fat	17 g
Carbohydrate	43 g
Fiber	12 g
Protein	12 g

Tip

When you are cleaning mushrooms, remember that water can make them soggy and rubbery. Use a damp paper towel or a soft brush to gently wipe any clumps of dirt off the mushrooms before use.

3. Add onion to the fat remaining in the pot and cook, stirring occasionally, for 5 minutes. Add garlic, carrots, celery, mushrooms, oregano and cinnamon; cook, stirring, for 3 minutes. Add parsley and basil; cook, stirring, for 2 minutes.

4. Stir in crushed tomatoes and diced tomatoes. Return beef and bacon (if using) to the pot, along with any accumulated juices, stirring well to combine; bring to a boil. Reduce heat and simmer, stirring occasionally, for 30 to 40 minutes to allow the deep tomato flavor to develop. Add reserved tomato juice as needed if the sauce gets too thick. Season to taste with salt and pepper.

5. Using a fork, scrape out the squash flesh into spaghetti-like strands. Divide among serving plates and top with Bolognese sauce. Sprinkle with additional parsley.

Nutrition Tip

One cup (250 mL) of cooked spaghetti squash has about 10 g of carbohydrates; 1 cup of cooked spaghetti made from wheat flour has about 35 g. And when you are having spaghetti, who eats just 1 cup? There are also wonderful nutrients like beta-carotene and lutein in spaghetti squash, but the biggest benefit for blood sugar management is the low carb count. Now you can have your spaghetti (squash) and eat it too.

Classic Skillet Burgers

Nothing hits the spot quite like a good burger, especially when it is spiced to perfection and keeps your blood sugar balanced. Serve with Portobello Mushroom Cap Buns (page 163), sliced tomatoes and pickles and a dollop of The Best Paleo Mayo (page 249).

Tips

You can substitute the fat of your choice for the bacon fat.

Use a light touch when handling ground meat. Overhandling can make the patties dense and tough.

Pressing a dimple into the middle of each patty helps prevent the meat from shrinking too much and forming a dense ball of cooked meat.

Resist the urge to move the meat around or press on it while it is cooking. Leaving it in one place allows the skillet surface to form a delicious sear.

- **Large cast-iron skillet (see tip, page 222)**

1 lb	ground grass-fed beef	500 g
	Sea salt and freshly ground black pepper	
1 tsp	Barbecue Spice Blend (page 260) (optional)	5 mL
1 tbsp	bacon fat	15 mL

1. Gently shape beef into 4 even patties, no more than 1 inch (2.5 cm) thick. Using two fingers, press a shallow dimple into the middle of each patty. Season both sides of each patty with salt, pepper and Barbecue Spice Blend (if using).

2. In the cast-iron skillet, melt bacon fat over medium-high heat. Add patties, in batches as necessary to avoid crowding them, and cook, turning once, for 4 to 6 minutes per side or until patties are no longer pink inside and an instant-read thermometer inserted horizontally in the center of a patty registers 165°F (74°C). Transfer burgers to a plate, tent with foil (see tip, page 223) and let stand for 5 minutes.

Nutrition Tip

Grass-fed beef is often higher in B vitamins, vitamin E, vitamin K, selenium, magnesium and beta-carotene (look for the yellow- to orange-tinged fat) than conventionally raised beef. This is because these cows eat a multitude of grasses, clovers, rushes and even some shrubs. Compare that to the less varied, predominantly grain diet of the conventionally raised cow, and it's no wonder the grass-fed meat is higher in micronutrients.

NUTRIENTS PER PATTY	
Calories	277
Fat	19 g
Carbohydrate	0 g
Fiber	0 g
Protein	24 g

Classic Rack of Lamb

No need to save this dish for a special occasion. Rack of lamb is quick and easy, and leftover chops can be easily heated up in a skillet and enjoyed again at another meal.

Tips

If you don't have fresh parsley or rosemary on hand, you can use 1 tbsp (15 mL) dried parsley and 1 tsp (5 mL) crushed dried rosemary in their place.

"Frenching" refers to the removal of the meat, fat and membranes from the tips of the rib bones, for the classic presentation of a roasted rack of lamb. Ask your butcher to do this for you if the rack of lamb is not already frenched.

Covering the ends of the bones with foil prevents them from burning and breaking, making for a nicer presentation of the cooked rack.

- Preheat oven to 450°F (230°C)
- Shallow roasting pan or rimmed baking sheet, lined with parchment paper

1	small clove garlic, minced	1
2 tbsp	minced fresh flat-leaf (Italian) parsley	30 mL
2 tsp	minced fresh rosemary	10 mL
½ tsp	sea salt	2 mL
2 tbsp	Dijon mustard (smooth or grainy)	30 mL
1 lb	rack grass-fed lamb (6 to 8 ribs), frenched (see tip, at left)	500 g

1. In a small bowl, combine garlic, parsley, rosemary, salt and mustard. Rub lamb all over with mustard mixture. Cover the ends of the bones with foil and place lamb, with ribs curving down, in prepared roasting pan.

2. Roast in preheated oven for 25 to 30 minutes for medium-rare or until cooked to desired doneness. Remove from oven, leaving the lamb in the pan, tent with foil (see tip, page 223) and let rest for 10 to 15 minutes, then cut into individual chops.

Variation

To prepare this recipe on the stovetop, cut the rack of lamb into individual chops. Coat each chop with mustard mixture and cook in a large skillet over medium-high heat, turning once, for 3 to 4 minutes per side or until cooked to desired doneness.

Nutrition Tip

Grass-fed lambs have a fat content about 15% lower than conventionally raised lambs. In addition, grass-fed meat has been shown to have at least 25% more omega-3 fatty acids than meat that is conventionally raised, resulting in a much more nutritious overall fat profile.

NUTRIENTS PER SERVING	
Calories	198
Fat	12 g
Carbohydrate	1 g
Fiber	0 g
Protein	23 g

Skillet–Grilled Lamb with Avocado Mint Sauce

You'll think you've been transported to the Mediterranean with this delicious family-friendly dish. The Avocado Mint Sauce adds a wonderful richness with the freshness of mint.

Tips

This lamb is best when cooked in a cast-iron skillet to keep it juicy, but you can also grill it on the barbecue as kebabs. If you are using wooden skewers for kebabs, soak them in water for at least 30 minutes before grilling.

The grilled lamb is great served in lettuce boats with chopped grape tomatoes and drizzled with the Avocado Mint Sauce.

$\frac{1}{2}$ tsp	dried oregano	2 mL
$\frac{1}{2}$ tsp	dried basil	2 mL
3 tbsp	extra virgin olive oil, divided	45 mL
2 tbsp	freshly squeezed lemon juice	30 mL
	Sea salt and freshly ground black pepper	
1 lb	boneless pasture-raised lamb loin or leg, cut into 1½-inch (4 cm) chunks	500 g
1 cup	Avocado Mint Sauce (page 246)	250 mL

1. In a large bowl, combine oregano, basil, 2 tbsp (30 mL) oil and lemon juice. Season to taste with salt and pepper. Add lamb chunks and toss to coat well. Cover and refrigerate for at least 1 hour or overnight.

2. In a large skillet (preferably cast-iron), heat the remaining oil over medium-high heat. Remove lamb from marinade, discarding marinade, and add lamb to the skillet. Cook, stirring often, for 8 to 10 minutes or until browned on all sides and cooked to desired doneness. Serve drizzled with Avocado Mint Sauce.

Nutrition Tip

As a rule, we want to stay as far away from trans fats as possible, but conjugated linoleic acid (CLA) is an exception. CLA naturally occurs in lamb, and studies show that this type of trans fat is associated with improved blood sugar regulation, maintenance of muscle mass and improved immune function. Be sure to look for grass-fed lamb, as it has nearly twice as much CLA as conventionally raised lamb.

NUTRIENTS PER SERVING	
Calories	323
Fat	19 g
Carbohydrate	5 g
Fiber	2 g
Protein	24 g

Sauces, Dressings and Spice Blends

Thai Almond Sauce

**Makes about
³/₄ cup (175 mL)**

This sauce is great
with both cooked and
raw vegetables, and
as a dressing for Thai
Zucchini Noodle Salad
(page 133).

Tip

Look for almond butter
that is made with roasted
almonds; it has a richer and
nuttier flavor that adds to
the overall deliciousness of
the sauce.

1	clove garlic, minced	1
½ tsp	hot pepper flakes	2 mL
½ cup	almond butter (see tip, at left)	125 mL
½ cup	full-fat coconut milk	125 mL
1 tbsp	organic gluten-free tamari or coconut amino acids	15 mL
½ tsp	unseasoned rice vinegar or apple cider vinegar	2 mL
	Juice of 1 lime	

1. In a small bowl, thoroughly whisk together garlic, hot pepper flakes, almond butter, coconut milk, tamari, vinegar and lime juice.

2. Store in an airtight glass container in the refrigerator for up to 3 days.

Nutrition Tip

When you can, eat your almonds with the skin on. A team of researchers at the Antioxidant Research Laboratory at Tufts University found that the unique combination of antioxidant flavonoids found in almond skins increased the vitamin E and flavonoid levels in the body. Both vitamin E and flavonoids are antioxidants that may help reduce the oxidation of fats in the bloodstream, which, in turn, has a positive impact on heart health.

NUTRIENTS PER 1 TBSP (15 ML)	
Calories	85
Fat	8 g
Carbohydrate	3 g
Fiber	1 g
Protein	3 g

Basic Marinara Sauce

Makes about 3 cups (750 mL)

Homemade marinara sauce is so much better than any commercial sauce, and almost as fast. It is delicious with Roasted Spaghetti Squash Noodles (page 168) and New Classic Meatballs (page 220), and is also a flavorful accompaniment for chicken or fish.

Tip

Making this marinara sauce in a skillet rather than a saucepan allows for a greater surface area for the evaporation of the water from the tomatoes. As a result, the tomato flavor becomes richer and more intense, for a more delicious sauce.

1	can (28 oz/796 mL) whole tomatoes, with juice	1
1 cup	filtered water	250 mL
3 tbsp	extra virgin olive oil	45 mL
1 cup	chopped onion	250 mL
5	cloves garlic, minced	5
1 tsp	sea salt	5 mL
¼ tsp	freshly ground black pepper	1 mL
Pinch	hot pepper flakes	Pinch
1 tbsp	chopped fresh parsley	15 mL
1 tbsp	chopped fresh basil	15 mL

1. Pour tomatoes into a large bowl and crush them with your hands. Pour 1 cup (250 mL) water into the can, rinse all the tomato bits out and reserve the tomato water.

2. In a large skillet (see tip, at left), heat oil over medium heat. Add onion and cook, stirring, for 4 minutes. Add garlic and cook, stirring, for 1 minute.

3. Stir in crushed tomatoes, tomato water, salt, black pepper and hot pepper flakes; bring to a boil over medium-high heat. Reduce heat and simmer, stirring occasionally, for about 15 minutes or until sauce has thickened. Stir in parsley and basil just before serving.

Nutrition Tip

The second ingredient listed on one of the big-name brands of tomato sauce is sugar, right after concentrated tomatoes. You can't tell exactly how much added sugar there is, because labels are not yet required to tell us what is added and what is naturally occurring. The label goes on to say that the product contains 78% concentrated tomatoes, which means 12% is *not* tomatoes. Going back to the ingredient list, after concentrated tomatoes and sugar, all that is listed are salt, citric acid and natural flavors, so it stands to reason that a lot of the 12% is added sugar. By the time you read and decode the underlying meaning of most labels, you could have made your own, and you would know exactly what is in it.

NUTRIENTS PER ½ CUP (125 mL)	
Calories	96
Fat	7 g
Carbohydrate	8 g
Fiber	3 g
Protein	1 g

Fresh Tomato Salsa

This bright, fresh salsa is fantastic with cold salmon, shrimp or sliced chicken. It is also a zesty accompaniment for scrambled eggs and the Basic Vegetable Frittata (page 175).

Tip

Leave the seeds and ribs in the jalapeño pepper if you like more heat in your salsa.

Variation

Add 1 chopped small mango for a delicious sweet twist.

4	plum (Roma) tomatoes, diced	4
1	small jalapeño pepper, seeded and minced (see tip, at left)	1
1	clove garlic, minced	1
½	small red onion, finely chopped	½
¼ cup	chopped fresh cilantro	60 mL
¼ tsp	ground cumin	1 mL
1 tbsp	freshly squeezed lime juice	15 mL
	Sea salt	

1. In a medium bowl, combine tomatoes, jalapeño, garlic, red onion, cilantro, cumin and lime juice. Season to taste with salt.

2. Store in an airtight glass container in the refrigerator for up to 3 days.

Nutrition Tip

The substance that gives jalapeño peppers their characteristic heat is called capsaicin. Capsaicin has been successfully studied for the treatment of pain associated with arthritis and diabetic neuropathy. Capsaicin inhibits the nerve-signaling molecule called substance P, which is associated with the inflammatory process.

NUTRIENTS PER ¼ CUP (60 ML)	
Calories	12
Fat	0 g
Carbohydrate	3 g
Fiber	1 g
Protein	0 g

Roasted Salsa

**Makes about 2 cups
(500 mL)**

Roasting the vegetables
first takes this favorite
condiment to a whole
new level. The taste is
rich and full — a real
crowd-pleaser. This
salsa is good both
warm and cold.

Tips

Leave the root end intact on
the onion when cutting it,
to keep the pieces together.
This allows some parts
of the onion to become
browned and crisp while
leaving other parts soft.
Both textures and tastes
add depth to the salsa.

Leave the seeds and ribs in
the jalapeño pepper if you
like more heat in your salsa.

- Preheat broiler, with rack set 4 inches (10 cm) from the heat source
- Baking dish or rimmed baking sheet, lined with parchment paper

12	plum (Roma) tomatoes, cut in half lengthwise, cored and seeded	12
2	large cloves garlic, peeled	2
1	large onion, cut into wedges (see tip, at left)	1
1	jalapeño pepper, halved and seeded	1
2 tbsp	extra virgin olive oil	30 mL
1/4 cup	chopped fresh cilantro	60 mL
1 tsp	ground cumin	5 mL
1/4 tsp	sea salt	1 mL
3 tbsp	freshly squeezed lime juice	45 mL

1. In prepared baking dish, combine tomatoes, garlic, onion and jalapeño. Drizzle with oil and toss well, making sure all vegetables are coated. Spread vegetables in a single layer so they char nicely.

2. Broil for 5 to 8 minutes, checking often so they don't burn, until vegetables are charred. Transfer the baking dish to a wire rack and let cool slightly or completely.

3. Coarsely chop vegetables. Transfer to a medium bowl and stir in cilantro, cumin, salt and lime juice.

4. Serve immediately or store in an airtight glass container in the refrigerator for up to 3 days.

Nutrition Tip

Tomatoes contain antioxidants in abundance, including vitamin C, beta-carotene, manganese and vitamin E. They are also near the top of the charts for lycopene, which is beneficial for heart and bone health. It turns out that it is not just red tomatoes that contain lycopene, but orange and tangerine-colored ones, too. The lycopene is better absorbed by the body when the tomatoes are cooked with a little oil, as in this recipe. All of the different types of tomatoes have their own special blend of antioxidants and nutrients, so try lots of different types with this salsa — they will all be delicious.

NUTRIENTS PER 1/4 CUP (60 ML)	
Calories	58
Fat	4 g
Carbohydrate	7 g
Fiber	2 g
Protein	1 g

Avocado and Papaya Salsa

**Makes about
2 cups (500 mL)**

This salsa is perfect with the Pumpkin Seed–Crusted Rainbow Trout (page 190) but also pairs nicely with any chicken or fish dish. Even though it's called a salsa, you will want to use it as a full-sized side.

Variation

Substitute mango for the papaya, and use pomegranate seeds in place of the red pepper.

1 cup	diced papaya	250 mL
1 cup	diced avocado	250 mL
1/4 cup	finely chopped red bell pepper	60 mL
3 tbsp	minced fresh cilantro	45 mL
2 tbsp	minced red onion (optional)	30 mL
1/4 tsp	sea salt	1 mL
1/4 tsp	cayenne pepper (optional)	1 mL
2 tbsp	freshly squeezed lime juice	30 mL
1 tbsp	extra virgin olive oil	15 mL

1. In a large bowl, combine papaya, avocado, red pepper, cilantro, onion (if using), salt, cayenne (if using), lime juice and oil, stirring gently so you don't mash the avocado or papaya.

2. Store in an airtight glass container in the refrigerator for up to 2 days.

Nutrition Tip

Papaya contains a unique protein-digesting enzyme called papain, which has been used for hundreds of years as a meat tenderizer in South America. Papain has been formulated into digestive aids and formulas used to treat inflammation. Papayas are an excellent source of vitamin C, carotenes and flavonoids — all antioxidants that promote the health of the cardiovascular system.

NUTRIENTS PER 1/2 CUP (125 ML)	
Calories	110
Fat	9 g
Carbohydrate	8 g
Fiber	3 g
Protein	1 g

Summer Salsa

The color of this salsa is like a fiesta in a bowl!

Tip

Even though this recipe is called a salsa, don't use it like a condiment. Instead of serving a lettuce salad with your protein, live it up a bit and serve this salsa that eats like a salad instead!

2	green onions, sliced on the diagonal	2
1 cup	firm blueberries	250 mL
1 cup	chopped pineapple (in pieces the size of the blueberries)	250 mL
1 cup	grape tomatoes, halved or quartered, depending on size	250 mL
¼ cup	minced fresh basil	60 mL
2 tbsp	minced fresh cilantro or parsley	30 mL
1	avocado, diced (to the same size as the blueberries)	1
	Juice of 1 lime	
	Sea salt	

1. In a large bowl, gently stir together green onions, blueberries, pineapple, tomatoes, basil and cilantro. Stir in avocado last so it doesn't get mushy. Drizzle with lime juice and season to taste with salt.

2. Store in an airtight glass container in the refrigerator for up to 2 days.

Nutrition Tip

Blueberries, especially wild ones, are well known for their high antioxidant levels. It's the anthocyanins that give the berries their wonderfully deep shades of blue, purple and red, but there are many other phytonutrients that also exert protection against oxidative stress. Although moderate on the glycemic scale, blueberries have a good amount of fiber, which helps them act like a lower-glycemic fruit in terms of blood sugar control.

NUTRIENTS PER ½ CUP (125 ML)	
Calories	63
Fat	4 g
Carbohydrate	8 g
Fiber	3 g
Protein	1 g

Spinach Hemp Pesto

**Makes about
2 cups (500 mL)**

This pesto is perfect for
tossing with Zucchini
Noodles (page 167),
Roasted Spaghetti
Squash Noodles
(page 168) or fish,
chicken, shrimp or eggs.

Tip

This pesto is so delicious
with so many things, it's
nice to have it on hand
all the time. Freeze any
leftovers in an ice cube
tray. Once frozen, store the
cubes in a freezer bag in the
freezer. This makes it easy
to thaw 1 or 2 cubes at a
time to dollop on chicken
or fish.

- **Food processor**

2	cloves garlic, roughly chopped	2
5 cups	baby spinach	1.25 L
1/2 cup	hemp seeds	125 mL
1/4 cup	nutritional yeast	60 mL
1/2 tsp	sea salt	2 mL
1/2 cup	extra virgin olive oil	125 mL
	Filtered water (optional)	

1. In food processor, combine garlic, spinach, hemp seeds,
   nutritional yeast and salt; process until a paste forms.
   With the motor running, through the feed tub, gradually
   drizzle in oil and process until creamy. If a thinner
   consistency is desired, add filtered water 1 tsp (5 mL)
   at a time until the desired consistency is reached.

2. Store in an airtight glass container in the refrigerator for
   up to 3 days or in the freezer for up to 1 month (see tip,
   at left).

Nutrition Tip

Eating hemp seeds will not cause a psychotropic
reaction, but will provide significant health benefits!
Hemp seeds are tiny powerhouses of nutrients. They
provide an anti-inflammatory 3:1 ratio of omega-
3:omega-6 fats, and they are high in gamma linoleic
acid (GLA), a fat that helps balance hormones. All of
the essential amino acids are present in hemp seeds,
making them a great plant-based source of protein.
They are also an excellent source of the relaxant
mineral magnesium.

NUTRIENTS PER 1/4 CUP (60 ML)	
Calories	186
Fat	5 g
Carbohydrate	16 g
Fiber	1 g
Protein	5 g

Creamy Avocado Pesto

Makes about 2¼ cups (550 mL)

Pesto is a wonderfully versatile sauce, and this version is no exception. This recipe makes a lot, so use any leftovers as a spread for Smoked Salmon Nori Rolls (page 188), Jerk Chicken Kebabs (page 202) or Classic Turkey Burgers (page 215).

Tip

To toast nuts or seeds, place them in a dry skillet over medium heat and stir occasionally until aromatic (about 2 to 4 minutes, depending on the nut or seed). At this point, reduce the heat to medium-low and cook, stirring constantly to ensure even browning, until nuts or seeds are evenly golden brown (about 2 to 5 minutes, depending on the nut or seed). Transfer to a plate or cutting board to cool. (If you leave them in the pan, they will continue to cook and may burn.)

NUTRIENTS PER 1 TBSP (15 ML)	
Calories	40
Fat	4 g
Carbohydrate	6 g
Fiber	3 g
Protein	3 g

- **Blender or food processor**

3	avocados, chopped	3
2	cloves garlic, chopped	2
½ cup	fresh basil leaves	125 mL
½ cup	pine nuts, toasted (see tip, at left)	125 mL
½ tsp	sea salt	2 mL
3 tbsp	freshly squeezed lemon juice	45 mL
	Filtered water (optional)	

1. In blender, combine avocados, garlic, basil, pine nuts, salt and lemon juice; blend until smooth and creamy, scraping down the sides of the blender as necessary. If a thinner consistency is desired, add filtered water 1 tsp (5 mL) at a time until the desired consistency is reached.

2. Store in an airtight glass container in the refrigerator for up to 2 days.

Nutrition Tip

Basil is a rich source of carotenoids, including beta-carotene, which can be converted to vitamin A in the liver to meet the body's needs. Beta-carotene is a powerful antioxidant that helps protect free radicals from oxidizing cholesterol in the blood. It is only after cholesterol is oxidized that the process of atherosclerosis begins, creating a buildup of cholesterol in the blood vessel walls.

Avocado Mint Sauce

Reminiscent of tzatziki, this sauce adds a delicious creamy coolness to grilled lamb.

Tips

You can process the sauce for longer or shorter depending on whether you want a smooth, creamy sauce or one that is coarser.

You may want to double the batch because this sauce makes a great dip for cut vegetables or a rich dressing for salads. Thin it out with more water if using it as a dressing.

- **Food processor or blender**

1	large ripe avocado	1
1	small clove garlic, minced	1
½ cup	chopped cucumber	125 mL
½ cup	tightly packed fresh flat-leaf (Italian) parsley leaves	125 mL
½ cup	tightly packed fresh mint leaves	125 mL
¼ tsp	sea salt	1 mL
3 tbsp	freshly squeezed lemon juice	45 mL
2 tbsp	extra virgin olive oil	30 mL
1 tbsp	filtered water (approx.)	15 mL

1. In food processor, combine avocado, garlic, cucumber, parsley, mint, salt, lemon juice, oil and water; process until well blended (see tip, at left). If a thinner sauce is desired, add more water as needed and process until blended.

2. Store in an airtight glass container in the refrigerator for up to 2 days.

Nutrition Tip

As with many herbs, the essential oil of mint has been shown to have antibacterial properties against various bacteria, including *Helicobacter pylori*, *Salmonella enteritidis* and *Escherichia coli 0157:H7*. It has also been shown to inhibit some types of fungi.

NUTRIENTS PER 1 TBSP (15 ML)	
Calories	20
Fat	1 g
Carbohydrate	1 g
Fiber	1 g
Protein	0 g

Classic Guacamole

Makes about 2½ cups (625 mL)

Some people like their guacamole really creamy, and others like it chunky. If your avocados are very ripe, you will end up with a much creamier guacamole. Serve with Belgian endive spears, rounds of cucumber or the crispy Seed Crackers (page 269) for a nice crunch.

2	ripe avocados, finely diced	2
¼ cup	minced sweet onion	60 mL
3 tbsp	minced fresh cilantro	45 mL
¼ tsp	sea salt (approx.)	1 mL
1 tbsp	freshly squeezed lime juice (approx.)	15 mL

1. In a medium bowl, combine avocados, onion, cilantro, salt and lime juice. Mash avocados with a fork until the guacamole reaches the desired consistency. Taste and adjust seasoning with salt or lime juice as desired.

2. Store in an airtight glass container in the refrigerator for up to 2 days.

Nutrition Tip

Avocados are definitely a high-fat food, there's no denying that, but the composition of the fat — over 65% monounsaturated fats, plus phytosterols — puts this food in a unique category. These fats provide anti-inflammatory benefits to the whole body, including the cardiovascular system. The cumulative benefits of eating avocados comes from eating them multiple times per week, which is not a problem when you use the recipes in this book!

NUTRIENTS PER ¼ CUP (60 ML)	
Calories	66
Fat	9 g
Carbohydrate	4 g
Fiber	3 g
Protein	1 g

Zucchini Wasabi Spread

Makes about 1 cup (250 mL)

This fresh and zesty spread is a perfect pairing with the Smoked Salmon Nori Rolls (page 188) or our crunchy Seed Crackers (page 269). It also makes a good dip for cucumber rounds, celery sticks and asparagus spears.

Tip

You can use 1 tsp (5 mL) or more wasabi powder mixed with an equal amount of filtered water instead of the wasabi paste.

Variation

Substitute 2 tsp (10 mL) grated gingerroot or fresh horseradish for the wasabi powder and water mixture.

- **Blender or food processor**

1 cup	finely chopped zucchini	250 mL
1 tbsp	chopped fresh cilantro or parsley	15 mL
½ tsp	sea salt (approx.)	2 mL
3 tbsp	extra virgin olive oil	45 mL
2 tbsp	freshly squeezed lime juice (approx.)	30 mL
1 tsp	wasabi paste (approx.)	5 mL

1. In blender, combine zucchini, cilantro, salt, oil, lime juice and wasabi paste; blend until smooth. Taste and adjust seasoning with salt, lime juice and wasabi paste as desired.

2. Store in an airtight glass container in the refrigerator for up to 3 days.

Nutrition Tip

Most of the wasabi pastes available commercially and in restaurants are a mixture of horseradish and Chinese mustard, likely because true wasabi root is very expensive. The glucosinolates in both horseradish and wasabi are responsible for the characteristic hot taste. When ingested, glucosinolates are broken down into isothiocyanates and indoles, which are potent anticancer compounds.

NUTRIENTS PER 1 TBSP (15 ML)	
Calories	27
Fat	3 g
Carbohydrate	1 g
Fiber	0 g
Protein	0 g

The Best Paleo Mayo

Makes about 1¼ cups (300 mL)

You'll never realize just how good mayonnaise can be until you make your own. When it comes to making mayonnaise, the immersion blender is a game-changer. It works every time.

Tips

Do not use extra virgin olive oil for this recipe; its flavor will be too strong for the mayo.

Use the blending container the immersion container came with, or use a tall glass jar with an opening big enough to fit the blender, such as a wide-mouth mason jar.

Make The Best Paleo Mayo every week and use bits of it all week for The Best Tartar Sauce (page 250), Ranch Dressing (page 252), Green Goddess Dressing (page 253) and Caesar Dressing (page 254).

- **Immersion blender**

1	large free-range egg	1
2 tbsp	freshly squeezed lemon juice	30 mL
1 tsp	Dijon mustard	5 mL
½ tsp	sea salt	2 mL
1 cup	light-tasting olive oil (see tip, at left)	250 mL

1. Place egg, lemon juice, mustard and salt in a tall container (see tip, at left). Place oil in a measuring cup with a spout for easy pouring.

2. Place the head of the immersion blender at the bottom of the container before turning it on. Blend, holding it to the bottom, for about 15 seconds. Slowly pour in oil in a steady stream. The emulsion will start to form in about 1 minute as you add the oil. Keep pouring the oil, moving the blender slowly up and down through the mixture as the emulsion forms. The whole process should take about 2 to 3 minutes.

3. Store in an airtight glass container in the refrigerator for up to 5 days.

Variations

Chive Mayo: Add 2 tbsp (30 mL) chopped fresh chives to the finished mayo and pulse a few times to blend.

Mustard Mayo: Stir an additional 1 to 2 tbsp (15 to 30 mL) Dijon or grainy mustard into the finished mayo.

Roasted Garlic Mayo: Add 1 tbsp (15 mL) puréed roasted garlic to the finished mayo and pulse a few times to blend.

Hot Mayo: Add 1 to 3 tsp (5 to 15 mL) of your favorite hot pepper sauce to the finished mayo and pulse a few times to blend.

NUTRIENTS PER 1 TBSP (15 ML)	
Calories	100
Fat	11 g
Carbohydrate	0 g
Fiber	0 g
Protein	0 g

Nutrition Tip

Commercial mayo is made with the inflammatory industrial seed oils, like canola oil, that we are trying to eliminate from our diets. These oils have been bleached, defoamed and deodorized, and contain very little, if any, of the phytonutrients present in the original oil. Commercial mayo also contains sugar — not a lot, but certainly more than needs to be there.

The Best Tartar Sauce

Once you taste how
rich and creamy The
Best Paleo Mayo is,
you'll never want to go
back to the commercial
stuff. It just gets better
when you make it into
tartar sauce.

Tip

If you don't have fresh dill
on hand, you can use $\frac{1}{2}$ tsp
(2 mL) dried dillweed in
its place.

1 tbsp	minced onion (yellow or red)	15 mL
1 tbsp	minced drained capers	15 mL
1½ tsp	minced fresh dill	7 mL
¼ tsp	sea salt	1 mL
¼ tsp	garlic powder	1 mL
1 cup	The Best Paleo Mayo (page 249)	250 mL
2 tsp	freshly squeezed lemon juice	10 mL

1. In a small bowl, combine onion, capers, dill, salt, garlic
   powder, mayo and lemon juice.

2. Store in an airtight glass container in the refrigerator
   for up to 4 days.

Nutrition Tip

Making your own tartar sauce means you know
what you are eating. There are 21 ingredients in one
big-name brand of tartar sauce, including high-
fructose corn syrup, modified cornstarch, "natural
flavor" and nanoparticles of titanium dioxide. There
are 9 ingredients in The Best Tartar Sauce, and none
of them are nanoparticles.

NUTRIENTS PER 1 TBSP (15 ML)	
Calories	125
Fat	14 g
Carbohydrate	0 g
Fiber	0 g
Protein	0 g

Easy Hollandaise

Makes about 1 cup (250 mL)

Hollandaise doesn't store well in the fridge, so we recommend making it fresh each time. It is so easy and delicious, you'll want to.

Tips

If your butter gets too hot in step 1, it could curdle the sauce. Make sure to melt it over medium-low heat so it doesn't bubble.

An immersion blender is the easiest way to make this sauce. Use the blending container it comes with or a tall glass jar with an opening big enough to fit the blender, such as a wide-mouth mason jar.

If you don't have an immersion blender, you can use a regular blender or a food processor to make the sauce. Drizzle in the warm butter through the feed tube.

Keeping the hollandaise warm over direct heat may cause it to split, so keep it warm indirectly in a glass jar set in a pan of hot water.

NUTRIENTS PER 1 TBSP (15 ML)	
Calories	84
Fat	9 g
Carbohydrate	0 g
Fiber	0 g
Protein	0 g

- **Immersion blender (see tip, at left)**

¾ cup	grass-fed butter	175 mL
2	large free-range egg yolks	2
1 tbsp	freshly squeezed lemon juice	15 mL
¼ tsp	cayenne pepper (optional)	1 mL
1 tbsp	warm water (if needed)	15 mL

1. In a small saucepan, melt butter over medium-low heat. Heat, swirling, until warm but not bubbling. Pour into a spouted measuring cup.

2. Place egg yolks, lemon juice and cayenne (if using) in a tall container (see tip, at left). Using the immersion blender, pulse about 10 times to combine. With the blender running, gradually drizzle in warm butter, blending until the sauce emulsifies and thickens (about 1 minute). If the sauce becomes too thick when all the butter is added, blend in warm water.

3. Serve immediately or transfer to a glass jar and keep warm in a hot water bath for up to 1 hour (see tip, at left).

Nutrition Tip

Grass-fed cows eat grass and hay year-round instead of being fed grain and soy. A grass diet improves the quality of the cow's milk and results in higher levels of omega-3 fats, vitamin E and beta-carotene than is present in dairy products from conventionally raised cows.

Ranch Dressing

There's nothing quite like creamy ranch dressing on cold, crisp romaine lettuce. Top it with grilled chicken, fish or steak, and you have a complete meal.

Tip

This dressing is delicious, thinned out at bit, as a drizzle for cooked vegetables. At the end of step 1, add cold filtered water, 1 tbsp (15 mL) at a time, until you reach your desired consistency. Try it on steamed or roasted asparagus, broccoli or cauliflower.

1	small clove garlic, crushed	1
2 tbsp	minced fresh dill	30 mL
1 tsp	finely chopped fresh chives	5 mL
¼ tsp	freshly ground black pepper	1 mL
⅛ tsp	paprika	0.5 mL
¼ cup	The Best Paleo Mayo (page 249)	60 mL
¼ tsp	grated lemon zest	1 mL
2 tsp	freshly squeezed lemon juice	10 mL
½ tsp	Dijon mustard	2 mL

1. In a small bowl, combine garlic, dill, chives, pepper, paprika, mayo, lemon zest, lemon juice and mustard.

2. Store in an airtight glass container in the refrigerator for up to 3 days.

Nutrition Tip

Compare the homemade ingredients above with the ingredients of a top commercial brand: vegetable oil (soybean and/or canola), water, egg yolk, sugar, salt, cultured nonfat buttermilk, natural flavors (milk, soy), spices, dried garlic, dried onion, vinegar, phosphoric acid, xanthan gum, modified food starch, monosodium glutamate, artificial flavors, disodium phosphate, sorbic acid and calcium disodium EDTA as preservatives, disodium inosinate, disodium guanylate. Need we say more?

NUTRIENTS PER 1 TBSP (15 ML)	
Calories	101
Fat	11 g
Carbohydrate	0 g
Fiber	0 g
Protein	0 g

Green Goddess Dressing

This paleo take on a classic creamy dressing is a natural for crispy salad greens, and it is also wonderful spread on chicken and wrapped in a crunchy romaine leaf. But don't stop there — use it as a dip for crudités or drizzle it on steamed vegetables.

Tip

You can make this dressing by hand, but it won't be as smooth. Mince the green onions, garlic and parsley as small as possible, almost like a paste, then mash them together with the avocado, salt, mayo, water and lemon juice.

- **Blender or food processor (see tip, at left)**

2	green onions, roughly chopped	2
1	small clove garlic, roughly chopped	1
½	avocado	½
¼ cup	tightly packed fresh parsley leaves	60 mL
⅛ tsp	sea salt	0.5 mL
¼ cup	The Best Paleo Mayo (page 249)	60 mL
¼ cup	filtered water	60 mL
4 tsp	freshly squeezed lemon juice	20 mL

1. In blender, combine green onions, garlic, avocado, parsley, salt, mayo, water and lemon juice; blend until smooth.

2. Store in an airtight glass container in the refrigerator for up to 3 days.

Nutrition Tip

The phrase "Always a bridesmaid, never a bride" fits parsley perfectly. But it's time parsley — and all herbs, for that matter — took center stage with all the other leafy green vegetables. Parsley is an excellent source of vitamin K, essential for bone and heart health, as well as the familiar antioxidant vitamin C. As with all herbs, parsley also contains volatile oils, such as myristicin, that show promising anticancer properties. So let's stop thinking of parsley and the other herbs as garnishes and use them as green vegetables to be incorporated into all of our salads (and more).

NUTRIENTS PER 1 TBSP (15 ML)	
Calories	37
Fat	4 g
Carbohydrate	1 g
Fiber	1 g
Protein	0 g

Caesar Dressing

**Makes about
1/3 cup (75 mL)**

Homemade dressings, this one included, will quickly become your favorites. If you prepare them ahead of time and let them stand in the fridge, the flavors have a chance to mingle.

Tip

You'll likely never use a whole can of anchovies at one time, so freeze them for a later date. Spread them out on a sheet of waxed paper so they are not touching and place them in the freezer for 2 to 3 hours. Once they are solid, you can pack them all together in a freezer bag without them sticking together, ready to go for the next round of Caesar Dressing.

1	anchovy (see tip, at left)	1
1	small clove garlic, finely minced	1
1/8 tsp	freshly ground black pepper	0.5 mL
1/4 tsp	Dijon mustard	1 mL
1/4 cup	The Best Paleo Mayo (page 249)	60 mL
1 tsp	filtered water (approx.)	5 mL

1. In a small bowl, using a fork, mash anchovies, garlic, pepper and mustard until a thick paste forms. Stir in mayo and water, mixing well. Add more water as needed for your desired consistency.

2. Store in an airtight glass container in the refrigerator for up to 3 days.

Nutrition Tip

If asked, most people will say they don't like anchovies, but when they are used correctly in recipes (especially in Caesar dressing), they impart a salty umami taste rather than a fishy one. Anchovies are brimming with anti-inflammatory omega-3 fats, calcium and protein, so give these little guys a chance.

NUTRIENTS PER 1 TBSP (15 ML)	
Calories	83
Fat	9 g
Carbohydrate	0 g
Fiber	0 g
Protein	0 g

Creamy Lemon Tahini Dressing

Serve this dressing drizzled on hot Roasted Broccolini (page 149) or Nori Egg Rolls (page 177). It is also delicious as a sauce for chicken or fish, as a dressing for coleslaw and even as a dip for crunchy vegetables.

Tips

Use the blending container the immersion container came with, or use a tall glass jar with an opening big enough to fit the blender, such as a wide-mouth mason jar.

To make this dressing without an immersion blender, whisk the ingredients in a small, deep bowl until smooth.

- **Immersion blender (see tips, at left)**

1	clove garlic, minced	1
2 tbsp	nutritional yeast	30 mL
¹/₈ tsp	sea salt	0.5 mL
¹/₂ cup	tahini	125 mL
¹/₄ cup	freshly squeezed lemon juice	60 mL
¹/₄ cup	cold filtered water (approx.)	60 mL
2 tsp	toasted (dark) sesame oil	10 mL

1. Place garlic, yeast, salt, tahini, lemon juice, water and sesame oil in a tall container (see tip, at left). Using the immersion blender, process until smooth, adding more water as necessary.

2. Store in an airtight glass container in the refrigerator for up to 5 days.

Nutrition Tip

Tahini is a paste made from ground sesame seeds and has the same health benefits as the seeds. It is rich in minerals like phosphorus, magnesium, potassium and iron, and vitamins including vitamin E and most of the B's. It also contains the amino acid methionine, which is important for the detoxification pathways in the liver. Instead of reaching for the peanut butter, give tahini a try.

NUTRIENTS PER 1 TBSP (15 ML)	
Calories	125
Fat	12 g
Carbohydrate	4 g
Fiber	2 g
Protein	3 g

Creamy Sesame Dressing

This dressing isn't just for salads. It is also delicious as a sauce for chicken or fish and as a drizzle for hot steamed vegetables.

2 tsp	grated gingerroot	10 mL
1/4 tsp	sea salt	1 mL
Pinch	cayenne pepper	Pinch
3 tbsp	tahini	45 mL
3 tbsp	unseasoned rice vinegar	45 mL
1 tbsp	organic gluten-free tamari or coconut amino acids	15 mL
1 tbsp	filtered water	15 mL
1 tbsp	freshly squeezed lime juice	15 mL
1/2 tsp	grated lemon zest	2 mL
1 tsp	freshly squeezed lemon juice	5 mL

1. In a small bowl, whisk together ginger, salt, cayenne, tahini, vinegar, tamari, water, lime juice, lemon zest and lemon juice until well combined.

2. Store in an airtight glass container in the refrigerator for up to 5 days.

Nutrition Tip
Sesame seeds, the main ingredient in tahini, contain nutrients called phytosterols (specifically beta-sitosterol) that may prevent or reduce the risk of heart disease, in part by helping to regulate cholesterol in the body. Sesame seeds have the highest level of phytosterols when ranked against 27 other seeds, nuts, legumes and grains.

NUTRIENTS PER 1 TBSP (15 ML)	
Calories	37
Fat	3 g
Carbohydrate	2 g
Fiber	0 g
Protein	1 g

Vinaigrette Basics

Store-bought salad dressings can be a Pandora's box of sweeteners, additives and hidden ingredients that can wreak havoc on blood sugar. Just when you are trying to eat more vegetables, including at least one salad every day, you read the labels of your favorite dressings to find they contain ingredients that can work against your health. Fear not! Once you learn the basic formula for making a vinaigrette, you can experiment with other ingredients and develop your own house dressing.

There are two main components to a basic oil-and-vinegar dressing, or vinaigrette: oil and acid (vinegar or citrus juice). The magic ratio of oil to acid is 3 parts oil to 1 part acid. Now that you know that, you can combine any healthy oil with any acid and discover wonderful flavors. Any combination of seasonings can then be added to the basic formula, including basic sea salt and freshly ground pepper, garlic, onions, herbs and spices. Add as many and as much as tastes good to you.

The following chart is a jumping-off point for you. Try different combinations and come up with your favorites.

Oils (3 parts)	Acids (1 part)	Seasonings (to taste)
Extra virgin olive oil Avocado oil Walnut oil Hazelnut oil Macadamia nut oil Hemp seed oil	Freshly squeezed lemon juice Freshly squeezed lime juice White wine vinegar Red wine vinegar Apple cider vinegar Balsamic vinegar Unseasoned rice vinegar	Minced shallots Minced garlic Dijon mustard Fresh or dried herbs (basil, parsley, dill, cilantro, mint, tarragon, etc.) Spices (salt, freshly ground pepper, cayenne pepper, etc.) Puréed fruit Organic gluten-free tamari or coconut amino acids

Classic Vinaigrette

**Makes about
1 cup (250 mL)**

Make a batch of this basic vinaigrette at least once a week, so you always have it on hand. It's not just a salad dressing, but also a marinade, a drizzle for fish or poultry both before and after cooking, and a sauce for simple steamed vegetables.

Tips

Don't worry if the vinaigrette separates — you are trying to mix oil and water (the acid), after all. Just shake well before serving.

When you store the vinaigrette in the fridge, the olive oil will harden and get cloudy, so take it out ahead of time and let it come to room temperature before serving.

²/₃ cup	extra virgin olive oil	150 mL
¹/₃ cup	freshly squeezed lemon juice	75 mL
1 tbsp	Dijon mustard	15 mL
¹/₄ tsp	sea salt	1 mL
¹/₄ tsp	freshly ground black pepper	1 mL

1. Place oil, lemon juice, mustard, salt and pepper in a glass jar with a tight lid. Seal the jar and shake well to combine.

2. Store in an airtight glass container in the refrigerator for up to 1 week.

Nutrition Tip

Olive oil and the Mediterranean diet go hand in hand, and olive oil is responsible for many of the cardioprotective effects of the diet. Thousands of studies have been conducted demonstrating the health benefits of the polyphenols in olive oil. But how do you make sure you are buying the right oil? The labeling can be a bit confusing, but look for "first cold-pressed extra virgin olive oil." This oil has the best chance of containing the highest phytonutrient and polyphenol content. Make sure it is in a dark glass bottle, and store it away from heat and light. Purchase only as much as you will use in about 1 to 2 months.

NUTRIENTS PER 1 TBSP (15 ML)	
Calories	80
Fat	9 g
Carbohydrate	0 g
Fiber	0 g
Protein	0 g

Strawberry Balsamic Vinaigrette

This vinaigrette is
wonderful with a
spinach salad of baby
spinach, chopped
fresh strawberries and
chopped walnuts. For
a smooth dressing,
this is best prepared
in a blender or food
processor (or with an
immersion blender).

Tip

For best results, thaw frozen
berries or use very, very
ripe fresh berries to make
the purée.

Variation

Use different berries for
different flavors; wild
blueberry is a knockout.

- **Blender or food processor**

8	medium strawberries, chopped (about ¹/₂ cup/125 mL)	8
¹/₂ tsp	roughly chopped or roasted garlic	2 mL
¹/₄ cup	extra virgin olive oil	60 mL
1 tbsp	balsamic vinegar	15 mL
¹/₂ tsp	Dijon mustard	2 mL

1. In blender, combine strawberries, garlic, oil, vinegar and mustard; blend until smooth.

2. Store in an airtight glass container in the refrigerator for up to 3 days.

Nutrition Tip

Strawberries are outstanding in terms of the
antioxidant and anti-inflammatory nutrients they
contain. They are an excellent source of both
vitamin C and manganese, an important antioxidant
mineral. The long list of phytonutrients, from
anthocyanins to quercetin, work synergistically
to provide significant cardiovascular benefits and
reduce inflammation in the body.

NUTRIENTS PER 1 TBSP (15 ML)	
Calories	65
Fat	7 g
Carbohydrate	1 g
Fiber	0 g
Protein	0 g

Barbecue Spice Blend

This spice blend gives you all the rich flavors of a good barbecue sauce without all the unhealthy oils and sugars.

3 tbsp	smoked paprika	45 mL
2 tbsp	chili powder	30 mL
1 tbsp	ground cumin	15 mL
1¹/₂ tsp	sea salt	7 mL
1 tsp	onion powder	5 mL
1 tsp	garlic powder	5 mL
1 tsp	freshly ground black pepper	5 mL

1. In a small bowl, combine paprika, chili powder, cumin, salt, onion powder, garlic powder and pepper.

2. Store in an airtight glass jar at room temperature for up to 6 months.

Nutrition Tip

Every blend of spices has a different total health effect depending on the quantities of each herb and spice and the resulting synergy. In this blend, chili powder and paprika have good antioxidant effects, and chili-containing meals have been shown to reduce hyperinsulinemia. No spice blend has been tested for its medicinal effects, but making your own food, including using a spice blend with no added preservatives or sweeteners, is a step in a healthy direction.

NUTRIENTS PER 1 TBSP (15 ML)	
Calories	19
Fat	1 g
Carbohydrate	3 g
Fiber	2 g
Protein	1 g

Italian Spice Blend

Makes about
1/3 cup (75 mL)

This blend adds wonderful Italian seasoning to any kind of ground meat, but is especially good with pork and turkey. For best results, use 1½ tbsp (22 mL) spice blend per 1 lb (500 g) ground meat. Combine the spices with the meat and refrigerate for about 30 minutes to let the flavors mingle.

1 tbsp	sea salt	15 mL
1 tbsp	fennel seeds, coarsely ground	15 mL
1 tbsp	garlic powder	15 mL
1 tbsp	onion powder	15 mL
1 tbsp	paprika	15 mL
2 tsp	dried oregano	10 mL

1. In a small bowl, combine salt, fennel, garlic powder, onion powder, paprika and oregano.

2. Store in an airtight glass jar at room temperature for up to 6 months.

Nutrition Tip

Like all herbs and spices, fennel contains its own unique combination of phytonutrients, which are the source of its health benefits. Fennel seeds are best known for their distinct anise flavor and their ability to aid digestion by reducing gas and bloating. This action is thanks to a number of volatile essential oils, including anethole and limonene, among others.

NUTRIENTS PER 1 TBSP (15 ML)	
Calories	20
Fat	0 g
Carbohydrate	4 g
Fiber	1 g
Protein	1 g

Garam Masala

**Makes about
4 tsp (20 mL)**

Garam masala is a spice blend common in Indian and Pakistani cuisine. Some say it is the Indian equivalent of the French herbes de Provence or the Chinese five-spice powder. You can purchase it ready-made, but once you make it yourself, you'll always have the best blend.

1½ tsp	ground cumin	7 mL
¾ tsp	ground coriander	3 mL
¾ tsp	ground cardamom	3 mL
¾ tsp	freshly ground black pepper	3 mL
½ tsp	ground cinnamon	2 mL
¼ tsp	ground cloves	1 mL
¼ tsp	ground nutmeg	1 mL

1. In a small bowl, combine cumin, coriander, cardamom, pepper, cinnamon, cloves and nutmeg.

2. Store in an airtight glass jar at room temperature for up to 6 months.

Nutrition Tip

All of the spices in garam masala have their own unique ability to impact our health in a positive way. In laboratory and human studies, cinnamon appears to have a beneficial effect on blood sugar. According to a 2012 study published in *Nutrition Research*, subjects had reduced hemoglobin A1c and fasting blood glucose levels after taking a cinnamon extract for 3 months.

NUTRIENTS PER 2 TSP (10 ML)	
Calories	13
Fat	1 g
Carbohydrate	2 g
Fiber	1 g
Protein	1 g

Extras

Spiced Roasted Almonds

**Makes 2 cups
(500 mL)**

When toasting nuts, set a timer for a little less time than is called for in the recipe. Nuts have different amounts of moisture in them, and they can go from perfectly roasted to burnt very quickly. Keep a close eye on them and remember they will crisp up a bit more after they are out of the oven.

- Preheat oven to 300°F (150°C)
- Rimmed baking sheet, lined with parchment paper

2 cups	whole raw almonds	500 mL
¾ tsp	ground cumin	3 mL
¾ tsp	ground coriander	3 mL
½ tsp	sea salt	2 mL
¼ tsp	cayenne pepper	1 mL
⅛ tsp	freshly ground black pepper	0.5 mL
Pinch	smoked paprika	Pinch
1 tsp	extra virgin olive oil	5 mL

1. Place almonds in a medium bowl. Add cumin, coriander, salt, cayenne, black pepper, paprika and oil, mixing until almonds are thoroughly coated with oil and spices. Transfer almonds to prepared baking sheet and spread out in a single layer.

2. Bake in preheated oven for about 25 minutes or until lightly toasted. Transfer to a plate and let cool completely.

3. Store in an airtight glass container at room temperature for up to 7 days (if they last that long!).

Nutrition Tip

For decades people avoided eating too many nuts, thinking that the high levels of fat in nuts were bad for the heart. We now know that isn't true, and a plethora of studies support the cardiovascular benefits of eating nuts. One of these studies, which examined the postprandial oxidative damage to fats in a high-glycemic diet, was published in the *Journal of Nutrition* in 2006. The subjects ate three different high-glycemic test meals, one of which contained almonds. The study found that the meal with almonds lowered postprandial glucose and decreased the oxidative damage to proteins and fats. This may be one mechanism by which nuts work to decrease the risk of heart disease.

NUTRIENTS PER ¼ CUP (60 ML)	
Calories	212
Fat	18 g
Carbohydrate	8 g
Fiber	4 g
Protein	8 g

Rosemary Pecans

**Makes 2 cups
(500 mL)**

It will be hard for everyone to resist grabbing a handful of these if you leave them out on the counter!

Variations

Use any combination of herbs and spices you prefer. Oregano makes a nice substitute for the rosemary.

Substitute walnuts for the pecans.

- **Preheat oven to 350°F (180°C)**
- **Baking sheet, lined with parchment paper**

1 tbsp	grass-fed butter	15 mL
2 tsp	dried rosemary, crumbled	10 mL
½ tsp	sea salt	2 mL
¼ tsp	dried thyme, crumbled	1 mL
¼ tsp	cayenne pepper (optional)	1 mL
2 cups	pecan halves	500 mL

1. In a small saucepan, melt butter over low heat. Stir in rosemary, salt, thyme and cayenne (if using). Add pecans and stir well to coat. Transfer pecans to prepared baking sheet and spread out in a single layer.

2. Bake in preheated oven for 10 minutes, stirring halfway through, until toasted and fragrant. Transfer to a plate and let cool completely.

3. Store in an airtight glass container at room temperature for up to 7 days.

Nutrition Tip

One of the trace minerals we need small amounts of every day is manganese, and pecans are an exceptional source. Manganese helps protect our skin against damage from ultraviolet light and is a cofactor (helper molecule) for manganese superoxide dismutase, a strong antioxidant produced in the body for protection against free radical damage. Trace minerals, although only required in small amounts, are nonetheless crucial for health.

NUTRIENTS PER ¼ CUP (60 ML)	
Calories	184
Fat	19 g
Carbohydrate	3 g
Fiber	2 g
Protein	2 g

Classic Kale Chips

The trick for delicious, crispy kale chips is to bake them slow and low. If the oven temperature is too high, the kale will turn brown and taste bitter. A longer time at a lower temperature allows the kale to dehydrate a bit and then bake to a perfectly crispy chip.

Tips

After the initial 15 minutes of baking, set a timer to check on the chips every 5 minutes. It is very easy to get involved in something else and end up with burnt chips.

If you don't store the chips in an airtight container, they will absorb whatever moisture is in the air and turn soggy. If that happens, place them on a parchment-lined baking sheet and bake at 250°F (120°C) for 3 to 5 minutes or until crispy again.

- Preheat oven to 250°F (120°C), with racks placed in the upper and lower thirds of the oven
- 2 baking sheets, lined with parchment paper

1	head curly or Lacinato kale	1
4 tsp	extra virgin olive oil	20 mL
	Sea salt	

1. Remove and discard the tough stems and ribs from the kale. Tear kale into 2-inch (5 cm) pieces. (You should have about 6 cups/1.5 L.) Rinse and dry well. (The drier the kale is to start, the sooner you'll have crispy chips!)

2. Place kale in a large bowl and drizzle with oil. Using your hands, rub the oil through the kale, coating each piece evenly. Sprinkle with salt. Arrange kale in a single layer, without overlapping, on prepared baking sheets.

3. Place one baking sheet on each oven rack and bake in preheated oven for 15 minutes. Switch the positions of the baking sheets on the racks and bake for 10 to 15 minutes or until chips are evenly crispy (see tip, at left). Let cool.

4. Store in an airtight glass container for up to 7 days (see tip, at left).

Variations

Sprinkle on ¼ cup (60 mL) nutritional yeast with the salt for a nice cheesy chip.

Using a total of ⅓ to ½ cup (75 to 125 mL) Creamy Cashew Cheese (page 273), lightly coat each piece of kale. You'll need to bake them for almost twice as long, but you'll be rewarded with a delicious cheesy ranch flavor!

Nutrition Tip

Kale demonstrates risk-lowering benefits for many different types of cancer, including colon, bladder, ovary, prostate and breast cancers. It is the isothiocyanates in kale, which support the detoxification system of the body, that are primarily responsible for these benefits. In addition, kale provides over 45 different flavonoids with both antioxidant and anti-inflammatory actions that also play an important role in cancer risk reduction.

NUTRIENTS PER SERVING	
Calories	54
Fat	9 g
Carbohydrate	4 g
Fiber	2 g
Protein	2 g

Leek Chips

**Makes about 2 cups
(500 mL)**

These delicious chips
are addictive just as
they are or as a topping
for almost anything.
Try them with Creamy
Broccoli Soup (page 121)
or Rich Mushroom Soup
(page 122). Store them
in an airtight container
at room temperature.
They will keep for about
a week (if they last
that long!).

Tip

If you don't store the chips
in an airtight container,
they will absorb whatever
moisture is in the air
and turn soggy. If that
happens, place them on a
parchment-lined baking
sheet and bake at 250°F
(120°C) for 3 to 5 minutes
or until crispy again.

- **Preheat oven to 250°F (120°C), with racks placed in the upper and lower thirds of the oven**
- **2 baking sheets, lined with parchment paper**

2	medium leeks	2
1 tbsp	extra virgin olive oil	15 mL
1/4 tsp	sea salt	1 mL

1. Remove and discard the dark green leaves and 1/4 inch (0.5 cm) of the root end of the leeks, leaving only the white and pale green parts. Cut leeks into 1/4-inch (0.5 cm) slices. Transfer to a large bowl of cold water and separate the slices into rings, washing away any sand caught in the layers. Transfer leeks to a colander and drain thoroughly, then pat very dry with a clean kitchen towel or paper towels.

2. Place leeks in a large bowl and drizzle with oil. Using your hands, toss leeks to make sure all rings are coated. Add salt, tossing well. Arrange leeks in a single layer, without overlapping, on prepared baking sheets.

3. Place one baking sheet on each oven rack and bake in preheated oven, stirring and switching the positions of the baking sheets on the racks every 10 minutes or so, until golden brown and crisp. Watch carefully, as some rings will be ready to come out sooner than others; transfer the chips to a plate as they are done. Some may be done in 30 minutes, others may take 60 minutes. Let chips cool completely and serve at room temperature.

4. Store in an airtight glass container for up to 7 days (see tip, at left).

Nutrition Tip

Along with onions and garlic, leeks are part of the Allium vegetable family, and they have many of the same beneficial compounds for cardiovascular health. Specifically, leeks contain the flavonoid kaempferol, which helps protect the lining of our blood vessels from damage, in part by increasing the production of nitric oxide, which helps the blood vessels to relax and dilate. To top it off, leeks also contain the bioactive form of folate, which can help protect against high homocysteine levels.

NUTRIENTS PER 1/4 CUP (60 ML)	
Calories	37
Fat	1 g
Carbohydrate	6 g
Fiber	1 g
Protein	1 g

Crispy Baked Zucchini Chips

These great veggie chips can really help satisfy the need to crunch something! You can't be in a hurry with these, though, as a low, slow oven is the key to crispy chips. You will be rewarded for your patience. These are best eaten the day they are made, which usually isn't a problem. Serve as is or with Creamy Cashew Cheese (page 273) or Ranch Dressing (page 252).

Tips

If you have a mandoline, you can use it to slice the zucchini, but do not use a food processor, as it will slice them too thinly.

If you don't store the chips in an airtight container, they will absorb whatever moisture is in the air and turn soggy. If that happens, place them on a parchment-lined baking sheet and bake at 250°F (120°C) for 3 to 5 minutes or until crispy again.

NUTRIENTS PER SERVING	
Calories	54
Fat	3 g
Carbohydrate	6 g
Fiber	2 g
Protein	2 g

- **Preheat oven to 225°F (110°C), with racks placed in the upper and lower thirds of the oven**
- **2 baking sheets, lined with parchment paper, paper lightly brushed with extra virgin olive oil**

2	medium zucchini, thinly sliced	2
1 tsp	extra virgin olive oil	5 mL
	Sea salt	

1. Place zucchini slices in a single layer on paper towels, with another layer of paper towels on top. Place a baking sheet on top and press down firmly but gently (don't squish them!) to squeeze out some moisture.

2. Arrange zucchini in a single layer, without overlapping, on prepared baking sheets. Very lightly brush the tops of the zucchini with oil. Sprinkle with salt.

3. Place one baking sheet on each oven rack and bake in preheated oven for 1 hour. Switch the positions of the baking sheets on the racks and bake for up to 1 hour more, until chips are the desired crispness. (Some chips will crisp up faster than others; watch carefully and remove the crisp ones so they don't burn, leaving the damp ones in until crisp.) Let chips cool on fresh paper towels to absorb any extra oil.

4. Store in an airtight glass container for up to 7 days (see tip, at left).

Variation

Add any spices you like, such as paprika, cumin, dried oregano, freshly ground black pepper or cayenne pepper, sprinkling them on with the salt.

Nutrition Tip

Zucchini, also known as summer squash, contains many nutrients that are helpful for blood sugar management, including fiber. Some of the 2.5 g of fiber in 1 cup (250 mL) of zucchini is pectin, which a number of animal studies indicate helps to keep metabolism and blood sugar levels in balance. Also present are many of the B vitamins, which are required for the metabolism of sugar, and zinc, which we need for the production of insulin.

Seed Crackers

These seed crackers are just the ticket when you want a healthy crunch that doesn't send your blood sugar through the roof. Try them with Creamy Cashew Cheese (page 273) or Rich Mushroom Soup (page 122).

Tip

If you don't store the chips in an airtight container, they will absorb whatever moisture is in the air and turn soggy. If that happens, place them on a parchment-lined baking sheet and bake at 250°F (120°C) for 3 to 5 minutes or until crispy again.

Variations

Herbed Seed Crackers: Add $1/2$ to 1 tsp (2 to 5 mL) dried oregano, thyme or dillweed to the seed mixture in step 1.

Spicy Seed Crackers: Add 1 to 2 tsp (5 to 10 mL) ground turmeric, chili powder or cayenne pepper to the seed mixture in step 1.

NUTRIENTS PER 4 CRACKERS	
Calories	171
Fat	15 g
Carbohydrate	8 g
Fiber	5 g
Protein	6 g

- **Preheat oven to 325°F (160°C)**
- **2 baking sheets, lined with parchment paper**

1 cup	raw sunflower seeds	250 mL
$1/2$ cup	raw sesame seeds	125 mL
$1/2$ cup	raw green pumpkin seeds (pepitas)	125 mL
$1/2$ cup	flax seeds	125 mL
3 tbsp	psyllium husks	45 mL
$1^1/2$ tsp	sea salt	7 mL
1 tsp	garlic powder	5 mL
2 cups	filtered water	500 mL

1. In a medium bowl, combine sunflower seeds, sesame seeds, pumpkin seeds, flax seeds, psyllium husks, salt and garlic powder. Add water and stir well. Let stand for 10 minutes to thicken.

2. Place half the seed mixture in the middle of a prepared baking sheet and smooth with a spoon, making sure there are no holes. Place another sheet of parchment paper on top and, using a rolling pin, flatten dough evenly to $1/4$ inch (0.5 cm) thick. Remove the top sheet of parchment paper.

3. Bake in preheated oven, rotating the baking sheet every 15 minutes, for 60 to 75 minutes or until very crispy. Let cool completely on pan, then break into pieces.

4. Repeat steps 2 and 3 with the remaining seed mixture.

5. Store in an airtight glass container for up to 1 month (see tip, at left).

Nutrition Tip

Fiber is one of the best tools when it comes to managing blood sugar and avoiding the blood sugar roller coaster. The best fiber sources that also help to control blood sugar are from vegetables, nuts and seeds. The psyllium husks in this recipe provide soluble fiber, which can slow the body's absorption of glucose from the intestines and at the same time keep the beneficial bacteria in the gut happy.

Almond Flax Crackers

Makes about 24 crackers

Savory and crisp, these crackers are the perfect nibble to go with Creamy Broccoli Soup (page 121) or Chilled Avocado and Cucumber Soup (page 120). What a treat to have a cracker so well balanced that your blood sugar remains stable.

Tip

Coconut oil can be solid or liquid depending on the temperature where it is stored. If your coconut oil is solid, melt some in the microwave or in a small bowl set over hot water.

- **Preheat oven to 350°F (180°C)**
- **Baking sheet, lined with parchment paper**

¾ cup	almond meal	175 mL
¾ cup	ground flax seeds (flaxseed meal)	175 mL
3 tbsp	nutritional yeast	45 mL
1 tsp	onion powder	5 mL
1 tsp	dried oregano	5 mL
½ tsp	baking soda	2 mL
½ tsp	sea salt	2 mL
¼ tsp	cayenne pepper (optional)	1 mL
2	large free-range egg whites, beaten	2
1 tbsp	melted coconut oil (see tip, at left)	15 mL

1. In a large bowl, combine almond meal, flax seeds, yeast, onion powder, oregano, baking soda, salt and cayenne (if using). Stir in egg whites and coconut oil. Form dough into a ball.

2. Place dough in the middle of the prepared baking sheet. Place another sheet of parchment paper on top and, using a rolling pin, flatten dough evenly to a 12- by 8-inch (30 by 20 cm) rectangle, about ¼ inch (0.5 cm) thick. Remove the top sheet of parchment paper. With a sharp knife, score the dough into 2-inch (5 cm) squares.

3. Bake in preheated oven for 15 to 20 minutes, rotating the baking sheet halfway through, until crisp. Let cool completely on pan, then snap along the scored lines to form crackers.

NUTRIENTS PER 4 CRACKERS	
Calories	177
Fat	14 g
Carbohydrate	7 g
Fiber	5 g
Protein	7 g

Variation

Substitute garlic powder for the onion powder and/or chopped dried rosemary for the oregano. Or develop your own blend of herbs and spices.

Nutrition Tip

Here's a prime example of how labeling laws prevent us from understanding the truth about what we are eating. A top brand of crackers has a big banner across the box declaring that the crackers are a "Sensible Solution" because they are low in saturated fat, have zero trans fat and are cholesterol-free. However, when you read the ingredients list, hydrogenated vegetable oil is the fourth ingredient, right behind enriched flour, soybean oil and sugar, and before high-fructose corn syrup. When you dig a little deeper online, you discover that 1 serving (5 crackers) has 0.4 g of trans fats, coming in just under the magic labeling cutoff of 0.5 g, after which the manufacturer has to declare the trans fats. Conceivably, someone could have 10 to 15 crackers in a sitting and end up eating a couple of grams of trans fats while thinking they have made a "sensible" choice. As for cholesterol, there is no cholesterol in plants, so anything made without animal products will be cholesterol-free — but that doesn't necessarily make it a healthy choice.

Oven-Baked Apple Chews with Cinnamon Nut Butter

**Makes about
24 slices and about
1 cup (250 mL) dip**

Sweet and chewy,
these baked apple
slices will be a hit with
the whole family. The
cinnamon nut butter
tops them off with rich,
delicious flavor.

Tips

For the apples, try
Honeycrisp, Fuji, Golden
Delicious or the variety of
your choice. Different types
of apples will produce very
different-tasting chips, so
have fun experimenting!

The apple chews can
be stored in an airtight
glass container at room
temperature for up to
7 days.

NUTRIENTS PER 6 APPLE SLICES	
Calories	58
Fat	0 g
Carbohydrate	15 g
Fiber	3 g
Protein	0 g

NUTRIENTS PER 1 TBSP (15 ML) DIP	
Calories	100
Fat	9 g
Carbohydrate	3 g
Fiber	2 g
Protein	3 g

- Preheat oven to 225°F (110°C), with racks placed in the upper and lower thirds of the oven
- 2 baking sheets, lined with parchment paper

2	large apples (see tip, at left)	2
1 cup	almond or cashew butter	250 mL
2 tbsp	coconut butter (or the fat from full-fat coconut milk)	30 mL
1 tsp	ground cinnamon	5 mL

1. Place each apple on its side and, using a very sharp knife or a mandoline, slice the apple as thinly as possible, right through the core. You can core each piece if you like, or just leave them as is, discarding any seeds. Arrange apple in a single layer, without overlapping, on prepared baking sheets.

2. Bake in preheated oven for 2 hours, turning apples over halfway through and switching the positions of the baking sheets on the racks. Turn the oven off and let apples cool in the oven, without opening it. (They will dehydrate better this way.)

3. In a small saucepan, heat almond butter and coconut butter over low heat, stirring until melted and combined. Remove from heat and add cinnamon, stirring well.

4. Serve apple chews with cinnamon nut butter as a dip.

Nutrition Tip

Apples help regulate blood sugar in a number of ways. Although they have a modest amount of total fiber, the pectin portion of that fiber works with other phytonutrients in the apple to exert effects that would normally be associated with much larger amounts of fiber. In addition, the polyphenols in apples stimulate the pancreatic beta cells to release insulin, and also reduce the absorption of glucose from the intestine. Another prime example of the synergy of nutrients in whole foods.

Creamy Cashew Cheese

This creamy nut cheese can be used as a dip for veggies, a coating for kale chips, a topping for Seed Crackers (page 269) or Almond Flax Crackers (page 270) or a sauce for Zucchini Noodles (page 167). So versatile!

Tips

To soak the cashews, place them in a small bowl, cover with water and let stand for 1 hour. If you are in a hurry, cover the cashews with boiling water and let stand for 30 minutes.

For added flavor, mince 1 tbsp (15 mL) of your favorite fresh leafy herbs and stir them in after blending. If using rosemary or thyme, mince 1 tsp (5 mL).

- **Blender or food processor**

1	clove garlic, chopped	1
1 cup	raw cashews, soaked (see tip, at left)	250 mL
1/2 cup	shelled dry-roasted pistachios (either salted or unsalted)	125 mL
1/3 cup	nutritional yeast	75 mL
4 tsp	freshly squeezed lemon juice	20 mL
1 tbsp	apple cider vinegar	15 mL
1 tbsp	Dijon mustard	15 mL
1/4 cup	filtered water (approx.)	60 mL
	Sea salt and freshly ground black pepper	

1. In blender, combine garlic, cashews, pistachios, yeast, lemon juice, vinegar and mustard; process until creamy, stopping to scrape down the sides of the bowl as needed. With the motor running, through the feed tube, add water a little at a time until the desired consistency is reached.

2. Transfer cheese to a bowl and season to taste with salt and pepper. Serve immediately or cover and refrigerate for a few hours until ready to serve, or for up to 5 days. (The cheese will harden a bit when chilled and will be easier to spread.)

Variations

Add 1/3 cup (75 mL) chopped olives (green or black) to the mixture before blending, or stir them in afterward for a chunkier version.

Add 1/4 cup (60 mL) chopped oil-packed or reconstituted sun-dried tomatoes to the mixture before blending, or chop them finely and stir in after blending.

NUTRIENTS PER 2 TBSP (30 ML)	
Calories	150
Fat	12 g
Carbohydrate	9 g
Fiber	2 g
Protein	6 g

Nutrition Tip

Commercial dips contain things like industrial seed oils, sugar, modified cornstarch, hydrolyzed corn and wheat gluten, monosodium glutamate (MSG), flavoring and artificial colors. Using this Creamy Cashew Cheese recipe as the base, you can have as many different dip flavors as you can dream up, all without any ingredients that negatively affect hormones and blood sugar.

Grilled Pineapple

Prepare to be transported to the tropics when you serve grilled pineapple with a dollop of Coconut Whip.

Variation

Substitute 3 peaches for the pineapple. Cut each peach in half and remove the pit. Grill the peach halves in the same way as the pineapple.

• **Preheat barbecue grill to high**

1	pineapple, peeled	1
	Coconut oil	
	Coconut Whip (opposite)	

1. Cut pineapple into 6 equal rings about 1 inch (2.5 cm) thick. (You can leave the core in or cut it out with a paring knife, but be careful to leave the rings intact.)

2. Grease preheated grill with coconut oil. Place pineapple rings on the grill, spacing them so that you can flip them easily. Grill, turning once, for 1 to 2 minutes per side or until you get nice grill marks.

3. Place each pineapple ring on a plate, add a dollop of Coconut Whip in the middle and serve immediately.

Nutrition Tip

Pineapples contain a substance called bromelain, best studied for its protein-digesting enzymes. When taken as a dietary supplement, bromelain may help reduce inflammation, and it has been studied for its potential ability to reduce tumor growth. Pineapple is also an excellent source of the antioxidant vitamin C, which is one key to a healthy immune system.

NUTRIENTS PER SERVING (WITHOUT COCONUT WHIP)	
Calories	75
Fat	0 g
Carbohydrate	20 g
Fiber	2 g
Protein	2 g

Coconut Whip

**Makes 6 to
8 servings**

Use full-fat coconut milk
for this recipe — "lite"
won't whip. Organic
coconut milk offers
the best consistency.
Avoid brands with guar
gum, as this causes the
cream and the water
to emulsify, which
is not what we want
for whipping.

Tips

Place the can of coconut
milk in the fridge the night
before you make this to
allow the coconut cream to
separate from the milk and
rise to the top of the can.

Keep a can or two of
coconut milk in the fridge
so you can make this
delicious whip anytime.

The coconut cream will
whip into peaks but will
not become airy and
increase in volume as
whipping cream does.

Chilling the beaters and
the bowl helps keep the
whip creamy.

| 1 | can (14 oz/400 mL) full-fat coconut milk, chilled (see tips, at left) | 1 |
| ½ tsp | vanilla extract | 2 mL |

1. Chill a medium, deep bowl and the beaters of an electric mixer in the refrigerator for 1 hour.

2. Without shaking the can of coconut milk, turn it over and open the bottom with a can opener. Pour out the coconut milk and reserve it for another use.

3. Scoop the coconut cream into the chilled bowl. Add vanilla and, using the electric mixer with chilled beaters, whip on high speed for 5 to 6 minutes or until soft peaks form. Serve immediately.

Variation

Substitute grated citrus zest, espresso powder, almond extract, ground cinnamon or other flavorings for the vanilla extract.

Nutrition Tip

Coconut milk is made from liquid extracted from the coconut meat, rather than the coconut water, which is the liquid in the middle of the coconut. The coconut meat and milk contain a specific saturated fat called lauric acid that is a medium-chain triglyceride (MCT). This fat is easily absorbed by the body and used for energy without producing a blood sugar or insulin spike.

NUTRIENTS PER SERVING (1 OF 8)	
Calories	51
Fat	5 g
Carbohydrate	1 g
Fiber	0 g
Protein	0 g

Coconut Banana Soft-Serve

Makes 4 servings

You won't be going back to commercial ice cream once you taste this! Plus, there's no added sugar, stabilizers or preservatives — just frozen real food. You'll need to plan ahead for this recipe, as it requires frozen ingredients.

Variation

Substitute 1 cup (250 mL) of any frozen sliced fruit for the bananas. Most fruit works well with coconut milk!

- Ice cube trays
- Baking sheet, lined with waxed paper
- High-power blender or food processor

1	can (14 oz/400 mL) full-fat coconut milk	1
2	bananas	2

1. Shake the can of coconut milk to make sure it is emulsified and the milk is smooth, without any lumps. Open the can and pour half of the milk into ice cube trays. Freeze until solid. (Refrigerate the remaining coconut milk in an airtight glass container for another use.)

2. Peel bananas and cut crosswise into 1-inch (2.5 cm) thick slices. Arrange in a single layer on prepared baking sheet and freeze until solid.

3. Add coconut milk cubes and frozen banana slices to the blender and process to the consistency of soft-serve ice cream, stopping the blender to stir as needed for even blending. Serve immediately.

Nutrition Tip

Making homemade ice cream or soft-serve this way really works best with a high-power blender. When you can freeze the coconut milk and then blend it until it is like a slushy, there is no need to add any sugar, and you can enjoy a frozen treat without throwing your blood sugar out of whack.

NUTRIENTS PER SERVING	
Calories	299
Fat	27 g
Carbohydrate	17 g
Fiber	2 g
Protein	3 g

References

Agricultural Marketing Service. United States Department of Agriculture. Grass fed marketing claim standard. Available at: ams.usda.gov/grades-standards/beef/grassfed.

Agricultural Marketing Service. United States Department of Agriculture. Pesticide data program. Available at: ams.usda.gov/datasets/pdp.

American Diabetes Association. Standards of Medical Care in Diabetes — 2015. *Diabetes Care*, 2015 Jan; 38 (Suppl 1). Available at: www.diabetes.teithe.gr/UsersFiles/entypa/STANDARDS%20OF%20MEDICAL%20CARE%20IN%20DIABETES%202015.pdf.

Animal Welfare Approved. First government approved food label for 100% grassfed meat introduced in Canada. Press release, 2013 Jul 22. Available at: animalwelfareapproved.org/wp-content/uploads/2009/06/Canada-Grassfed-FINAL.pdf.

Atkinson FS, Foster-Powell K, Brand-Miller JC. International tables of glycemic index and glycemic load values: 2008. *Diabetes Care*, 2008 Dec; 31 (12): 2281–83.

Ayas NT, White DP, Al-Delaimy WK, et al. A prospective study of self-reported sleep duration and incident diabetes in women. *Diabetes Care*, 2003 Feb; 26 (2): 380–84.

Barański M, Srednicka-Tober D, Volakakis N, et al. Higher antioxidant and lower cadmium concentrations and lower incidence of pesticide residues in organically grown crops: A systematic literature review and meta-analyses. *Br J Nutr*, 2014 Sep 14; 112 (5): 794–811.

Barkeling B, Rössner S, Björvell H. Effects of a high-protein meal (meat) and a high-carbohydrate meal (vegetarian) on satiety measured by automated computerized monitoring of subsequent food intake, motivation to eat and food preferences. *Int J Obes*, 1990 Sep; 14 (9): 743–51.

Bassioni G, Mohammed F, Al Zubaidy EAH, Kobrsi I. Risk assessment of using aluminum foil in food preparation. *Int J Electrochem Sci*, 2012 Apr; 7: 4498–509.

Basu S, Yoffe P, Hills N, Lustig RH. The relationship of sugar to population-level diabetes prevalence: An econometric analysis of repeated cross-sectional data. *PLoS One*, 2013; 8 (2): e57873.

Biswas A, Oh PI, Faulkner GE, et al. Sedentary time and its association with risk for disease incidence, mortality, and hospitalization in adults: A systematic review and meta-analysis. *Ann Intern Med*, 2015 Jan 20; 162 (2): 123–32.

Bland JS. *The Disease Delusion: Conquering the Causes of Chronic Illness for a Healthier, Longer, and Happier Life*. New York: Harper Wave, 2014.

Canadian Diabetes Association. "Full Guidelines." *Clinical Practice Guidelines*. Available at: guidelines.diabetes.ca/fullguidelines.

Centers for Disease Control and Prevention. Insufficient sleep is a public health problem. Available at: www.cdc.gov/features/dssleep.

Centers for Disease Control and Prevention. Phthalates. Fact Sheet. Available at: www.cdc.gov/biomonitoring/Phthalates_FactSheet.html.

Charles D. Are organic vegetables more nutritious after all? *The Salt* (NPR), 2014 Jul 11. Available at: npr.org/sections/thesalt/2014/07/11/330760923/are-organic-vegetables-more-nutritious-after-all.

CNN. MRSA Fast Facts. Updated 2016 Jun 9. Available at: www.cnn.com/2013/06/28/us/mrsa-fast-facts.

Cooper C. CFIA approves grassfed label. *Food in Canada*, 2013 Jul 30. Available at: www.foodincanada.com/food-safety/cfia-approves-grassfed-label-112145.

Cordain L. *The Paleo Diet: Lose Weight and Get Healthy by Eating the Foods You Were Designed to Eat*. New York: Houghton Mifflin Harcourt Publishers, 2011.

Daley CA, Abbott A, Doyle PS, et al. A review of fatty acid profiles and antioxidant content in grass-fed and grain-fed beef. *Nutr J*, 2010 Mar 10; 9: 10.

de la Monte SM, Wands JR. Review of insulin and insulin-like growth factor expression, signaling, and malfunction in the central nervous system: Relevance to Alzheimer's disease. *J Alzheimers Dis*, 2005 Feb; 7 (1): 45–61.

Diabetes Prevention Program Research Group. Long-term effects of lifestyle intervention or metformin on diabetes development and microvascular complications over 15-year follow up: The Diabetes Prevention Program Outcomes Study. *Lancet Diabetes Endocrinol*, 2015 Nov; 3 (11): 866–75.

Donga E, van Dijk M, van Dijk JG, et al. A single night of partial sleep deprivation induces insulin resistance in multiple metabolic pathways in healthy subjects. *J Clin Endocrinol Metab*, 2010 Jun; 95 (6): 2963–68.

Eberhardt MV, Lee CY, Liu RH. Nutrition: Antioxidant activity of fresh apples. *Nature*, 2000 Jun 22; 405: 903–4.

Eddy D, Schlessinger L, Kahn R, et al. Relationship of insulin resistance and related metabolic variables to coronary artery disease: A mathematical analysis. *Diabetes Care*, 2009 Feb; 32 (2): 361–66.

Emanuele NV, Swade TF, Emanuele MA. Consequences of alcohol use in diabetics. *Alcohol Health Res World*, 1998; 22 (3): 211–19.

Enders G. *Gut: The Inside Story of Our Body's Most Underrated Organ.* Vancouver: Greystone Books, 2015.

Esposito K, Ciotola M, Carleo D, et al. Post-meal glucose peaks at home associate with carotid intima-media thickness in type 2 diabetes. *J Clin Endocrinol Metab*, 2008 Apr; 93 (4): 1345–50.

Gagnière J, Raisch J, Veziant J, et al. Gut microbiota imbalance and colorectal cancer. *World J Gastroenterol*, 2016 Jan 14; 22 (2): 501–18.

Gebauer SK, Chardigny JM, Jakobsen MU, et al. Effects of ruminant trans fatty acids on cardiovascular disease and cancer: A comprehensive review of epidemiological, clinical, and mechanistic studies. *Adv Nutr*, 2011 Jul; 2 (4): 332–54.

Gillam C. FDA to start testing for glyphosate in food. *Time*, 2016 Feb 17. Available at: time.com/4227500/fda-glyphosate-testing.

Guyenet S. What's the ideal fasting insulin level? *Whole Health Source*, 2009 Dec 22. Available at: wholehealthsource.blogspot.ca/2009/12/whats-ideal-fasting-insulin-level.html.

Healy GN, Dunstan DW, Salmon J, et al. Breaks in sedentary time: Beneficial associations with metabolic risk. *Diabetes Care*, 2008 Apr; 31 (4): 661–66.

Healy GN, Dunstan DW, Salmon J, et al. Objectively measured light-intensity physical activity is independently associated with 2-h plasma glucose. *Diabetes Care*, 2007 Jun; 30 (6): 1384–89.

Hoffman-Snyder C, Smith BE, Ross MA, et al. Value of the oral glucose tolerance test in the evaluation of chronic idiopathic axonal polyneuropathy. *Arch Neurol*, 2006 Aug; 63 (8): 1075–79.

Hyman M. Systems biology, toxins, obesity, and functional medicine. *Altern Ther Health Med*, 2007 Mar–Apr; 13 (2): S134–39.

International Agency for Research on Cancer. World Health Organization. IARC Monographs evaluate consumption of red meat and processed meat. Press release, 2015 Oct 26. Available at: iarc.fr/en/media-centre/pr/2015/pdfs/pr240_E.pdf.

Johnston CS, Kim CM, Buller AJ. Vinegar improves insulin sensitivity to a high-carbohydrate meal in subjects with insulin resistance or type 2 diabetes. *Diabetes Care*, 2004 Jan; 27 (1): 281–82.

Jönsson T, Granfeldt Y, Ahrén B, et al. Beneficial effects of a Paleolithic diet on cardiovascular risk factors in type 2 diabetes: A randomized cross-over pilot study. *Cardiovasc Diabetol*, 2009 Jul 16; 8: 35.

Khaw KT, Wareham N, Bingham S, et al. Association of hemoglobin A1c with cardiovascular disease and mortality in adults: The European prospective investigation into cancer in Norfolk. *Ann Intern Med*, 2004 Sep 21; 141 (6): 413–20.

Kohlstadt I, ed. *Advancing Medicine with Food and Nutrients*, 2nd ed. Boca Raton: CRC Press, 2013.

Lee DH, Lee IK, Song K, et al. A strong dose-response relation between serum concentrations of persistent organic pollutants and diabetes: Results from the National Health and Examination Survey 1999–2002. *Diabetes Care*, 2006 Jul; 29 (7): 1638–44.

Leheska JM, Thompson LD, Howe JC, et al. Effects of conventional and grass-feeding systems on the nutrient composition of beef. *J Anim Sci*, 2008 Dec 5; 86 (12): 3575–85.

Leproult R, Copinschi G, Buxton O, Van Cauter E. Sleep loss results in an elevation of cortisol levels the next evening. *Sleep*. 1997 Oct; 20 (10): 865–70.

Leproult R, Van Cauter E. Role of sleep and sleep loss in hormonal release and metabolism. *Endocr Dev*, 2010; 17: 11–21.

Lieb CW. The effects of an exclusive, long-continued meat diet. Based on the history, experiences and clinical survey of Vilhjalmur Stefansson, Arctic explorer. *JAMA*. 1926 Jul 3; 87 (1): 25–26.

Lindeberg S. The Kitava study. Available at: staffanlindeberg.com/TheKitavaStudy.html.

Liu RH. Potential synergy of phytochemicals in cancer prevention: Mechanism of action. *J Nutr*, 2004 Dec; 134 (12 Suppl): 3479S–85S.

Massin P, Lange C, Tichet J, et al. Hemoglobin A1c and fasting plasma glucose levels as predictors of retinopathy at 10 years: The French DESIR study. *Arch Ophthalmol*, 2011 Feb; 129 (2): 188–95.

McAfee AJ, McSorley EM, Cuskelly GJ, et al. Red meat from animals offered a grass diet increases plasma and platelet n-3 PUFA in healthy consumers. *Br J Nutr*, 2011 Jan; 105 (1): 80–89.

Mesci B, Oguz A, Sagun HG, et al. Dietary breads: Myth or reality? *Diabetes Res Clin Pract*, 2008 Jul; 81 (1): 68–71.

Miller M. The epidemiology of triglyceride as a coronary artery disease risk factor. *Clin Cardiol*, 1999 Jun; 22 (6 Suppl): II-1–6.

National Geographic Magazine. What the world eats. Interactive web page. Available at: nationalgeographic.com/what-the-world-eats.

National Heart, Lung and Blood Institute. National Institutes of Health. The Atherosclerosis Risk in Communities Study (ARIC). Updated 2014 Jul. Available at: nhlbi.nih.gov/research/resources/obesity/population/aric.htm.

National Institute of Diabetes and Digestive and Kidney Diseases. National Institutes of Health. Insulin resistance and prediabetes. Available at: www.niddk.nih.gov/health-information/health-topics/Diabetes/insulin-resistance-prediabetes/Pages/index.aspx.

National Institute of Environmental Health Sciences. National Institutes of Health. Bisphenol A (BPA). Available at: niehs.nih.gov/health/topics/agents/sya-bpa.

National Institute on Aging. National Institutes of Health. 2014–2015 NIH Alzheimer's Disease Progress Report. 2015 Dec. Available at: d2cauhfh6h4x0p.cloudfront.net/s3fs-public/2014-2015_alzheimers-disease-progress-report.pdf?maJSMEv2CY5HS8MnjFt2RTujfgTu1a1e.

Nedeltcheva AV, Kessler L, Imperial J, Penev PD. Exposure to recurrent sleep restriction in the setting of high caloric intake and physical inactivity results in increased insulin resistance and reduced glucose tolerance. *J Clin Endocrinol Metab*, 2009 Sep; 94 (9): 3242–50.

O'Dea K. Marked improvement in carbohydrate and lipid metabolism in diabetic Australian Aborigines after temporary reversion to traditional lifestyle. *Diabetes*. 1984 Jun; 33 (6): 596–603.

O'Dea K. Traditional diet and food preferences of Australian aboriginal hunter-gatherers. *Philos Trans R Soc Lond B Biol Sci*, 1991 Nov 29; 334 (1270): 233–40; discussion 240–41.

Paddock C. Type 2 diabetes revealed by gut bacteria. *Medical News Today*, 2012 Sep 27. Available at: www.medicalnewstoday.com/articles/250742.php.

Peck P. ADA: Diabetic retinopathy detected in pre-diabetes patients. *MedPageToday*, 2005 Jun 13. Available at: medpagetoday.com/Endocrinology/Diabetes/1185.

Pepino MY, Tiemann CD, Patterson BW, et al. Sucralose affects glycemic and hormonal responses to an oral glucose load. *Diabetes Care*, 2013 Sep; 36 (9): 2530–35.

Polhill TS, Saad S, Poronnik P, et al. Short-term peaks in glucose promote renal fibrogenesis independently of total glucose exposure. *Am J Physiol Renal Physiol*, 2004 Aug; 287 (2): F268–73.

Pullen LC. Environmental toxins associated with diabetes, obesity. *Diabetes Care*. 2014; 37: 1951–58.

Qin J, Li Y, Cai Z, et al. A metagenome-wide association study of gut microbiota in type 2 diabetes. *Nature*, 2012 Oct 4; 490 (7418): 55–60.

Rock A. How safe is your ground beef? *Consumer Reports*. Updated 2015 Dec 21. Available at: www.consumerreports.org/cro/food/how-safe-is-your-ground-beef.

Scrafford CG, Tran NL, Barraj LM, Mink PJ. Egg consumption and CHD and stroke mortality: A prospective study of US adults. *Public Health Nutr*, 2011 Feb; 14 (2): 261–70.

Sevastianova K, Santos A, Kotronen A, et al. Effect of short-term carbohydrate overfeeding and long-term weight loss on liver fat in overweight humans. *Am J Clin Nutr*, 2012 Oct; 96 (4): 727–34.

Singleton JR, Smith AG, Bromberg MB. Increased prevalence of impaired glucose tolerance in patients with painful sensory neuropathy. *Diabetes Care*, 2001 Aug; 24 (8): 1448–53.

Siri-Tarino PW, Sun Q, Hu FB, Krauss RM. Meta-analysis of prospective cohort studies evaluating the association of saturated fat with cardiovascular disease. *Am J Clin Nutr*, 2010 Mar; 91 (3): 535–46.

Spiegel K, Leproult R, Van Cauter E. Impact of sleep debt on metabolic and endocrine function. *Lancet*, 1999 Oct 23; 354 (9188): 1435–39.

Spijkerman AM, Dekker JM, Nijpels G, et al. Microvascular complications at time of diagnosis of type 2 diabetes are similar among diabetic patients detected by targeted screening and patients newly diagnosed in general practice: The Hoorn Screening Study. *Diabetes Care*, 2003 Sept; 26 (9): 2604–8.

Średnicka-Tober D, Barański M, Seal C, et al. Composition differences between organic and conventional meat: A systematic literature review and meta-analysis. *Br J Nutr*, 2016 Mar; 115 (6): 994–1011.

Stephens BR, Granados K, Zderic TW, et al. Effects of 1 day of inactivity on insulin action in healthy men and women: Interaction with energy intake. *Metabolism*, 2011 Jul; 60 (7): 941–49.

Stocks T, Rapp K, Bjørge T, et al. Blood glucose and risk of incident and fatal cancer in the Metabolic Syndrome and Cancer Project (Me-Can): Analysis of six prospective cohorts. *PLOS Med*, 2009 Dec; 6 (12): e1000201.

Stubbs RJ, van Wyk MC, Johnstone AM, Harbron CG. Breakfasts high in protein, fat or carbohydrate: Effect on within-day appetite and energy balance. *Eur J Clin Nutr*, 1996 Jul; 50 (7): 409–17.

Sumner CJ, Sheth S, Griffin JW, et al. The spectrum of neuropathy in diabetes and impaired glucose tolerance. *Neurology*, 2003 Jan; 60 (1): 108–11.

Talbott S. *The Cortisol Connection: Why Stress Makes You Fat and Ruins Your Health — And What You Can Do About It*. Alameda, CA: Hunter House, 2007.

Tilg H, Moschen AR. Microbiota and diabetes: An evolving relationship. *Gut*, 2014 Sep; 63 (9): 1513–21.

U.S. Department of Health and Human Services. Centers for Disease Control and Prevention. Antibiotic resistance threats in the United States, 2013. Available at: www.cdc.gov/drugresistance/threat-report-2013/pdf/ar-threats-2013-508.pdf.

Veerman JL, Healy GN, Cobiac LJ, et al. Television viewing time and reduced life expectancy: A life table analysis. *Br J Sports Med*, 2012 Oct; 46 (13): 927–30.

Weinberg SL. The diet–heart hypothesis: A critique. *J Am Coll Cardiol*, 2004 Mar 3; 43 (5): 731–33.

The White House. National strategy for combating antibiotic-resistant bacteria. 2014 Sep. Available at: www.cdc.gov/drugresistance/pdf/carb_national_strategy.pdf.

Wilcox G. Insulin and insulin resistance. *Clin Biochem Rev*, 2005 May; 26 (2): 19–39.

Index

Green Beans with Shiitakes, Shallots and Toasted Almonds, 144
Green Goddess Dressing, 253
greens (leafy), 65, 160. *See also* kale; lettuce
    Detox Vegetable Soup, 117
    Easy Sautéed Greens, 160
    Greek Chicken Salad, 210
    Modern Cobb Salad, 139
    Modern Tuna Salad with Avocado and Ginger, 191
    Nori Egg Rolls, 177
    Pan-Seared Sea Scallops, 192
    Roasted Asparagus Salad with Arugula and Hazelnuts, 126
Guacamole, Classic, 247
gut (intestines), 55–57
Guyenet, Stephan, 20

H
haddock, 184
HbA1c (hemoglobin A1c), 24–25
    test for, 18–19, 20
heart disease, 24–25, 34, 36
hemp seeds, 244. *See also* seeds
herbs (fresh), 65, 99. *See also specific herbs*
    Asian Cabbage Crunch, 131
    Eggs in a Hole, 172
    Lemon and Herb Sardines, 189
    Meatballs, New Classic, 220
    Paleo Mayo, The Best (variation), 249
    Rack of Lamb, Classic, 235
    Ranch Dressing, 252
    Salmon Cakes, 187
    Spaghetti Squash Bolognese, 232
    Summer Salsa, 243
high-fructose corn syrup, 95
Hollandaise, Easy, 251
homeostasis, 9, 57
hormones, 50–51, 58. *See also* insulin
hot pepper sauce, 69
    Paleo Mayo, The Best (variation), 249

hunter-gatherers, 29–30
hydration, 99
hygiene (excessive), 57
hypoglycemia, 37
hypothalamus, 58

I
indigenous peoples, 29–30
indole-3-carbinol (I3C), 151
industrial seed oils, 44, 85, 88
inflammation, 9, 21
insulin, 14–15, 17–21, 58
insulin resistance, 15–16, 20, 36, 54, 58
intestines (gut), 55–57
Inuit, 29
inulin, 126, 165
iodine, 192
Italian Spice Blend, 261

J
Jerk Chicken Kebabs, 202
jicama, 135
    Cooked Shrimp Ceviche, 196
    Jicama, Avocado, Radish and Orange Salad with Cilantro, 134
juice (fruit), 96
junk food, 64

K
kale, 137, 266
    Classic Kale Chips, 266
    Detox Vegetable Soup, 117
    Kale and Sweet Potato Sauté, 161
    Shredded Kale Salad with Pecan Parmesan, 136
ketchup, 69
Keys, Ancel, 34
kidney disease, 23–24
Kitavans, 30
kitchen
    pantry staples, 66–71, 72
    stocking, 64–71
    tools and equipment, 60–63

L
lamb, 235
    Classic Rack of Lamb, 235
    Skillet-Grilled Lamb with Avocado Mint Sauce, 236
lauric acid, 275
leaky gut, 55–56
Leek Chips, 267
legumes, 84, 88
Leifert, Carlo, 77
lemon
    Classic Vinaigrette, 258
    Creamy Lemon Tahini Dressing, 255
    Creamy Sesame Dressing, 256
    Easy Hollandaise, 251
    Lemon and Herb Sardines, 189
    Lemon Pepper Chicken Wings, 212
    Paleo Mayo, The Best, 249
    Ranch Dressing, 252
leptin, 49
lettuce
    Asian Chicken Lettuce Cups, 208
    Buffalo-Inspired Chicken Lettuce Wraps, 207
    Fish Tacos (tip), 180
    Modern Cobb Salad, 139
    Taco Salad, 231
lifestyle, 16, 47–59
Light and Breezy Coleslaw, 129
lignans, 131
lime
    Beet and Carrot Salad with Toasted Cashews, 127
    Creamy Sesame Dressing, 256
    Summer Salsa, 243
    Thai Almond Sauce, 238
    Watermelon Salad, 141
    Zucchini Wasabi Spread, 248
Lindeberg, Staffan, 30
lipogenesis, 16, 26
Liu, Rui, 40
liver disease, 16, 26
lunches, 99–100
Lustig, Robert, 42
lutein, 138, 176
lycopene, 140, 166

Library and Archives Canada Cataloguing in Publication

Hillhouse, Jill, author
The paleo diabetes diet solution : manage your blood sugar with 125 recipes plus a 30-day meal plan / Jill Hillhouse, CNP ; with Lisa Cantkier, CHN.

Includes index.
ISBN 978-0-7788-0548-9 (paperback)

1. Diabetes—Diet therapy—Recipes. 2. Low-carbohydrate diet—Recipes. 3. High-protein diet—Recipes. 4. Prehistoric peoples—Nutrition. 5. Cookbooks. I. Cantkier, Lisa, author II. Title.

RC662.H55 2016   641.5'6314   C2016-904429-7